The Pyramid of Game Design

Designing, Producing and Launching Service Games

Nicholas Lovell

CRC Press
Taylor & Francis Group
Boca Raton London New York

CRC Press is an imprint of the
Taylor & Francis Group, an **Informa** business

AN A K PETERS BOOK

CRC Press
Taylor & Francis Group
6000 Broken Sound Parkway NW, Suite 300
Boca Raton, FL 33487-2742

© 2019 by Taylor & Francis Group, LLC
CRC Press is an imprint of Taylor & Francis Group, an Informa business

No claim to original U.S. Government works

Printed on acid-free paper

International Standard Book Number-13: 978-1-138-29889-7 (Paperback)
International Standard Book Number-13: 978-1-138-29899-6 (Hardback)

Library of Congress Cataloging-in-Publication Data

Names: Lovell, Nicholas, 1972- author.
Title: The pyramid of game design : designing, producing and launching service games / Nicholas Lovell.
Description: Boca Raton: Taylor & Francis, CRC Press, [2018] | Includes bibliographical references and index.
Identifiers: LCCN 2017061432| ISBN 9781138298897 (pbk. : alk. paper) | ISBN 9781138298996 (hardback : alk. paper)
Subjects: LCSH: Computer games industry. | Computer games.
Classification: LCC HD9993.E452 L68 2018 | DDC 794.8068/5--dc23
LC record available at https://lccn.loc.gov/2017061432

**Visit the Taylor & Francis Web site at
http://www.taylorandfrancis.com**

**and the CRC Press Web site at
http://www.crcpress.com**

Printed and bound in the United States of America by Sheridan

The Pyramid of Game Design

To Catherine, Alasdair and Lucy.

Contents

CHAPTER 17 ■ THE PYRAMID OF GAME DESIGN AFTERWORD   279

Author

Nicholas Lovell is a game designer, consultant and writer.

His books include *The Curve* (Portfolio Penguin), *The F2P Toolbox* (GAMESbrief), *Design Rules for F2P Games* (GAMESbrief) and *How to Publish a Game* (GAMESbrief). Since 2008, he has advised more than 50 companies on adapting to service games, with a particular focus on free-to-play. Clients have included Bandai Namco, Bohemia Interactive, CCP, Exient, Firefly Studios, Madfinger, nDreams, Rebellion, Rovio, Square Enix and Supersaurs. Since 2017, Nicholas has been Design Director at Electric Square.

Nicholas runs a website dedicated to the business of games at www.gamesbrief.com. He lives in London with his wife, two children and a cat.

CHAPTER 1

The Pyramid

G AMES ARE CHANGING.
We have vast experience crafting polished, enjoyable and profitable games. Yet people who have worked on those games often struggle to make a successful transition to service games. The tools and frameworks that help to make better boxed games are less helpful when making service games.

The Pyramid of Game Design provides a new framework and new tools to help you make better service games. *Better* means **more fun**, **more profitable** and with **less risk**. *Service games* means games that offer **compelling, ongoing experiences** to players and an **ongoing source of revenue** for the game makers. That covers free-to-play (F2P), as well as a new generation of AAA games with a product heritage and a service mentality.

WHY IS FREE-TO-PLAY SO DOMINANT IN TWENTY-FIRST CENTURY GAME DESIGN

Free-to-play games have two fundamental advantages over traditional boxed products:

- **Widening the funnel**: Being free reduces the barrier to entry, **increases the potential audience** and makes it easier to get people to try your game. Just being free is not enough to get customers, particularly on mobile. Whether you choose to be free or stick with paid, you are competing with free, and you need a plan to win that contest.

- **Enabling Superfans**: Service games embrace a **variable pricing** model that enables players who are heavily engaged with your game to spend lots of money on it. This has always been possible. Just think of the thousands of dollars that fans of *RuneScape* or *EVE Online* or *World of Warcraft* have spent on flights, hotels and food when they attend Runefest or FanFest or Blizzcon. The difference now is that the game company, rather than third parties, receives the money from Superfans.

The poster children of the industry are household names that have become billion-dollar franchises. *League of Legends* has 140 million Monthly Active Users (MAUs) and generated $1.9 billion in 2016.[1] Supercell generated $1.3 billion from *Clash of Clans* and $1.2 billion from *Clash Royale* in 2016, and the studio was acquired by Chinese internet giant Tencent in June 2016 at a valuation of more than $10 billion. *Fortnite* launched as a free-to-play rival to *PUBG* and other battle royale-style games and trounced its competition, generating $1 billion in revenue in its first year. *Candy Crush Saga* had 93 million Daily Active Users (DAUs) and generated $1.5 billion in revenue in 2013, the year before parent company King's stock market flotation.[2] King was eventually acquired by Activision Blizzard in November 2015 for $5.9 billion. It's not just about new companies. Nintendo, Niantic and the Pokémon Company saw phenomenal success with *Pokémon Go*, which reached the billion-dollar milestone in early 2017.[3] Valve has seen success with both free and paid service games like *Team Fortress 2*, *Dota 2* and *Counter-Strike: Global Offensive*.

Established companies have embraced free-to-play, sometimes without the "free" part. Digital distribution has enabled ongoing direct relationships with players, in a way that was impossible—or not cost-effective—in a physical era. Publisher Paradox, the master of grand strategy games, offers dozens of downloadable content (DLC) packs for games like *Europa Universalis* and *Crusader Kings*. Blizzard embraced free-to-play with its collectible card game *Hearthstone*. With a year to go until launch, Blizzard had not decided whether *Overwatch* was going to be a paid game or a free game, which is why it looks like a free-to-play game that decided at the last minute to charge upfront.[4]

Electronic Arts (EA) has added a component to its *FIFA* series, *FIFA Ultimate Team*, in which gamers assemble teams by buying or trading packs of soccer players. EA announced at a Morgan Stanley investor conference in March 2017 that the *Ultimate Team* addition to its sports franchises generated $800 million a year in revenue. About 75% of gamers who buy EA's sports games join Ultimate Team and about half spend some money, an impressive lifetime conversion rate in the region of 35%.[5] That revenue is highly profitable because digital content generates higher margins than physical content. With 30% of EA's full game sales now in digital form,

GAAP VERSUS GAAS

GAMES AS A PRODUCT (GAAP) OR PRODUCT GAMES

Traditional PC and console model. Fire-and-forget games that are complete when they launch. The marketing team focuses on a big launch splash and has little ongoing relationship with players. Sales weighted towards the first month.

Examples: *The Last of Us, Dear Esther, Grand Theft Auto.*

GAMES AS A SERVICE (GAAS) OR SERVICE GAMES

The free-to-play model. Games that are continually developed. Many features not developed at time of release to public. The marketing team focuses on user acquisition over time. Often free, with a variable pricing model such that different players spend different amounts in the game.

Examples: *Clash Royale, Gardenscapes, Crossfire, League of Legends.*

HYBRID GAMES

The distinction between the two models is blurring. Both sides of the Industry are learning and adopting the best, most successful of each other's techniques. This is not without controversy. Electronic Arts withdrew microtransaction from *Star Wars Battlefront II* on the day before release following a consumer backlash and an intervention from *Star Wars* licence owner Disney.[9]

Examples: *Destiny, Overwatch, FIFA Ultimate Team.*

together with extra digital content, Jorgenson said EA's gross margins had grown from "the low 50s to now, this year, the low 70s."[6]

The new service model has also enabled indies to thrive, whether it is the pixel-art Nimblebit, makers of *Tiny Tower* and *Pocket Planes*, or PC castle-building specialists Firefly, makers of *Stronghold Kingdoms*. British developer Lockwood Publishing created social virtual world *Avakin Life* on mobile. It has 2.5 million MAUs and reached $1 million in monthly revenue in November 2016.[7] Many of the techniques that service games require are percolating through the games industry. Kickstarter campaigns, open development, Early Access, downloadable content, retention hooks, microtransactions and loot boxes all draw on the two advantages of the digital age: direct access to customers and a variable pricing strategy that allows **those who love what you do to spend lots of money on things they really value.**[8]

The transition to service games has not been entirely positive. There have been significant casualties, notably studios who make double-AA quality games for console or PC as well as narrative games as a genre. There are ethical considerations to the variable pricing model, and it is my belief that service games will be regulated by government. We will discuss ethical issues throughout the book.

I think F2P is one of the best things that has happened to games. This book will focus on how YOU can make better, more enjoyable, more successful and more profitable games.

PRODUCT versus SERVICE GAMES

The Pyramid and the other tools that I introduce in this book improve both product and service games. They are much more *important* for service games.

Imagine two different scenarios:

> Maria has heard good things about *Generic Shooter 3: This Time It's Personal*. Everyone she knows is excited for it, and the pre-order offer looks sweet. She goes to collect it from her local GameStop on launch day and plays it over the weekend. The graphics are amazing, but the gameplay, well, let's just say that she's seen it before. By Monday, she's less enamoured, and over time, the shooter stays un-launched, as Maria returns to *Destiny* or replays *Uncharted* for the third time.

> Kyle clicked on an ad and downloaded *Generic Farming Simulator 3*. It's a litany of "press here, click there" instructions, littered with large green arrows to indicate each interaction he must complete to level up, to harvest his crops and to buy new agricultural machinery. The game is well crafted and keeps him playing for a few sessions of half an hour each, but his interest wanes and, before long, he is no longer playing it. It lasts another week before he deletes it from his phone.

The scenarios seem similar, but there is a fundamental difference. Maria paid $60 for her pre-ordered copy of *Generic Shooter 3*. The retailer, the publisher and the developer all received revenue from her, even though she didn't enjoy the game much and stopped playing after a few hours. Kyle also didn't enjoy the game much and quit after a few hours as well. No-one made any money from Kyle. He was able to try out—and, in this case, reject—the game without any money changing hands.

FREE-TO-PLAY IS NOT SHAREWARE OR A DEMO

DEMO

Play part of the game to experience what it is like. Demos are often stand-alone: no progress is carried on from the demo into the game if you choose to buy it.

SHAREWARE

Popularised by Apogee Software in the early 1990s and how the first copies of *Doom* were distributed. Players can play the initial experience, often with lots of content, for free, but must pay to unlock the rest of the game. Progress is carried over from the free content into the paid content. For example, *Doom* consisted of three episodes when it was launched on December 10, 1993. Within five months, the first, free episode had been downloaded 1.3 million times and developer id Software was raking in $100,000 per day from players paying to get the remaining two episodes.[10]

FREE-TO-PLAY

In a free-to-play game, players can play the entire game for ever without spending money. In contrast to a demo or the shareware model, there is not an abrupt "pay up or stop playing temporarily" moment. Some F2P games monetise aggressively with paywalls demanding that players pay now or leave, but almost all let players come back after a while and resume playing.

Demo and shareware models are free trials of a product game. Service games are not a free trial; they are the game, and rarely slam down an impassable paywall.

Service game makers have no choice but to keep their players engaged in the game if they want to become a commercial success. They can't rely on pre-order campaigns, on vast marketing budgets or on popular licences to drive revenue. For a service game, those techniques can only drive downloads. The game itself must be good enough to keep users playing for a long time and for some of those users to turn into payers.

The techniques these games use vary, from being awesomely fun like *Crossy Road* to being shamelessly manipulative like *Pirate Kings*. Service games put "keep players playing" at the top of their to-do list, whereas product games put "make players want to buy it" at the top of theirs. Product games have lengthy marketing-driven feature lists (multiplayer *Tomb Raider* or that level where you jump from jeep to truck to jeep again in *Uncharted 2*) that bloat the budget, but fulfil some need—real or imaginary—to make the gaming public and the gaming press pay attention to the game.

The evolution of the industry also explains the demise of a staple of the PlayStation and PlayStation 2 console generations: the licensed game. Big publishers licensed major movies during the early stages of the console cycle and then kids' products during the later stages as consoles percolated through families into the hands of younger children. The logic was that if players recognised the brand, be it *Spider-Man* or *SpongeBob SquarePants*, they would be more likely to open their wallets and buy the game. Never mind that movie tie-ins are nearly always rushed, because game licences are usually not agreed until movie production is underway, or that children's games are often underfunded and hamstrung by the demands of the rights holders. Licenced games were a good business when the primary success criterion of a game was that it was purchased, not that it was enjoyed.

Licences have their place in service games. Glu Mobile turbocharged their successful game *Stardom Hollywood* by slapping Kim Kardashian's name on it to create *Kim Kardashian: Hollywood*. *Pokémon Go* would not have taken off so fast without the *Pokémon* brand and depth of intellectual property (IP). On the other hand, service games are a graveyard of well-loved franchises attached to game designs which have not embraced the principles of successful service-game design. Who is still playing Lara Croft's endless runner, *Tomb Raider: Relic Run*?

Many amazing games were developed during the product-only era of video games. Game developers took professional pride in crafting deep, engaging experiences for their players. Executives understood that although it was possible to make money by slapping a licence on any old rubbish, the games that made huge amount of money were the ones that were reviewed well by critics, that scored higher than 90% on review aggregation website Metacritic, and that were recommended by players to their friends.[13]

Yet, at a commercial level, it is not a complete disaster for a product game if no one plays it, or if they all give up after the first 15 minutes, as long as they bought it. The publisher has the money and can fund the next cynical brand tie-in title. They can fund *Little Britain: The Video Game* (*Eurogamer*, 1/10) or *Charley's Angels* (*GameSpot*, 1.9/10) and no matter how they bad they are, they will still generate revenue, although perhaps not a profit, from users who purchase the games on the strength of the licence alone.[14]

In contrast, service games live and die by their *retention*. They succeed by keeping people playing them, and spending money on them. That is why *World of Warcraft* has had so many expansions and updates, despite being 15 years old. It's why mobile and browser games have regular, large updates, which can add whole new mechanics or game features to a title which has been out for years. It is also why the top charts of mobile games are so stagnant, with titles like *Candy Crush Saga*, *Clash of Clans* and *Game of War* remaining in the Top 10 year after year.

VARIABLE PRICING: THE REASON WHY FREE-TO-PLAY GAMES ARE NOT FREEMIUM

Venture capitalist Fred Wilson, an investor in businesses such as Twitter, Tumblr, Zynga, Etsy and Meetup, describes the freemium model as "Give your service away for free, possibly ad-supported but maybe not, acquire a lot of customers very efficiently through word of mouth, referral networks, organic search marketing, etc., then offer premium-priced, value-added services or an enhanced version of your service to your customer base."[11] Many people think that free-to-play games follow a similar business model to that of freemium business. This is not true.

The freemium model only addresses the first part of what makes F2P successful—widening the funnel—but not the second part—enabling Superfans. Typically, freemium services offer a free tier and a higher tier that costs a few dollars a month or a few tens of dollars. Freemium becomes a volume business where companies only have two levers they can pull: having more users in total or increasing the number of users who choose to pay. Freemium is a business model that focuses more on audience size and conversion rate than on Average Revenue Per User (ARPU).

In free-to-play games, we have a third lever to pull: ARPU. I am an avid player of collectible card game *Hearthstone* and have played it for about three years. I have spent approximately £1,000 in the game, buying new packs of cards to enable me to experience the full range of deck archetypes and even buying some female heroes after my six-year-old daughter wondered why there were only two girls out of nine characters.[12] Blizzard, the developer of *Hearthstone*, has three commercial levers it can pull:

- The number of players it has (MAU)
- The number of players who spend money (conversion)
- Creating compelling content to encourage players to keep spending (ARPU)

Blizzard is very good at pulling that last lever.

Free-to-play games are not like freemium because they offer **variable pricing**. Variable pricing enables you to let the players who love what you do spend lots of money on things they really value. This gives the developers many ways to improve the Lifetime Value (LTV) of a customer, which makes it a better business model than traditional freemium.

Variable pricing is why it is possible to have a successful free-to-play game with a tiny audience. Many people assume that the success of F2P is about having a mass-market game played by a vast audience, and then persuading a tiny proportion of them to spend money. This is viable, but it is not the only strategy. If you build a game that has great retention and committed players, then you can have a successful and long-lived title with fewer than 50,000 MAUs. Of course, if you have great retention, committed players and a vast audience, you can make enormous amounts of money, like Riot Games (*League of Legends*), Supercell (*Clash of Clans*) or Smilegate (*Crossfire*).

WHY I PREFER MICROTRANSACTIONS TO SUBSCRIPTIONS

- **Subscriptions have one chance to convert**
  If you offer me a 30-day trial to a product, then in exactly 720 hours, I will be told to decide whether to pay up or push off. I might not have got round to trying the product yet. It may be nearly payday and I may be short of money. I may have something else on my mind: a child won't sleep, or I have a hot date this evening. Whatever the reason, a subscription business with a trial goes to enormous effort to get me into the service, then throws me away without a thought. It's wasteful.

  In contrast, a free-to-play game lets you play the game for free forever. This gives the designers many opportunities to offer you the chance to pay for something you value, which varies from player to player.
- **Subscriptions don't offer variable pricing**
  A subscription is generally for a fixed price, for example, $15 for *World of Warcraft* or $9.99 for Xbox Live Gold. It offers predictable revenue to the developers, but it does not enable those who love what you to do to spend lots of money on things they value. Developers can only put effort into getting more players, not into creating more things that players might pay for.
- **You are fighting for a subscription slot**
  Most consumers have a short-term memory for seven items and are uncomfortable having more subscriptions than they can remember. That means that if their subscription "slots" are full, you need to kick another subscription out. That is a high bar.[15]

FRAMEWORKS FOR SUCCESS: THE PYRAMID, THE SESSION AND THE GEARBOX

I have worked with dozens of companies on their service-game strategy since 2008, as well as delivering more than 75 masterclasses on how to make money from free-to-play games. The companies have ranged from one-person indies to some of the biggest publishers in the world. In the course of that work, I have identified several frameworks that help game makers to developer successful service games: The Session, the Pyramid and the Gearbox.

The Session

The fundamental unit of service success is the Session (Figure 1.1).

A Session involves the player choosing to come back to your game *now*, despite the variety of competing entertainment choices that exist on their smart device, PC or console. It involves them doing some fun, rewarding activity. Successful game developers signal when it is a good time to leave and plant strong Return Hooks to bring each player back for the next Session.

This is the biggest shift from product development, where Playtime is the primary focus. Playtime remains important, but it is not sufficient to ensure success in a service world. Developers need to devote much more attention to making it easy for players to choose to come back into the game, to leave elegantly and to have strong reasons to return.

You may find the analogy of films versus television to be useful. Old-style boxed product games were like blockbuster movies: huge budgets,

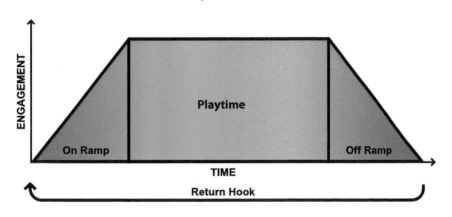

FIGURE 1.1 The Session.

massive spectacle, single-purchase experiences. New-style service games are like television: typically, lower initial budgets but with continuous development, where commercial success comes from ensuring that viewers return episode after episode and season after season.

The Pyramid

The Pyramid is a lens for viewing the components of service success (Figure 1.2).

- The *Base Layer* is the heart of the game. It is the moment-to-moment gameplay. It is a match in *Team Fortress 2*, a level of *Candy Crush Saga* or a narrative level of *Uncharted*.

- The *Retention Layer* is what keeps players playing for days and weeks and months and years. It is progress and unlocks and tech trees and narrative and achievements and leaderboards and more.

- The *Core Loop* connects the Base and Retention Layers and can usefully be thought of as a Gearbox.

- The *Superfan Layer* is where the game has become a hobby for a subset of players. They play this game more than any other game, and it occupies a huge amount of their time and possibly money.

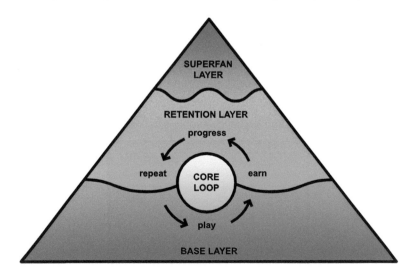

FIGURE 1.2 The Pyramid.

In product games, a good Base Layer is the heart of the success. In service games, the Retention Layer is what will mark out whether a title will be a long-term, profitable, fun game. We need new techniques and tools to help us make successful Base, Retention and Superfan Layers.

THE PYRAMID OF DISCO ZOO

Disco Zoo has a Base Layer based on the classic gameplay of *Battleships* (Figure 1.3). Players have a limited number of "shots" to rescue animals and take them back to the zoo.

In the collection Retention Layer, rescued animals are placed in the player's zoo where they earn coins while they are awake. Players must return often to wake the animals up or pay with hard currency to start a disco party. The Base Layer would soon get dull without the collection mechanic and the joy of rescuing dozens of animals to build your own thriving zoo. (I think *Disco Zoo* could work without the Base Layer, or with a different Base Layer. The Base Layer makes the game more fun, but it is not essential to the mechanics of its Retention Layer.)

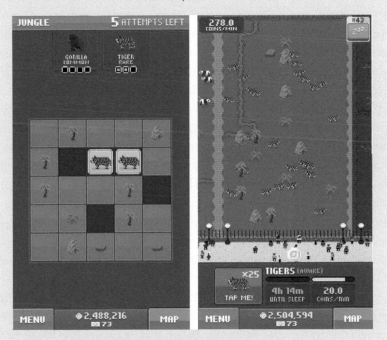

FIGURE 1.3   The *Battleships*-style Base Layer and the Retention Layer of *Disco Zoo*.

In 2017, I visited a client who was just starting a new project in an established genre. They said, "We are about to start making a new game. We will be prototyping and building the Retention Layer here, in the head office of the company, where our innovation was born. We are outsourcing the Base Layer to a studio—in another country—that has made this type of gameplay over and over again."

The client believes that the Base Layer is a known problem: a challenging thing to build and execute, but where the parameters of success are clear. The Retention Layer is an unknown problem: the development team needs to iterate, to experiment, and to prototype to build a successful Retention Layer.

That client has embraced the Pyramid.

The Gearbox

The Gearbox encapsulates the techniques that connect the Base and Retention Layers. For service games, a well-designed Gearbox is the difference between success and failure.

The easiest way to visualise the Gearbox is to consider the Pre- and Post-Event Screens. Imagine the car setup before a racing game; the hero and weapon selection before a first-person deathmatch; or the screen where a player selects which powerups to take into a Match-3 level. Then imagine the corresponding victory screen at the end of the Base Layer experience, where the player learns what rewards she earned from the event she just completed. The Gearbox enables players to understand the value (over and above "fun") of playing the Base Layer, which gives the developer more techniques with which to craft fun, rewarding gameplay.

Some of the Gearbox is invisible to players. It is the information that is passed into the Base Layer based on the choices or progress that the player has made in the Retention Layer, such as difficulty balancing data, the chance of encountering certain enemies or allies, rewards that are dependent on the player's level and so on. Some of it is visible: loadout screens, the selection of boosts or just information on what the player can expect to encounter in the Base Layer.

Games have different levels of Gearbox. Endless runner *Rodeo Stampede* fires the player out of a cannon to reach the Base Layer of lassoing and riding wild animals. There is no explicit Pre-Event Screen, although players can select which animal they wish to ride and which hat they wish to wear before they launch. *Overwatch* has a team assembly page where players choose their heroes and see the choices of their teammates. *Marvel Contest of Champions* has a selection screen where players choose the composition of their fighting squad based on the enemies they expect to meet, whereas *XCom: Enemy Unknown* allows players to customise every aspect of their loadout. These games seek a connection between the moment-to-moment fun of the Base Layer and the long-term progression enjoyment of the Retention Layer.

There is an overlap between the concepts of the Pyramid and traditional game concepts of "gameplay" systems and "progression systems."[16] The Pyramid does not seek to replace these ideas. Instead, it offers a lens to design and hone your service game, where the demands of the Session put pressure on traditional short, medium and long-term engagement techniques.

ADAPTING TO SERVICE-GAME DESIGN

Every spring, tens of thousands of video games developers descend on San Francisco for the Game Developers Conference, known as GDC. For a week, the hotels and bars within a ten-block radius of the Moscone Conference Centre overflow with developers wearing branded T-shirts and hoodies, taking a week out of making games to catch up with old friends and new developments in the industry. The city also plays host to the Game Developers Choice Awards, where the industry recognises and celebrates the greatest achievements in game development during the previous 12 months.

In 2010, GDC General Manager Meggan Scavio took to the awards stage to announce a new category that recognised the growing importance of games played by non-traditional players on non-traditional platforms: Best New Social/Online Game. Nominees included a 3D online role-playing game from Sony Online Entertainment called *Free Realms*, *Bejewelled Blitz* from PopCap and Nexon's *Dungeon Fighter Online*. The winner was a game that at its peak had more than 80 million daily players, *Farmville*.[17]

Studio General Manager Bill Mooney ambled onto stage in combat trousers, a *Farmville* T-shirt and a ragged hoodie. In an acceptance speech that misjudged the mood in the room, Mooney said that *Farmville*-developer Zynga was an indie, and he encouraged other indies to bring their games to social networks or even to apply for one of the 200 open positions at Zynga.[18] He was booed and heckled. One developer even shouted, "*Farmville* is not a game."[19]

This is a challenge as we try to advance the art and the craft of video game design. Many gamers and many game developers have a particular notion of what makes something into a game. There are many different definitions, and many smarter people than me have attempted to come up with a definition.[20]

Raph Koster, lead designer on *Ultima Online* and author of *A Theory of Fun*, says the definition that most people use, particularly non-professionals, is something like "a form of play that has rules and goals."[21] By that definition, *Farmville* is clearly a game, but it suffers from severe dislike from some parts of the industry. Koster explains:

> "If you look at the AAA game world today, you can trace just about everything in it to the early core gamer market. Video games got going with sports, dragons, robots, guns, jumping & climbing, and cars. Those were the first big ideas. And here we are now, decades in, and they are still the big ideas. Many other ideas have come along since, but somehow, they have always been quirky, "outside the mainstream"—like, say, when *Rollercoaster Tycoon,* or *Guitar Hero*, or *The Sims* came along. **The only way something like "playing house" can possibly be "outside the mainstream" is if there's a subculture in charge."** (Raph's emphasis.)[22]

Not only were early video games centred on male power fantasy themes, they also focused on Base Layer gameplay. The waves of *Space Invaders*. The mazes of *Pac-Man*. The matches of *Pong*. Because memory and graphics resources were scarce, developers focused on polishing the Base Layer as a competitive advantage. A generation of gamers grew up with an expectation that the Base Layer was the heart of gameplay.

There were exceptions. Space exploration and dogfighting title *Elite* combined impressive 3D space battles with a trading and exploration layer that would hold up today. As the industry developed, we developed role-playing games with character progression and deep lore such as the *Ultima* series. But in most cases, players, developers and critics would look at the Base Layer gameplay to see the fun, and treat the Retention Layer as a bolt-on afterthought.

This problem is amplified by the greenlight process in AAA game development. Many greenlight meetings focus on the "vertical slice," a piece of gameplay that is supposed to show all the important systems of the game to a senior management team who may only spend 20 minutes reviewing the title. They might play, for example, a single level of a game like *Uncharted*. If they like it, they can approve the game on the assumption that the finished title will include 15 such levels. Instead of a deep Retention Layer, they have chosen to daisy-chain a series of Base Layer experiences together to satisfy the needs of a boxed product.

This is fine for many, although not all, product games. The challenge lies when a game's Retention Layer is not as easy to understand as "just 15 more vertical slices." When it involves layers of complexity revealed to the player over time. When it involves the exploration of a range of interlocking systems that offer progression or new gameplay experiences over time. These systems are harder to see in a vertical slice.

As a result, many AAA game studios tend to view retention as being primarily an asset-creation problem. If you have enough skilled artists, coders and level designers, you can create enough content to keep players engaged for the 20 hours or so which is the minimum needed to justify a $60 price. In contrast, service games view retention as a system-design problem: how do we create interesting systems that evolve to give players meaningful choices, experiences and progression for a very long time without the prohibitive costs of high-quality asset generation?

Assets remain vital to the success of a service game, but their role has changed. They are no longer our primary retention tool; they now act as amplifiers to the emotions that are evoked by the game. They provide context and meaning to the progression of the game and give strong, joyful feedback. They keep the player playing not by giving her something to see but by making her feel good for the exploration, progression or experiences she is having within the game.

In my masterclass, I identify games that have successfully used free-to-play mechanics, ranging from *Team Fortress 2* and *World of Tanks*, to *Subway Surfers* and *Angry Birds Transformers*, to *Candy Crush Saga* and *Gardens of Time*. There are many games that, even if they are not free-to-play, show the hallmarks of having been inspired by the techniques and systems that help to make a successful service game. *Destiny*, a first-person shooter game from Bungie, has appointment mechanics and time-based Return Hooks to keep the player coming back. *Skylanders*, Activision's toys-to-life product that combines physical toys with console gameplay, has a model where gamers can spend hundreds of dollars to collect all the toys. Here are just a few examples of the genres that have been transformed (or created) by the free-to-play era:

- First person shooters: *Team Fortress 2, Crossfire*

- Collectible card games: *Rage of Bahamut, Hearthstone, Duelyst, Clash Royale*

- Idle games: *Adventure Capitalist, Nonstop Knight, Clicker Heroes*

- Multiplayer online battle arenas (MOBAs): *League of Legends, Vainglory, Dota 2*

- Resource management: *Hay Day, Farmville, Dragon City*

- Strategy: *Mobile Strike, Clash of Clans, Game of War*

- Match-3: *Candy Crush Saga, Bejewelled Blitz, Gardenscapes*

- Fighting: *Marvel Contest of Champions, Skullgirls, Dungeon Fighter Online*

- Role-playing: *The Old Republic, Path of Exile, Fire Emblem Heroes*

- Building sims: *Tiny Tower, Fallout Shelter, Virtual Villagers*

- Action: *World of Tanks, Warframe*

- Sport: *FIFA Ultimate Team, New Star Soccer*

- Racing: *CSR Racing, Real Racing 3, Kartrider*

- Hidden object: *Criminal Case, Gardens of Time, Pearl's Peril*

These games, and many others, show that not only do AAA product-design techniques inspire F2P design, but that inspiration flows in the other direction as well. Product and service games can learn from each other to make better, more enjoyable and more profitable games.

In the following pages, I will introduce the frameworks and techniques you need to be successful. In Chapters 2–4, I cover the heart of the Pyramid: The Base Layer, the Retention Layer and the Core Loop Gearbox that connects the two. In Chapters 5 and 6, I look at the Session, the central unit of service-gaming experience. Chapter 7 covers the Superfan Layer, and Chapter 8 looks at what players will pay for when developers are giving away their content for free.

Chapters 9–12 focus on production issues. Service games are ongoing experiences that are developed and iterated even once they have millions of players and are receiving vast amounts of data on the behaviour of those players. They are well suited to Agile technological and Lean commercial techniques that focus on validated learning to deliver high-quality products with less risk than traditional approaches. I will explore the difference between a Minimum Viable Product, a Minimum Feasible Product and a Minimum Desirable Product, how to prototype the Retention Layer and when to pivot. I will also look at the difference between concept, pre-production, production and live operations, and how to manage your teams when you have different features in all four stages of development at the same time.

Chapter 13 focuses on managing creativity in a service organisation, Chapter 14 covers how to launch your game in a competitive market and Chapter 15 looks at the role of metrics in a modern game. Finally, in Chapter 16, I discuss the ethics of free-to-play.

THERE IS NO RIGHT ANSWER, ONLY TRADE-OFFS

This book aims to be helpful to makers of all games, from the most casual of mobile games to the most core of PC or console titles. It draws together ideas, advice, techniques and frameworks from the whole game-development spectrum.

As a result, it is impossible to put forward recommendations on the "right" way to address a problem. The broad themes of acquisition, retention and monetisation; the structure of the Base Layer, the Retention Layer, the Core Loop and the Superfan Layer; and the concepts of the Session and the Gearbox are universally applicable. Specific advice is not.

That is OK because it is representative of game development. For much of what we do, there is no right answer, only trade-offs. Shiny graphics help initial downloads and marketing, but they slow down loading times, which hurts the On-Ramp and hence retention, and they don't work on older devices, reducing your potential audience size. Aggressive monetisation can generate revenue, but it risks alienating some of your players, which leads to reduced audience size and may lead to bad reviews or word of mouth, which leads to increased user acquisition costs. We can ship on time, or we can take more time and money to tackle bugs and add polish. The issues that you prioritise will depend on your artistic preference, your commercial ambitions and your funding imperatives.

Making successful service games is a messy business. It involves compromise and flexibility. Throughout this book, I will make recommendations and suggestions. I will give you a set of tools that will make it easier for you to achieve your objectives and ambitions. Along the way, you will see how these tools or suggestions conflict. You will get a clearer idea of the consequences of the decisions you take. Remember: there is no right way and wrong way—only trade-offs.

With that explanation out of the way, let's dive into the Base Layer.

CHAPTER 2

The Base Layer

A TARI'S SEMINAL ARCADE GAME, *Pong*, was released in 1972, the year that I was born. It is a two-player arcade game based on table tennis, where each player controls a paddle and must return the ball to the other side. If a player misses the ball, he or she concedes a point to the other side. The first person to score 11 points wins.

Atari's second employee was an engineer called Al Alcorn. According to the account of the early days of Atari in Stephen Kent's detailed *The Ultimate History of Video Games*, founder Nolan Bushnell told Alcorn that his first project, a simple game based on ping pong with "one ball, two paddles, and a score ... nothing else on the screen," was needed to fulfil a contract that Atari had signed with General Electric. In truth, there was no contract. Bushnell didn't want Alcorn to believe that he was just making a journeyman game to learn the ropes. He feared that if Alcorn thought his work would be thrown away at the end of the project, it would demotivate him.[1]

Alcorn exceeded his brief. He added features to the game, such as dividing each paddle into eight notional segments and making the angle at which the ball flew off vary depending on which segment it hit. He created a prototype using a cheap black and white television and a wooden cabinet. Bushnell named the game *Pong*, and they installed the prototype in Andy Capp's Tavern, a shabby bar in California's Sunnyvale—a small town that, at the time, had not yet felt the growth of Silicon Valley.

The results were phenomenal. Two weeks after they installed the prototype, Alcorn received a call from bar manager Bill Gattis, who told him that the Pong machine wasn't working, and he might want to fix it soon because it had become quite popular. "I went to fix the machine, not knowing what to expect," said Alcorn. "I opened the coin box to give myself a free game and, lo and behold, this money gushed out. I grabbed handfuls of it, put in my pockets, gave the manager my business card and said, 'Next time this happens, you call me at home right away. I can always fix this one.'"[2]

Alcorn rushed to tell Bushnell that the new machine had stopped working because the quarters had overflowed. Before long, *Pong* was taking in $200 a week, where most other coin-operated machines collected $40 or $50 a week.[3] It was a financial sensation.

It was also a game that kept people coming back for more. When Alcorn went to fix the prototype at Andy Capp's Tavern, Gattis told him, "Al, this is the weirdest thing. When I opened the bar this morning, there were two or three people at the door waiting to get in. They walked in and played that machine. They didn't buy anything. I've never seen anything like this before."

Pong and similar arcade titles still have an influence over game design decisions nearly half a century later. In the early days of video games, when arcades ruled supreme and technology was limited, designers sought out high-quality, repeatable gameplay that was fun and rewarding. Some consider this "pure" gameplay: *Space Invaders* and *Pong*. *Gauntlet* and *Frogger*. *Time Crisis* and *Dance Dance Revolution*. This is what I call the *Base Layer*.

The Base Layer is the heart of many, although not all, games. It is the enjoyable, repetitive action that players do over and over again. It can be short or long. Some examples:

- A raid or quest in *World of Warcraft*

- A match in *FIFA*

- Playing *Space Invaders* until you die

- Completing a level in a narrative action game like *Uncharted* or *Tomb Raider*

- Surviving as far as you can in *Crossy Road*

- Clearing all the bubbles in *Bubble Witch Saga*

- Winning a battle in *Summoners War*

The examples are many, but it can be hard to come up with a precise definition for the Base Layer because it depends so much on the genre, audience and nature of the game. One shorthand is "How do you describe the game to your audience?" Your answer—first-person shooter (FPS), Match-3, hidden object, card battler—will give a strong clue to your Base Layer.

When you participate in a game jam, you are likely to create a Base Layer. If you are developing an arcade game, or a game inspired by one, you are focusing on the Base Layer. Anna Anthropy's excellent book *A Game Design Vocabulary* focuses on the skills a game maker needs to make a strong Base Layer. The Base Layer is well-suited to prototyping, for early testing with a real audience—"Here's my prototype, do you find it fun?"—and for understanding the nature of the game that you are making. For service games, the Base Layer can be important, but it is rarely sufficient.

A successful Base Layer for a service game has the following characteristics:

- It is *fun*, for some value of fun.

- It is *replayable* (like the maps of a first-person shooter or the procedurally-generated experience of an endless runner) or cheap to develop (like the designed levels of a Match-3 game).

- It can *connect with the Retention Layer* to give the player a sense of progression.

- It has elements of choice, randomness, skill, interacting systems or other players to create *unpredictability* (although many successful service games choose to downplay skill, particularly on mobile).

FUN

"Being really fun" is a good starting point for your Base Layer. Our product is an entertainment product and making something that players enjoy playing is crucial. Fun is in the eye of the beholder, and what I find fun may not be the same as what you find fun.

Not all games are fun. I've enjoyed playing *Papers, Please*, Lucas Pope's dystopian take on running a fictional, Soviet border crossing. It is a game with high levels of empathy, encouraging players to understand the human challenges of being a bureaucrat in a difficult situation, trying to do the right thing while also protecting his family, keeping his job and not being arrested. It is an excellent game, and is, on some level, fun. On the other hand, it is a serious game, making players think about serious topics, and is rightly cited as an example of games as an art form. It is nevertheless a "good" game, with smart mechanics and a strong sense of narrative and setting. That, for me, is close enough to fun to pass this test. Because *Papers, Please* is a paid game, it is not trying to get players to play it for a long period of time. It can afford to be more thoughtful, perhaps even less "fun" than other games because its commercial success does not depend on it being fun to play for a year or more.

The Base Layer is limited in what it can achieve in a service game. If you have a Base Layer in your game, it is necessary that it be fun but not sufficient. While I always recommend that developers seek to maximise the fun in their game, I am uncomfortable on relying on "be super fun" as your primary strategy for ensuring a long life for your games. We need more techniques, as we will cover when we discuss the Retention Layer in the next chapter.

REPLAYABILITY

In the world of product games, we have some games that are best enjoyed once, such as many action adventure, narrative or role-playing games (RPGs). We also have many games with high replayability, such as sports games and real-time strategy (RTS) games.

Service games need replayability because their commercial success comes from retention. They must keep players engaged for months or years during which time they can generate sufficient revenue to cover development costs, ongoing operational costs and the costs of acquiring customers. This means that they have tended to use some of the following elements:

Multiplayer: A multiplayer game is expensive to build and maintain. It requires a critical mass of players to maintain liquidity. On the other hand, other humans are a wonderful source of variety and unpredictability. Many of the most successful service games are multiplayer, such as *League of Legends, Crossfire* and *Hearthstone*.

Multiplayer on PC or console tends to be synchronous, where multiple players play on the same map or level at the same time. On mobile, we tend to see more games with asynchronous gameplay, where players take turns to interact, such as the battles in *Clash of Clans* or the turn-based gameplay of *Words with Friends* and *Draw Something*.

Procedural Generation: Endless runners, such as *Temple Run, Subway Surfers* or *Jetpack Joyride*, often use pre-designed sections of the level that are chained together to create an infinite length of track for the player to explore. *Angry Birds Transformers* uses a similar procedural generation system, although its levels are finite.

Reasons to Play Again: Level-based games such as *Angry Birds* and *Candy Crush Saga* use a variety of techniques to make players choose to replay a level, such as star systems or high score leaderboards. These are covered in more detail in Chapter 3: The Retention Layer.

Cheap Content: Some games eschew replayability in favour of cheap content drops. *Angry Birds*, *Candy Crush Saga* and *Gardenscapes* are all examples of games in which the replayability is less important than cheap level creation. Many AAA studios struggle with this point, and end up making Base Layers that take advantage of the expensive skills that these studios have developed in art, animation, audio and level design. This is fine in a multiplayer game in which players will revisit the same Base Layer level multiple times, but it is commercially unsustainable if players only visit a level once or twice.

The importance of replayability is why narrative games struggle in the service era. A narrative game like *Dear Esther*, sometimes pejoratively called a walking simulator, offers an unusual and uncomfortable narrative experience that can be completed in two hours. Although it has some replayability, it is unlikely that players will play it dozens of times, and most will only play it once. A free game that puts expensive narrative at its heart will find it difficult to generate a commercial return.

CONNECTING WITH THE RETENTION LAYER

Most successful service games have a strong connection between the Base and Retention Layers, a topic we will cover in Chapter 4: The Core Loop and the Gearbox. Even games with simple Base and Retention Layers achieve this. Let's take the example of one of the earliest endless runners, *Temple Run*, first released in 2011.

- Players run as far as they can.

- They collect coins and powerups.

- They get a multiplier based on the number of achievements they have earned.

- Their final score involves points per metre run and coin collected, multiplied by their achievement multiplier.

To increase your multiplier, you need to get more achievements, which require skill (Run 5,000 metres), grind (Collect 100,000 lifetime coins) or purchase (Unlock four characters, which can be done using currency that can be purchased with real money or earned by collecting it in the Base Layer). It is a clever system that connects actions in the Base Layer to progress in the Retention Layer, encouraging players to use achievements and the in-game store to attain the overall goal of getting a better score.

THE ROLE OF SKILL IN THE BASE LAYER

Back in the heyday of Facebook games, one publisher received a pitch from a developer. In essence, the pitch was "we are going to make a game like those Facebook games out there, but with more skill." To which the publisher replied, "I don't understand. Why would you put skill into a game?"

There is no right answer to how much skill your service game needs. Free-to-play games and the emergence of smartphones and tablets as important gaming devices have widened the potential audience beyond the traditional 15- to 30-year-old male. The gaming audience now encompasses all ages and genders. The value of skill in your game design depends on the target audience and genre. Successful service games exist with Base Layers that range from the hyper-skilful gameplay of first-person shooters (FPS) like *Counterstrike: Go* to the skill-less roulette wheel of *Pirate Kings*.

Determining whether your target audience values twitch or decision-making skills more is an important service-game decision. Most twitch-based games focus on competition as a motivator. As gamers age, they value competition less. Analyst firm Quantic Foundry has collected data from 300,000 gamers who have completed its Gamer Motivation Profile. It defines "competition" as the appeal of competing with other players in duels, matches, or team-versus-team scenarios. Co-founder and analytics lead Nick Yee has determined that competition is a primary motivation for the under-25 age group, particularly males, but that it drops steadily over time.[4] (See Figure 2.1.)

As players age, their reflexes slow down, and they may no longer be as good as they once were at twitch-based gameplay. For some players, it may be that their preferences change. For others (and I include myself in this), the decline in competition as a primary motivation may be because they are no longer good enough at these games to be competitive, so they choose other genres. Without practice, their (or should I say my?) skills atrophy, and the cycle accelerates.

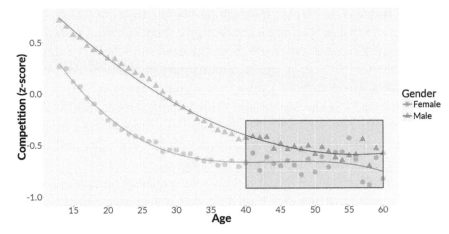

FIGURE 2.1 How players value "Competition" by age.[5]

Some service games care more about the perception of skill than the actual skill required. In *Marvel Contest of Champions*, a skilful player can win the beat 'em-up Base Layer more easily than an unskilled player, but most of the time, the outcome is decided by the statistics of the two characters who are fighting one another. These statistics are determined in the Retention Layer. The key for the designer is to make sure that players *feel* as if their actions in the Base Layer matter. Perception is more important than reality.

In *Fundamentals of Game Design*, designer Ernest Adams distinguishes between intrinsic skill and stress.

- Intrinsic skill is the level of skill needed to surmount the challenge if the player had an unlimited time in which to do it. An archer needs a certain amount of skill to hit its target; trivia games require factual knowledge.

- Stress is when you increase the pressure on a player's skill by applying additional factors, such as the constant arrival of new tetrominoes, the blocks found in *Tetris*, or the need to prioritise targets in a light gun game such as *Time Crisis*.

I tend to use the word *intensity*. Many service games, particularly on mobile, are lean-back entertainment, closer to light entertainment on television than high-octane blockbuster movies. If a game is too intense for too long, it risks not only losing players from this session but making them disinclined to come back next time.

Make sure you have a plan for the intensity of your games. High intensity is fine, if that is your audience, but give them respite. *Clash Royale* games have a fixed duration of three minutes, and the last minute is intense because the rate at which resources are delivered is doubled for both players. Tower defence games have waves of enemies. Match-based games such as FPSs and Multiplayer Online Battle Arenas (MOBAs) give players respite between matches. Even endless runners have moments when there are no imminent hazards and players can relax and regain their composure before the intensity rises again.

If you want to achieve the largest possible audience, be cautious about making a game that requires high skill and is also high intensity. As a developer, you need to be aware that competition only appeals to a subset of players, and as those players age, the desire for competitive gameplay decreases. Some players never lose it and are always motivated by competition, whereas others were always alienated by it. That is not to say you can't do it at all; there are many successful skill-based service games, particularly on PC. But be aware of the trade-offs you are making when you make these design decisions.

As Ken Wong, designer of *Monument Valley*, says, "The feeling that games need to function as a sport, with a focus on skill and goals, led to a certain culture where only some games were marketed and talked about as 'real games.' We are now seeing a diversification in the kinds of games people want to play and create."[6]

THE ROLE OF UNPREDICTABILITY IN THE BASE LAYER

Unpredictable outcomes make games more fun and more replayable. Unpredictability comes from three main sources: random chance, other human players, and emergent properties of the game systems.[7] Although unpredictability is good, when that unpredictability is driven too heavily by randomness, players feel that their actions have little impact on the game.

Multiplayer games can achieve all the unpredictability that they need from the actions of the other players. The map and the placement of all the power-ups might be known to all players, but whether a sniper will be waiting to pick off any player who tries to grab the health pack is unknown.

Each level of *Angry Birds* has uncertainty because of the physics engine that drives the game. When a player catapults a bird into the structure that they must destroy, exactly what happens next is determined by tiny variations in the speed and angle that the bird hits the structure. In a Match-3

BOOKS TO HELP YOU MAKE A BETTER BASE LAYER

- Ernest Adams, *Fundamentals of Game Design*
- Anna Anthropy and Naomi Clarke, *A Game Design Vocabulary*
- Raph Koster, *A Theory of Fun*
- Katie Salen and Eric Zimmerman, *Rules of Play*
- Jesse Schell, *A Book of Lenses*

game like *Bejeweled*, success is influenced by the random drops of new jewels whenever a player matches three or more jewels in a row, combined with the potential emergent behaviour of cascading matches.

Your goal is to make players enjoy your Base Layer enough that they want to play it again. Unpredictability is a key component of replayability. Deciding how much skill your Base Layer is going to require, whether that skill requirement is based on physical skill or decision making and how you are going to ensure sufficient, enjoyable unpredictability, are key design tasks when creating a successful Base Layer.

DO YOU EVEN NEED A BASE LAYER?

In Chapter 1, I talked about the developers who heckled Bill Mooney with shouts of "it's not a game" during his acceptance speech when *Farmville* won the Best Online/Social Game award at the 2010 Game Developers Choice Awards. I have spent a lot of time thinking about why a certain group of developers were so negative towards a game that was popular with tens of millions of players and that I, who consider myself a core gamer, enjoyed playing—a lot.

My conclusion is that *Farmville* does not have a Base Layer. *Farmville* has loops of planting and harvesting, with an eye towards efficiency and, for some players, decoration. There is no fail state in *Farmville*, or in the many similar games in its genre. You never see a Game Over screen. You cannot lose. For a subset of people, that means that *Farmville* can never be a game. They see a "spreadsheet" that just ticks up, and that has no meaningful gameplay.

There are whole genres of games that are just "spreadsheet" games, from resource managers like the *-ville* series of games to idle games like *Nonstop Knight, Clicker Heroes* or *Adventure Capitalist*. Those games are built around progression, achievement, unlocks and levelling up. They are not Killer games in the Bartle taxonomy, but Achiever games (see Bartle Types: Killers, Achievers, Explorers and Socialisers on p. 28). They appeal to a different type of player.

BARTLE TYPES: KILLERS, ACHIEVERS, EXPLORERS, AND SOCIALISERS (FIGURE 2.2)

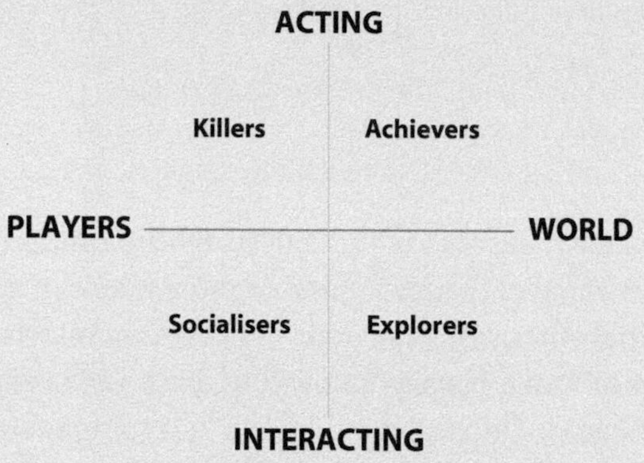

ACTING

Killers   Achievers

PLAYERS ———————————————— **WORLD**

Socialisers   Explorers

INTERACTING

FIGURE 2.2   The Bartle Player Types.[9]

Killers: Get their satisfaction from *acting* on *other players*. Motivated by competition, the joy of winning and human interaction. A subset of Killers, such as trolls and griefers, enjoy making other players miserable.

Achievers: Get their satisfaction from *acting* on the *game world*. They enjoy making progress, levelling up, earning achievements and getting their *World of Warcraft* character to level 60. Gamification works well on Achievers.

Explorers: Get satisfaction from *interacting* with the *game world*. Explorers want to know more about the game world. This can be technocratic: how can I do odd things in the game, like rocket-jumping in *Quake* or driving cars off tall buildings in *Grand Theft Auto?* It can also be story-driven, either through narrative-centric design of games like *Dear Esther, Depression Quest* and *The Last of Us* or lore-driven, such as when a player chooses to seek out and read the backstory to every item in a role-playing game.

Socialisers: Get satisfaction from *interacting* with *other players*. For these players, time spent in a virtual world is best spent socially. They often play the games that other people are playing because that maximises the chance for social interaction, or they treat games as chat rooms, rather than places where they must strive for progress.

All players are a bit of everything, although usually one or two Bartle types are more dominant. Very roughly, the gaming population is equally split between the types, although Killers have more games made for them and are also easier to monetise. For more information on the types, see Professor Richard Bartle's Book, *Designing Virtual Worlds*.[8]

The biggest challenge to accepting the position of the hecklers that *Farmville* is not a game is that there are many traditional games that have a Base Layer and a Retention Layer but where it is possible to choose not to engage with the Base Layer at all.

The *Total War* series of games from Creative Assembly involves fighting tactical battles on 3D battle maps while vying with AI opponents for control of a strategic map. My favourite of the many *Total War* games is *Medieval 2*, released in 2006. In that game, you fight to secure domination of the whole of Europe, starting in 1066, against rival nations including the Moors, the French, the Rus and the Arabs. When I start playing, I fight the tactical battles because they are evenly matched. I am not yet able to field an army of such overwhelming force that my victory is inevitable. As soon as I can, I start using the autoplay option: I am more interested in the grand strategy across the map of Europe, Asia and North Africa than in the tactical combat of the individual battles. My focus and enjoyment has shifted from the Base Layer to the Retention Layer.

A simple way to think about it is to consider football (soccer for US readers). Electronic Arts publishes *FIFA*, a Base Layer–focused game where players take control of virtual soccer stars to compete in football matches. Sega publishes *Football Manager*, a Retention Layer–focused game that is focused on everything but the match—training, recruitment, tactics, finance and more. Both are football games, but in *Football Manager*, the football match is simulated, not played. As I discussed in the previous chapter, EA has now added a Retention Layer, *FIFA Ultimate Team*, to a franchise that was previously focused on a Base Layer experience. The Retention Layer gameplay has become so popular that players have demanded that Electronic Arts adds a button that lets them complete matches automatically, without having to play them.

Let me just repeat that: A Base Layer game like *FIFA* has added a mode that is popular, profitable and has players clamouring *not* to play the Base Layer. That suggests that there is something they value in the new mode, and that the Base Layer gameplay is no longer the only thing that draws their attention.

Resource management games like *Hay Day* or *SimCity* have no meaningful Base Layer. Their gameplay resides in a different place, a more strategic layer that I call the *Retention Layer*. The gamers who hate these types of games, or deride them as not even being games, are gamers for whom Base Layer gameplay is more fun and enjoyable than Retention Layer gameplay. That is fair enough for them, but that does not mean that Retention Layer gameplay is not important for many millions of gamers in the world. A game can have Base Layer gameplay, Retention Layer gameplay or both.

CHAPTER 3

The Retention Layer

THE RETENTION LAYER KEEPS people playing your game for days, weeks, months and years. You can think of the Retention Layer as the systems and feedback that we give the player to know that she is making progress. It forms the *strategy* of how you design your game to encourage players to return regularly over a long period of time. (In contrast, Return Hooks, which I address in Chapter 6, are the *tactics* you use to get a player to come back next time.) There is no "right" way of doing a Retention Layer. The nature of a Retention Layer varies with genre, and its complexity must be adapted for the target audience. In PC and console development, the Retention Layer provides depth and long-term engagement. In mobile games, it is the Retention Layer that enables titles to move from being snackable fun into enduring experiences that keep players engaged for months or years.

Candy Crush Saga developer King built the case for its initial public offering and subsequent sale to Activision on the strength of its Retention Layer. In the S-1 Registration Statement that King filed to go public, it stated its primary strategy was "designing high quality game IP, selecting the most popular ones through our tournament portal and adapting them into our *Saga* format for launch on mobile and social platforms." In Pyramid terms, King tested the Base Layer on its website. If it proved to be compelling, King added its proven Retention Layer—the "*Saga* format"— and released the combined package on mobile and Facebook.[1] It used the technique on games including *Candy Crush Saga*, *Pet Rescue Saga*, *Farm Heroes Saga* and *Bubble Witch Saga*.[2]

In the rest of this chapter, I set out 18 techniques that you can use in your Retention Layer, ranging from the basic (high scores and levels) to the profound (appointment mechanics, nested loops and stars as currency). The chapter should be read in conjunction with the chapters on the Session.

RETENTION LAYER 1: BE REALLY FUN

Fun is important. Some games have little beyond "be really fun" as a strategy to bring players back. This is a risky strategy. I recommend you try to be really fun but that you also employ other techniques to draw players back in as well.

Sometimes novelty is enough to deliver the fun. When Atari released *Pong*, many people had never had the type of experience that *Pong* offered before. We recently saw two waves of expansion of the games audience, as first Facebook games (also known as social games) and then mobile games on iOS and Android made games accessible to new audiences, many of whom had rarely played games before. When players are exposed to novelty, it is possible to grab their attention with simple, enjoyable games that would sink without trace on traditional platforms. This creates a temporary gold rush when simple games flourish, drawing more game makers onto the platform, which pushes up the threshold for success. We are just at the end of one of those waves.

As the industry has developed, so has the audience. We must keep looking for new additions to the Retention Layer to satisfy their demand for novelty and to strengthen our ability to deliver games with enduring value for our players.

RETENTION LAYER 2: HIGH SCORE

In *Pong*, the Retention Layer consisted of nothing more than "being really fun," together with six words printed on an instruction card:

Avoid missing ball for high score.

Remember that *Pong* had novelty and a powerful Base Layer going for it. It is risky to rely on this strategy alone in a crowded market.

A modern game like the hyper-difficulty puzzler *Super Hexagon* goes for the same approach.

RETENTION LAYER 3: PERSISTENT HIGH SCORE

Making players *remember* their last high score is a weak Retention Layer. These days, a computer does that work. In *Crossy Road*, the player's best score is shown in the top left corner of the mobile screen. The desire to keep playing to get the highest score possible is increased by a reminder that you have a personal best to beat.

This works well when paired with a strong, repeatable Base Layer. It is a classic system from the era of arcade games that still holds up well in the 21st century. Its primary weakness is that, as the player improves, so the probability of beating her high score decreases because her existing score is already high. She will need many attempts to improve. Her willingness to keep trying to improve the score, despite a decreasing probability of achieving it, will eventually hit a wall and she will leave your game.

RETENTION LAYER 4: LEADERBOARDS

For some players, it is not enough to beat themselves; it is better to beat other people (Bartle Achievers compared with Bartle Killers—see Bartle Types: Killers, Achievers, Explorers, Socialisers on p. 28).

In the days of *Pong*, before games kept high scores, players did it themselves in a lo-fi way. Andy Beaudoin, design director at Turn 10, reminisced: "the chalkboard of high scores was the makeshift Retention Layer at my local coin-op arcade when I was growing up. Getting my name on that chalkboard was more important than girls … for the years before high school, at least."

Early arcade games built on the success of "one more go" gameplay by allowing players to enter three initials to immortalise their score (Figure 3.1).

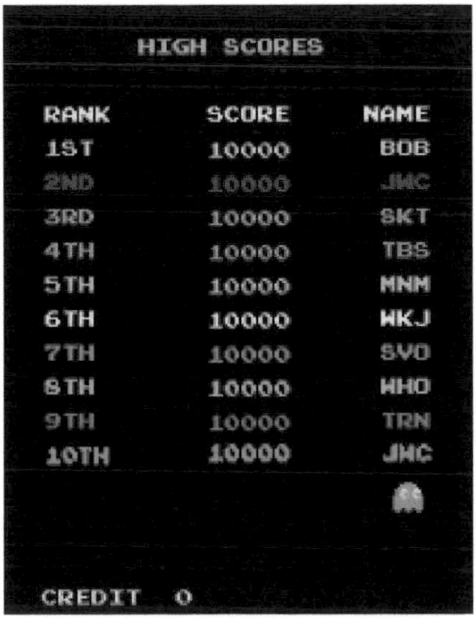

FIGURE 3.1   The high score table, or leaderboard, in *Pac-Man*.

Leaderboards struggle with the problem that they become demotivating once an exceptionally skilled—or lucky—player gets an outlandish score, placing them at the top of the leaderboard and out of reach of most players. Arcade games handle this by resetting the high scores when the machine is turned off at the wall. (Did you ever do that? No one ever admits to it.) Modern games like *Bejeweled Blitz* take a different approach by using seasons.

RETENTION LAYER 5: SEASONS

Bejeweled Blitz is a fast-paced Match-3 game developed by Popcap. Players have 60 seconds to earn the highest score they can by matching three or more jewels in a row. The jewels explode, new jewels cascade down from above in a random pattern that offers the potential for more matches, leading to a chain reaction of explosions, bonuses and power-ups. The game, by definition, can only last for 60 seconds, or a few seconds more with certain power-ups. Players always have time for one more go.

Bejeweled Blitz on Facebook uses a season mechanic. A player can see how his best score that week ranks with those of his friends. The high score table is reset every week. Whenever one of the player's friends beat his high score, he is notified, giving him a nudge to bring him back to the game. The weekly reset means that a player has the chance to be at the top of the leaderboard again because the skilled or lucky player does not get to stay at the top of the leaderboard forever.

Collectible card game *Hearthstone* uses a similar system. Each calendar month, players try to climb the ladder to reach the coveted Legend status. This is not a leaderboard, in that players don't have to be the best, but they must have beaten enough people on the ladder to be granted the achievement of reaching Legend. At the end of each month, progress is reset, so players can attempt to reach the top again. By zeroing the leaderboards, Blizzard encourages committed players to work towards Legend status every month, and less committed players can be reassured that the rankings are reset every month. And if they haven't made much progress towards Legend this month, they can try again next time with the benefit of having honed their skills and earned additional cards in the meantime.[3]

THE IMPORTANCE OF CEREMONY

When a player destroys a row of jewels in *Bejeweled Blitz,* the ensuring cascade of explosions is gorgeous, showcasing PopCap's skills in animation, art and audio. The same is true in the success animations at the end of each level of casual game *Peggle;* as the last ball approaches the last peg on the bagatelle table, time dilates, Beethoven's *Ode to Joy* plays and the player is rewarded with a feast of visual and aural rewards.

This "PopCapification" is part of the charm and success of these games. Amplifying the emotion a player is already feeling with ceremony is an important part of service-game success.[4]

RETENTION LAYER 6: LEVELS

I cut my gaming teeth on a home computer called the ZX Spectrum. It was launched in 1982, with 16 Kb of memory, later upgraded to 48 Kb, and boasted colour output as well as a strange rubber keyboard. It was a huge success, outselling both the Commodore 64 and, according to Tristan Donovan, author of *Replay,* "for a brief moment, it was thought to be the world's bestselling computer. Such was its success that Britain's Prime Minister Margaret Thatcher even showed the Spectrum to the visiting Japanese premier as an example of the UK's technological superiority."[5]

One of the most iconic games for the ZX Spectrum was developed by teenage programmer Matthew Smith. *Manic Miner* was a platform game where players had to complete 20 levels of jumping from platform to platform, avoiding deadly hazards and surreal enemies that included mutant telephones and aggressive toilets (Figure 3.2).

Manic Miner was hard in a way that few games would dare to be in the 21st century. At the start of the game, the player has three lives. When players touch a fixed hazard or a moving enemy, they lose a life and go to the start of the level. Completing a level requires a combination of knowing the successful route from start to exit together with pixel-perfect jumping and exquisite timing to avoid the moving enemies. With all three lives gone, players were back at the beginning—not to the beginning of the level, but to the beginning of the entire game.

Manic Miner had a finite set of 20 fiendishly-challenging levels. The original *Angry Birds* game now has about 500 levels. *Gardenscapes* has

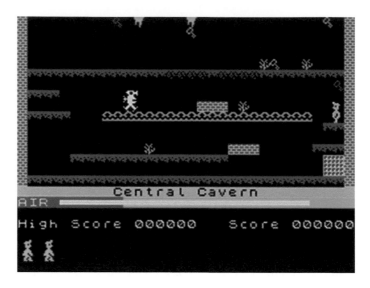

FIGURE 3.2 *Manic Miner* on the ZX Spectrum.

more than 1,500, and *Candy Crush Saga* has more than 3,000. It's not infinite, but it feels like it when you first start.

The motivation to see what's in the next level is a powerful driver of retention.

RETENTION LAYER 7: GETTING TO THE END

Not all games have an end. In fact, for a free-to-play (F2P) game, most experts (including me) recommend that your game is endless; it should offer enjoyable, repeatable gameplay for many years to come.

Many product-based games do have an end. *Manic Miner* had 20 levels, which I completed. (I cheated. Before you loaded the game, you could type "POKE 35136,0" to get infinite lives. Look, it was bloody hard, alright?) *Bubble Bobble* had 100 levels, which I also completed. (This time with no cheating.)

Having an end is a trade-off. It may damage the long-term retention and monetisation of your game, but it is a powerful motivator for many people.

RETENTION LAYER 8: LEVELLING UP

For many humans, it can be hard to tell if you achieved much in a given day. Did you do well at work? At school? At home? Did you make progress in your life? Was today a move-forwards day, a move-backwards day or a stand-still day? At the end of the day, have you achieved anything more than keeping your job or getting your children through school, the evening meal and into bed with no more than the usual number of scrapes and bruises?

Video games are not like that. Video games are full of feedback. If you spend an hour hitting a wall with a pickaxe in *Ultima Online*, your Mining skill increases, and you are a step closer towards the Grand Master title. If you fight using your warrior in *Dragon Age*, you earn experience points, level up and unlock a range of new abilities or powers. You make *progress*.

In a graduation speech at the University of Chicago in 2016, economist Erik Hurst drew a startling conclusion: video games are so much better at delivering a sense of progress, achievement and autonomy that low-skilled (that is anyone with less than a bachelor's degree) male workers are choosing to play video games rather than engage with the labour market. Hurst found that in 2015, 22% of lower-skilled men aged 21–30 had not worked at all during the prior 12 months. On average, men in that cohort had gained four hours per week of leisure time between the early 2000s and 2015; three of those hours were now spent playing computer games.[6] Typically being unemployed leads to dissatisfaction with life, but this cohort do not seem to be suffering from such an outcome. Hurst concludes that video games are better than a terrible job. "These technological innovations have made leisure time more enjoyable. This acts like an increase in an individual's reservation wage. For lower-skilled workers, with low market wages, it is now more attractive to take leisure."

Hurst argues that video games are better at providing positive feedback and a sense of advancement than the real world of jobs, relationships and commitments. His arguments chime with the principles of Self-Determination Theory (SDT), a framework to explain why people play video games, which was proposed by researchers Andrew Przybylski, Scott Rigby and Richard Ryan. SDT posits that people engage in voluntary behaviour like play or enjoy their work more to the extent that it satisfies three elements:

- **Competence:** feeling like they are doing well and making progress.

- **Autonomy:** having meaningful choices over what to do and confidence that those choices matter.

- **Relatedness:** having a meaningful connection with other players or even non-player characters.[7]

Levelling up delivers against the need for competence and progression, which Hurst identified as often lacking in the workplace. Competence can encompass many facets. It includes the twitch-style physical skill needed in the Base Layer, strategic mastery in the Retention Layer or simply making good decisions. When those decisions are meaningful and have consequences that matter, it is even more motivating to players.

Levelling up is at the heart of the fun in many idle games. In 2016, Nick Yee of Quantic Foundry carried out research into the audience of idle game players using their data set of 300,000 gamers. For the idle games Yee analysed (*Adventure Capitalist*, *Clicker Heroes* and *Crusaders of the Lost Idols*), the audience is *gamers*. Seventy per cent of the players of these games identify as core gamers, 20% as hardcore gamers and 10% as casual gamers, a distribution that matches the baseline data for all the gamers in their data set. Among the games that were disproportionately popular amongst these idle game players were core role-playing game (RPG) titles like *Diablo III* and *Fallout 4*, and massively multiplayer online (MMO) games like *The Elder Scrolls Online* and *EVE Online*.

Yee also looked at what motivated the gamers, using his gamer motivation analysis.[8] Yee found that idle game players were most motivated by Completion (collecting stars, completing all missions) and Power (levelling up, getting powerful gear) and least motivated by Excitement (fast-paced, thrilling, surprises) and Fantasy (being someone else, somewhere else).

As Yee explains, "Idle Clickers attract core gamers (especially core RPG gamers) because they isolate the power progression and accumulation mechanics from the typical trappings of AAA RPGs. These are the gamers who enjoy the levelling up and power accumulation in RPGs, but are less interested in big-action combat or elaborate fantasy settings that often come bundled together in an RPG."[9]

Or to put it another way, you get all the joyful feedback that you are making progress and doing well without any of that messy combat or story or world-building. For some players, the progression of the idle game is min-maxing in its most joyful form. For others, particularly Bartle Explorers, the idle game is the boring grind of an RPG bereft of the lore, narrative and characterisation that makes RPGs worthwhile in the first place.

Yet again, there is no right or wrong, only consequences.

MIN-MAXING

TV Tropes defines min-maxing as, "the art of optimizing a character's abilities during creation by maximizing the most important skills and attributes, while minimizing the cost. Seen from a purely mathematical and gamist perspective, it's an elegant process of minimum expenditure for maximum result. Seen from a more narrativist perspective, the process may end up creating a character with absolutely no unifying reason to have the abilities that it does." In video games, a min-maxer is a player who gets "innate satisfaction from playing the game 'optimally'."[10]

RETENTION LAYER 9: MAKING PROGRESS ACROSS A MAP

What is better than a number going up in a video game? Seeing that number go up as you make progress across a map!

Figure 3.3 shows the *Candy Crush Saga* map. When a player completes a level, as well as feeling the sense of achievement from his level number rising from 112 to 113, he sees his train moving forward through the fantasy candy land on the swirling, brightly-coloured map.

- The map rewards players with visual progression to complement the increase in level number.

- The non-linear design allows players to see up to 50 levels on the same screen.

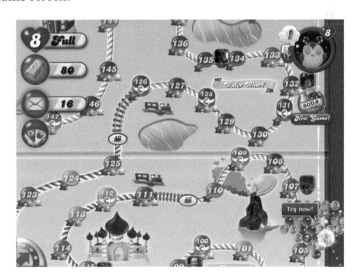

FIGURE 3.3   The map screen from *Candy Crush Saga*.

HOW FACEBOOK CHANGES GAME DESIGN

The *Saga* format created by King is dying as Facebook changes the way it interacts with games. When the *Saga* format emerged in 2012, the cheapest and most-effective ways of acquiring new customers was to use the built-in virality of the Facebook platform. Games were able to post notifications to many places within Facebook and offered rewards to players for connecting to Facebook (if they were playing outside the Facebook platform, for example on mobile) and inviting their friends.

Virality has been on the decrease ever since. Fewer players are choosing to connect their mobile game to Facebook, perhaps as a result of increasing social stigma from spamming their friends' timelines. Facebook has also dialled back the virality, for two reasons:

- Spam from games was a negative user experience that hurt Facebook overall.
- Facebook generates its revenue from ads. It would rather sell users to game companies than give them users for free.

The *Candy Crush Saga* map remains a masterpiece of design, but as the platform environment changes, developers must find new ways to attract and engage their players on a social level.

- It grabs pictures of friends from Facebook, providing social proof.

- It is a leaderboard hidden in plain sight: To Bartle Killers, the map is obviously a leaderboard; to everyone else, the map shows progress and that their friends are playing *Candy Crush Saga* too.

Many developers "innovate" by making their version of the *Candy Crush Saga* map more high-fidelity: 3D, more animation and more high-tech. In the process, they often lose the 50 levels, the social proof, the leaderboard hidden in plain sight and the pull-through of the swirly progression path. It is an innovation that lacks almost everything that made the original great.

The *Candy Crush Saga* map is a visual, spatial and numerical recognition of achievement that shows the player that he is making progress. It is good to tell people when they level up; it is better to show them.

RETENTION LAYER 10: LOOPS

Humans like to finish what they've started. Most of us are trained from an early age to be "finishers": to keep our promises and to demonstrate "consistency," a term coined by psychologist Robert Cialdini in his seminal

ROBERT CIALDINI'S SIX PRINCIPLES OF *INFLUENCE*

Robert Cialdini is professor of Marketing and professor of Psychology at Arizona State University. That is a dangerous combination. In 1985, Cialdini published *Influence*, in which he identified six principles that all compliance professionals—by which he means anyone in sales, marketing or negotiation—use to persuade people.[11] These six principles have stood the test of time and are visible in many successful games.

Social proof: People are likely to behave like other people around them. It's why people form queues (yes, I'm British) or stare at the sky if other people do so.

Reciprocity: If you do someone a favour, they feel they owe you. Salespeople will harness this by offering you a coffee at the start of the conversation or by negotiating a discount on your behalf from their boss.

Commitment and consistency: The importance of keeping your promises is a core tenet of most human societies. Games harness this technique with appointment mechanics: if you plant crops in a resource-management game, you are implicitly promising that you will return at a particular time in the future to harvest them.

Likeability: There is a reason that salespeople are friendly, good-looking and well-dressed. People find it easier to like attractive, friendly people and are more likely to buy from them or to do as they ask.

Authority: When you are too old (or unattractive) to use likeability as your sales technique, it is time to resort to authority. Wear a suit and tie, cultivate an air of knowledge and expertise, and you will be more able to persuade people to do what you want.

Scarcity: If all else fails, invoke a sense of urgency. Closing down sale. Must end soon. "I can only offer this deal until the end of the financial quarter." Scarcity makes people buy things right now. Anyone who has ever bought a game in a Steam sale understands the value of scarcity in making people buy things.

book, *Influence* (see Robert Cialdini's Six Principles of *Influence*). Many games build a set of nested loops to harness this human preference and to create games that keep players coming back for more.

One way to think about it is to have short, medium and long-term goals. In a role-playing game, the short-term goal might be "avoid being killed by these orcs." The medium goal might be to complete a mission that involves rescuing half a dozen villagers from said orcs. The long-term goal might be to discover your heritage as the long-lost king and kick the evil orcs out of your land. These nested loops keep players engaged.

Some service games, particularly ones that focus on the Retention Layer, have many nested loops inside each other. In farming game *Hay Day*:

- Players have crops growing that will be ready to be harvested at different times.

- They have basic farming machinery like dairies that turn milk into cream, and sugar presses that convert sugar cane into sugar or maple syrup.

- Advanced machines combine cream, sugar and wheat into cream cakes.

- Animals need to be fed and milked, or have their eggs collected.

- Other loops include a delivery boat that needs certain products once every 16 hours, and non-player characters (NPCs) who have requests for multiple items that players need to fulfil.

Psychologist Jamie Madigan points out that these uncompleted loops are compelling because of two related psychological phenomena:

- The *Zeigarnik effect* describes how we tend to find it easier to recall a task and the details surrounding it, when we have begun to undertake it but were unable to complete it. It is named after Russian psychologist Bluma Zeigarnik who observed that waiters seem able to remember the details of complex orders until they are fulfilled, at which point the information vanishes from their memory.

- The *endowed-progress effect* means that if you give people a feeling of advancing towards a goal, they're more likely to try harder to reach that goal, even relative to people who have to put in the same effort but have no sense that they have started. The classic example is when two customers are given a loyalty card. One card has eight blank spaces. The other has ten blank spaces but two are already stamped. Both cards require eight more actions to complete. In an experiment at a car wash, researchers found that 19% of people with the blank card came back to redeem it, but 34% of people with the "I've started, so I'll finish" card returned.[12]

Nested loops encourage people to close them while giving players a sense of competence and autonomy, which are two of the three components of self-determination theory. No matter how challenging their life in the physical world may be, in this game world, there are clear rules, predictable behaviours and certainty that if you do the right thing, you will get your just reward.

RETENTION LAYER 11: REAL TIME

A defining feature of service games is the use of real time. Whether it is the energy gating of early Zynga games, the implicit commitment to return to a game of *Words with Friends,* the length of time that it takes to raise a dragon in *Dragon City* or the monthly seasons of *Hearthstone*, the passing of real time is a key component of successful free-to-play games.

In the old world of boxed products, time was often something that you could fast-forward. *XCom* enabled you to run time at high speed until you spotted an alien incursion. Service games often make time more significant. In *Candy Crush Saga*, you regain a life every ten minutes. In *Tiny Tower*, it takes real time for the tiny people in the game to complete their tasks. Sometimes these games use the local clock, which makes it easy for players to cheat; other games use a server. (I know that *Tiny Tower* uses the clock on my phone because I once cheated by moving my clock forward until it was running 3.5 days ahead of time. Then I missed an important meeting because my calendar alarm didn't alert me. I have stopped doing this now.)

Successful service games use the existence of a server-side clock to create new gameplay patterns, loops, and rewards that make less sense in an offline world. Understanding when and how to harness real-world time for your game is a crucial element of building a successful Retention Layer.

RETENTION LAYER 12: APPOINTMENT MECHANICS

The appointment mechanic is one of the most important elements of service-game design. Not all games have them, but they are at the heart of many successful genres. Zynga was an early master of the system, and the appointment mechanic in *Farmville* was critical to its success.

Farmville attracted a new type of gamer. The audience skewed female. It skewed older than age 30. It was an audience of everyone, but it had a high proportion of mothers and housewives.[13] In an (imagined, stereotypical)

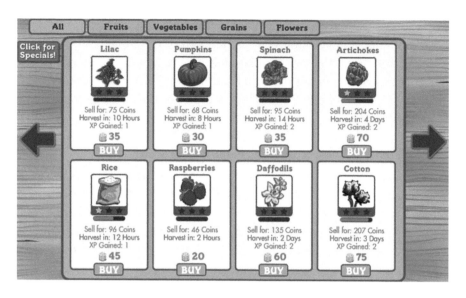

FIGURE 3.4 The planting screen in *Farmville*, which is the game's appointment mechanic.

day, such a housewife might wake before her family. She has a few moments before she must rouse them and hustle them out of the house to school. She checks Facebook. While she is there, she visits her *Farmville* farm and looks at the screen shown in Figure 3.4 to decide which crops she might plant. If her chores today include doing the laundry, grocery shopping and picking the kids up from school, she might decide that she will have some spare time at around 3 o'clock in the afternoon, about eight hours from now. Looking at the available crops, she could choose pumpkins because they will be ready at that time.

Now her chore list has extended: she must do the laundry, pick up the groceries, collect the kids from school and *harvest pumpkins*. She made the appointment with the game; the game did not make it for her. As psychologist Robert Cialdini has shown, humans are conditioned to feel bad if they don't keep their promises.[14] Zynga used that conditioning to encourage players to return at the appointed time, even to the extent of punishing them by making the crops wither and die if they didn't return on time (although this mechanic has subsequently fallen out of favour.)

An appointment mechanic is not a Tamagotchi, the digital pet launched in 1996 by Japanese toy maker Bandai. A Tamagotchi is a small, keychain-sized toy with a screen containing a game of hatching virtual pets and raising them to adulthood. Tamagotchis are demanding: players must feed them, train them, stroke them and heal them when they are ill. Criticisms of the toy led to it being banned from schools. Children sneaked the toy in anyway because a Tamagotchi left alone for a day would die.

The key difference between a Tamagotchi and an appointment mechanic is *agency*. In the original Tamagotchi design, the player had little agency over when a pet needed attention. If it was hungry, ill or desperate for the toilet, it demanded its owner's attention, even if that was at a time that was disruptive to school, work or sleep. In the *Farmville* appointment mechanic, players have much more agency over when they must return to the game to complete tasks or to collect rewards.

I can't emphasise enough the difference between an appointment mechanic and a Tamagotchi. Some games choose not to let players have the choice: the free crystals in *Marvel Contest of Champions,* which appear every 4 and 24 hours, are simple rewards for logging in. An appointment mechanic has a deeper pull on players. It gets them to think about their own time commitments, to make a promise to return in the future, and due to human nature, make them feel guilty if they don't return to make good on that promise.

RETENTION LAYER 13: NARRATIVE

"What happens next?" is perhaps the oldest trick in the book for getting people to come back to your entertainment. Television shows end on cliff-hangers. Novels end each chapter with something dangling to keep the reader reading. Video games have a narrative that leaves you wanting more.

Wait, what? Video games have narrative?

In April 2017, video-game academic Ian Bogost wrote an opinion piece in *The Atlantic* entitled "Video Games Are Better without Stories" and a subheading that proclaimed, "Film, television and literature all tell them better. So why are game still obsessed with narrative?"[15] Bogost argues that "the best interactive stories are still worse than even middling books and films," and makes the case that video games are strongest when they don't try to emulate the narrative forms of cinema, television or novels. Bogost believes that, "If there is a future of games, let alone a future in which they discover their potential as a defining medium of an era, it will be one in which games abandon the dream of becoming narrative media and pursue the one they are already so good at: taking the tidy, ordinary world apart and putting it back together again in surprising, ghastly, new ways."

Bogost's view is controversial. Developer Brianna Wu argued in response that Bogost's view is male-centric, and that perhaps story is more important to a female audience than to a male audience.[16] Perhaps men enjoy taking the world apart and putting it back together more than women do. Cambridge scientist Simon Baron-Cohen thinks so. In his book, *The Essential Difference*, he describes a difference between how male and female brains work: "The female brain is predominantly hard-wired for empathy. The male brain is predominantly hardwired for understanding and building systems."[17]

Marketers Jane Cunningham and Philippa Roberts run a consultancy focused on helping businesses connect to a female audience called Pretty Little Head. They rephrase Baron-Cohen's research. "Men understand the world by constructing systems: breaking a thing down into its component parts, in order to establish how it works and what underlying principles govern its behaviour. Women, on the other hand, understand the world by putting themselves in the shoes of others, feeling what they're feeling and seeing what they're seeing."[18]

Narrative is a compelling, powerful driver of enjoyment in video games and deployed well, it can cause players to feel something that no literary form can achieve. My go-to example of this strength is Season 1 of Telltale's *The Walking Dead* where, over five episodes, players inhabit the role of Lee, a convict whose routine transfer to prison is interrupted by a zombie outbreak. Lee joins together with a band of survivors and takes on the role of parent to Clementine, a 12-year-old girl. The season finale was a fabulous example of how a game enables a player to inhabit a role and experience certain emotions which would be hard to evoke in any other medium. For the sake of spoilers, I will say no more.

On the other hand, narrative in video games is often done badly. In *A Game Design Vocabulary*, designer Anna Anthropy says, "When I mention 'story' in a game to most players and developers, what they think of is cutscenes: an interruption of a game to show a five-minute movie, directed in obvious imitation of a Hollywood production. Or they think of a wall of expository text that the player has to stop and read or, more likely, skip annoyedly past…. The truth is that we already have all the tools we need to tell stories in games—to tell real stories, not exposition—but we don't understand those tools."[19]

Anthropy is focused on the Base Layer and prefers to use the tools of Base Layer design to drive her narrative. Much AAA development is in thrall to Hollywood production values and wishes to tell stories in a way that is familiar to cinema goers. Neither are the "correct" view, although both have a place; neither are the "correct" view because there is no such thing. For service games, the truth is more prosaic: making a game that relies on narrative for its primary retention device is likely to be prohibitively expensive.

AAA narrative costs a lot of money. Whether it is cutscenes with lengthy voiceovers by famous actors or levels designed to showcase an element of the narrative, the process requires many skilled, expensive people. When the objective is to create a finite experience that lasts for between 5 and 200 hours, that expense might be justified. When the objective is to get people playing every day for several years, it is difficult to make the financial case for that type of narrative stack up.

Service developers are experimenting with new, profitable forms of narrative. *Episode* is a narrative free-to-play game that offers short, teen-friendly stories told using snippets of dialogue that are rarely longer than a tweet. Each episode lasts between two and five minutes. There are a limited number of free episodes per session, and the first episode of a new story is always free. Readers can pay to read more, or they can pay to enhance their involvement in the storyline. I'm playing through *Mean Girls*, a sequel-of-sorts to the 2004 movie starring Lindsay Lohan. The writing is fantastic and pithy ("[My Mum] picked half my genes based on the donor's alumni status"), and the plotline revolves around getting to Yale ("I never knew anything about my father. All I had was a folder, with like, a first name and a bullet list of info … 6'1". No family history of diabetes. Yale graduate."), managing relationships and vying with arch rival Regina. Along the way, players can choose to pay with the premium currency to have coffee with boyfriend-material Micah or to buy a fancy dress for a party.

Episode seems to me to scratch the same itch as soap operas do for television watchers. That is not a criticism; although soap operas may not be high art, they require their viewers to understand a complex web of interactions between dozens of characters and a single scene lasting only a few minutes can advance multiple different plotlines. As Celia Brayfield, bestselling novelist and author of *Bestseller: Secrets of Successful Writing*, says, "I was fascinated by the fact that television viewers, who my (book) editors considered to be morons, could hold 35 storylines of a series in their heads for three months even if they missed half the episodes."[20] Those viewers are being retained by the narrative, and the human brain is a highly-tuned machine for understanding human interactions and relationships: exactly the topics that *Episode* focuses on.

Narrative games are proving to be financially successful. *Episode* has been consistently in the top-20 grossing games in the United Kingdom and the top 40 in the United States. In November 2017, Korean publisher

Nexon acquired Pixelberry Studios, developer of *Choices: Stories You Play* and other story-focused smartphone games popular with women in North America and Europe. The valuation was not disclosed, but Nexon CEO Owen Mahoney said Pixelberry was generating "tens of millions of dollars" in revenue per year and is "double-digit profitable."[21]

It is not that narrative *can't* work in a F2P game. It is that it is so expensive, relative to repeatable, scalable systems, that you must be sure that narrative is worth it before you use it. Seek out the repeatable, scalable systems first, and use narrative, like art, as an amplifier of emotion, not as the primary driver of retention.

RETENTION LAYER 14: THE STAR SYSTEM

Angry Birds, like many games, has a three-star system for completing levels as shown in Figure 3.5. When you complete a level, you are awarded one, two or three stars depending on how successful you were. Different games use different criteria for how many stars are awarded: How quickly was the game completed? What was the score? Did it use fewer attempts than normal, or fewer resources?

The objective of a star system is to bring players back into the game to replay previous levels, which is cheaper than building new levels. The weakness of the system is that it only appeals to a sub-type of players. Even an arch-completionist like me has not bothered to go

FIGURE 3.5   The three-star system in *Angry Birds*.

back to previous levels of *Angry Birds* to get three stars on every level. Making progress through the visual stages can be more rewarding than redoing previous stages. When the design encourages players to look forward rather than back, it puts pressure on the developer to churn out new levels to keep players engaged. The content treadmill is worth avoiding if you can. Be aware of this if you add star systems to your game.

RETENTION LAYER 15: STARS AS CURRENCY

Some games take the star system and make it work harder. *Kingdom Rush* is a paid, tower defence game that uses its star system as a currency.

Figure 3.6 shows the *Kingdom Rush* map. The player's progress is shown along a linear campaign path. Each node is a separate tower defence level and the player can earn up to three stars for completing it, as well as two bonus stars that can be earned by completing different modes of gameplay on the same level.

Figure 3.7 shows the upgrade screen for *Kingdom Rush*, where players spend the stars that they have earned on upgrades for their towers and special powers. Making the stars a currency is a genius move. Players value stars not just as a marker of their completionist commitment, but as a resource that needs to be harvested to make progress in the game. Players

FIGURE 3.6   The map in *Kingdom Rush*.

FIGURE 3.7   Upgrades in *Kingdom Rush.*

are encouraged to go back and replay previous levels to get the highest number of stars so that they can spend them on upgrading archer towers, reinforcements or a variety of other game systems. Stars-as-resources also acts as a difficulty balancing system. Players who are finding the game too hard are less likely to quit in frustration and never return if they are shown a clear route to making progress. When a player is stuck on a Base Layer level, she now has a choice over how she attempts to get past it; she can attempt new tactics on the same level or go back to an earlier level to earn more stars, upgrade her towers and reinforcements and try again with more powerful tools at her disposal.

It is an elegant solution to the problem of how to make it fun and rewarding to replay early levels whilst also making the star system more valuable to players.

RETENTION LAYER 16: CHALLENGES

Challenges and Achievements look similar; both involve the player receiving a task from the game, completing the task and being rewarded, whether with a quick "Well Done," a statistic-based reward such as Experience Points (XP) or currency, or a marker that recognises their success.

I define **Challenges** as tasks or objectives that a player can do many times, earning new rewards each time. **Achievements** are tasks that can only be completed once, like the trophies in a PlayStation game or Xbox Achievements. An objective to shoot 100 enemies or harvest 100 watermelons is a Challenge if it can be completed many times. If the player is only rewarded for *the first time* she shoots 100 enemies or he harvests 100 watermelons, it is an Achievement. These terms are not universally agreed across the games industry. Most people know what an Achievement is, but the term Challenge, which can also be an Objective, Quest, Task or Mission, is not established.

Achievements and Challenges deliver on the requirements of self-determination theory. They provide a permanent record of competence. They allow players to exercise autonomy in choosing which Achievements or Challenges they choose to complete, and potentially in how they complete them. Surprisingly, they may also deliver on *relatedness*, the desire of players to have a meaningful connection with other people. Researchers Przybylski, Ryan and Rigby claim that completing a quest that earns the adoration of NPCs is close enough to the real thing.[22]

Fallout Shelter, Bethesda's mobile take on its popular *Fallout* franchise, makes extensive use of a Challenge system, which they call Objectives, to drive Retention. The goal of the game is to develop an underground vault, dug into the mountainside following a nuclear apocalypse. Players allocate dwellers to appropriate jobs; breed them to get new dwellers; manage the resources of power, water and food; and develop new weapons and clothing. It is a resource-management game in the vein of *Tiny Tower* or *Hay Day*.

In Figure 3.8 I have three objectives. I can collect 4,400 power, a simple Challenge that just takes time, and will happen automatically if I engage with the game in a normal way. I can deliver 20 babies, a Challenge that is double-edged, because if I have too many children in the vault, the balance of workers to hungry mouths is upended, and all my dwellers might starve. I can also collect 11 outfits, which involves participating in a mini-exploration game based on an idle game mechanic.

Fallout Shelter's objectives are drawn from a randomised list of similar tasks. When I collect 4,400 power, a new objective will immediately appear in the list in its place: it might be to collect a random amount of power, water or food. It might be to manufacture a few weapons or outfits. It might be to send a random number of dwellers exploring in the nuclear wasteland.

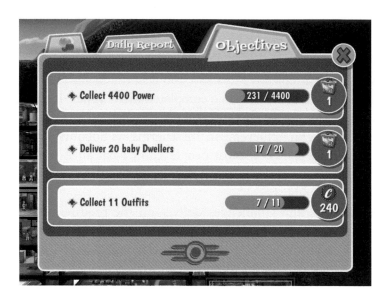

FIGURE 3.8   Objectives in *Fallout Shelter*.

The objective system has two clear purposes: to give me goals created by the game (as opposed to goals that I set myself) and to provide a mechanism of delivering currency and loot crates, which *Fallout Shelter* calls Lunchboxes, to players.

These objectives are not Achievements. None of them are memorable enough to be part of water-cooler conversations about my enjoyment of the game. They are not long-term, challenging, goals.

Fallout Shelter's objective system demonstrates the boxed product legacy of the design team. As a Bartle Achiever, I enjoyed the system, but it tended to extend my session lengths, an ambition that harks back to product design, rather than encouraging me to return to the game (i.e., improving number of sessions per day or day-by-day retention), a design objective of a service game.

In contrast, *Hearthstone's* Challenge system, which it calls quests, is a retention system, because if you complete your available quests today, you don't receive any new ones until tomorrow. *Hearthstone* is a collectible card game in which players compete in matches against other players using decks of 30 cards. The cards are a valuable resource in the game and are gained primarily by buying packs of five cards, using either real money or in-game gold. A card pack costs 100 gold.

FIGURE 3.9   *Hearthstone*'s quest system.

Each day, *Hearthstone* gives players a new mission. The player is granted a new quest each day until their three quest slots are full. Figure 3.9 shows an example quest log.

- *Day 1*: Win 2 games with Druid or Rogue; earn 40 gold.

- *Day 2*: Win 5 games with Paladin or Warrior; earn 60 gold.

- *Day 3*: Win 3 games with any class; 40 gold.

- *Day 4*: No new quests granted until you have cleared space in your quest log by clearing at least one of the previous quests.

The quests are the primary means by which *Hearthstone* gives players free currency. A quest is worth an average of about 50 gold, which equates to half a card pack. Regular players can earn a free card pack every two days or so. The quests do not expire, but a player can only have three active quests at any time.

Hearthstone is signalling that each day, it would be sensible for a player to return to the game and win between two and five matches, which would take between two and ten attempts, or about an hour of play time. If she doesn't turn up, that's fine, but from day three, she starts "losing" about

LOSS AVERSION

Loss aversion is a phrase used in economics and behavioural psychology referring to the tendency of humans to prefer to avoid losses rather than to seek gains of equivalent value. It was first identified by Amos Tversky and Daniel Kahneman in 1984, and they subsequently argued that the fear of loss is exactly twice as powerful as the prospect of gain.

A simple example is that, for most people, possessing $100 and losing it in a game is twice as emotionally painful as suddenly receiving $100 in a game is emotionally rewarding. Traditional economists regard this as irrational: in each case, your economic situation is changing by $100, so it should be irrelevant whether you already owned it. Behavioural psychologists and marketers, on the other hand, are convinced that it is a real, observable effect. I agree with them, for many reasons, not least of which is that I think that economists arguing that humans are perfectly rational are deluded. For more evidence of that position, I recommend Daniel Kahneman's *Thinking Fast and Slow* and Dan Ariely's *Predictably Irrational*.

half a pack of free cards for each day that she doesn't play, because she gets no more quests until she has cleared a slot. The mechanic is elegant and simple, triggering loss aversion to make the player come back, while still feeling generous on Blizzard's part.

Challenges are an easy system to implement and can be tweaked to meet certain objectives. They can be designed such that they extend session length or make players come back frequently. They can deliver resources into the game and make the game feel generous. They can provide purpose before players have learned to set goals themselves.

They also can be retrofitted after launch. Unless the Challenge system is the primary way in which you are delivering currency or progression into the game, they are strong candidate for releasing during soft launch, or even later, a topic I will return to in Chapter 12: Production.

RETENTION LAYER 17: ACHIEVEMENTS

Achievements are like Challenges, but they are permanent, not temporary. A player can only earn a given Achievement once.

Different Achievement implementations have different objectives. Some focus on anchoring performance expectations and giving players clear goals. Others exist to showcase elements of the game that players may not have explored, or to provide a form of social comparison in a game that lacks other social features. I divide Achievements into three main archetypes.

Pointless Achievements

Pointless Achievements exist because some platform holders insist that games should have Achievements. Some designers can't be bothered to invest time and effort into designing these systems. They only make them because they must be able to check the "Achievements" box on the specification sheet. They go through the motions. You know the ones: Shoot one enemy in the head. Shoot 10 enemies in the head. Shoot 100 enemies in the head. These Achievements are things that will happen as you play the game, whether you intend to earn them or not.

The primary value of these achievements is to signpost to achievement-centric players that the Achievement system even exists. They are underwhelming.

Reverse Achievements

Reverse Achievements are designed to enable developers to reuse expensive assets that have already been created. They encourage players to play the game in a different way. In endless runner *Jetpack Joyride,* the normal objective is to stay alive for as long as possible. Missions offer twists on this objective. "Have five near misses with missiles" encourages players to take more risks. A difficult mission requires a player to die between, for example, 1,000 and 1,100 metres. He must avoid hazards as normal for the first 1,000 metres and then seek hazards out to ensure he dies within the next 100 metres. *Plants versus Zombies* offers an Achievement for completing a night-time level without using mushrooms, plants which are specially designed to be used at night. Players would be unlikely to behave like this without the nudge from the Achievement system.

Challenging Achievements

The third type of Achievement is one that is hard. It is a genuine achievement, something that requires significant investment of time and effort. In *Hay Day*, managing to harvest 100 crops in 30 minutes requires significant planning. In *Kingdom Rush*, earning the Imperial Saviour achievement by completing the Citadel level with three surviving imperial guards requires concentration and focus. In *Red Dead Redemption*, Rockstar's take on the classic Western, you earn the Dastardly trophy by kidnapping a woman, tying her to a railroad track and watching as the locomotive runs her down.[23] Most players are unlikely to discover this achievement by accident (or maybe I'm just too nice).

Be wary about making Challenges or Achievements central to your design. One of my clients has recommended that I don't use them in my initial design work: "Nicholas, you are an achievement junkie. Only about a quarter of players are like you. If we design our game loops focused on Achievements, it will satisfy 25% of our audience and leave the rest bored or frustrated." He is right. It is vital to make sure that your game is fun and rewarding without the crutch of Achievements. They are fun, enjoyable elements that can add longevity to your game and satisfy a subset of your players. Achievements can be retrofitted easily. They may not belong in the game until you are sure you have found the fun in the core experience.

Whether you implement a rotating Challenge system, or focus on long-term Achievements, or both depends on your design goals. There is no right answer. Think about what they are for. They can be effective ways of drip-feeding currency into the economy. *Fallout Shelter* rewards players with "Caps," the game's main currency, or "Lunchboxes," which is the mechanism by which the game grants players new characters or weapons. They can encourage different ways of playing, as in *Plants versus Zombies* or *Jetpack Joyride*. They can enable developers to reuse assets by challenging completionist players to collect every item in a level or enabling Achievers to replay the games in a different way. There is no right way to use Achievements.

But try not to make them boring.

RETENTION LAYER 18: SOCIAL

Social is a powerful driver of retention. It can draw on a range of human social desires because it focuses on the interaction between humans and other humans, not between humans and the game.

In a turn-based, two-player game such as *Words with Friends* or *Draw Something*, players take turns to create a word out of tiles or to draw a picture for a friend to recognise. That friend is then notified via Facebook or the mobile app. If the friend fails to respond, he is not just letting the game down; he is breaking an implicit promise that once he starts playing, he commits to taking his turn regularly and swiftly until the game is over.

This is one of Robert Cialdini's *Influence* principles: commitment and consistency. There is a social contract to keep playing. The notification the player receives on his phone or from Facebook is a trigger to return to the game so that he can keep his promise to his friend.

A variety of connected games use this technique in different ways:

- In *World of Warcraft*, you must log in to Azeroth at the time that you promised so you can participate in a planned raid. If you don't, your guild mates may take a long time to forgive you.

- In *Game of War*, if you are not active, you will be kicked out of your alliance.

- In *Candy Crush Saga*, my cousin-once-removed, Sheila, keeps asking me for extra lives. When I was playing *Candy Crush Saga* a lot, I kept asking Sheila for extra lives and unlocks, which she kept supplying. These days, the only I reason I load *Candy Crush Saga* is to pay Sheila back. (Triggering another of Cialdini's principles: reciprocity).

- At its height, *Farmville* would encourage players to send each other's gifts of trees or farm animals. This worked brilliantly until players concluded that Zynga was harnessing their human desire not to let their friends down in a way that felt deceitful and annoying.[24]

Building a Retention Layer based on social features is expensive and challenging. A developer can either harness an existing social graph, like that of Facebook, or attempt to a build a new one, the route many MMO games take. In the former case, there is an implicit "Facebook tax," the cost of maintaining the integration and systems even as Facebook moves the goal posts. In the latter, you must build your own networking and communication tools and create ways for players to find existing friends and to make new ones. This is expensive and hard to achieve. It can be done, as many MMO games can attest, but unless it is at the core of your game, you should think very hard before embarking on this expensive route.

Done well, a social layer is one of the most compelling retention tools in existence. Players are still playing *World of Warcraft* and *EVE Online* 15 years after they were first released because of the social relationships they have made there. A good social experience can drive long-time retention and, as I will discuss shortly, is often a prime component of the Superfan Layer.

RETENTION LAYERS IN BOARD GAMES

I've focused on the Retention Layer in video games, but we are also seeing it emerge in board games. *Beasts of Balance* is a hybrid digital/physical game. The physical game is a "balance things on top of other things" game, a variant of Jenga with odd-shaped animal objects. Each object contains a radio frequency identification (RFID) chip that is scanned before you place it. This enables the physical Base Layer to interface with an iPad app, unlocking a digital Retention Layer. Players can unlock new animal hybrids, explore their bestiary and earn Achievements (Figure 3.10).

Board game designer Matt Leacock has added a Retention Layer to his board game, *Pandemic*. In *Pandemic Legacy*, players open a one-use card each time they play the game. This permanently changes the ruleset for the game. This can involve writing on cards, ripping them up or marking a character as eliminated from the game. The game can now be played as a "season" which can involve as many as 24 separate play-throughs of the main game.

FIGURE 3.10 *Beasts of Balance* combines a physical Base Layer with a digital Retention Layer.

On the other hand, merely connecting your game to Facebook, Twitter or another social network of your choice does not create a social experience. If you are adding "social" just to allow people to post updates to their newsfeed, you may be better to spend your engineering time on other, more substantial, retention tools. There is little point in just adding in a lightweight social feature so you can tick the social box if you don't have a clear understanding of how and why it will improve the core experience of the game for the majority of your users.

We have discussed the Base Layer of the game, where repeatable actions that are enjoyable and rewarding take place over and over again. The Retention Layer sits on top, encouraging players to play for days, weeks, months and years. The Core Loop connects the two.

CHAPTER 4

The Core Loop and the Gearbox

THE CORE LOOP IS a much-used and ill-defined term in the games industry. Many developers use the term to refer to the Base Layer, the core activity that players repeat multiple times as they play the game. I don't view that as the Core Loop; it is the Base Layer.

In the previous chapter, we discussed the role of nested loops: actions that the player has started and will now wish to finish, whether that be rescuing 10 slaves from the pirates, waiting to harvest a field of pumpkins or completing an Achievement. These are loops, but they are not, to my mind, the Core Loop.

My definition is that **the Core Loop takes players from the Base Layer into the Retention Layer and back again**.

Figure 4.1 shows the Pyramid with the Core Loop included. A player plays the Base Layer to have fun and get rewards. Those rewards enable the player to progress through the Retention Layer. As the player advances through the Retention Layer, she wants to progress more, so she returns to the Base Layer to have more fun and get more rewards. This is a loop that, when done right, can keep a person playing for a very long time.

In hidden object game *Criminal Case*, players engage with a light narrative centred around forensic investigations of murders. A player might visit the crime scene: a gruesome dismemberment in a dirty bathroom. The Base Layer involves hunting for hidden objects in the 2D image.

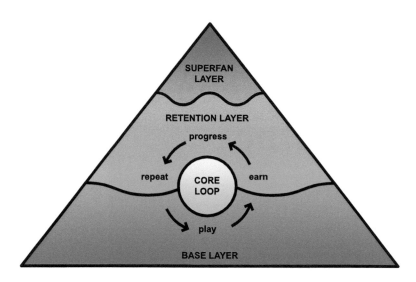

FIGURE 4.1   The Core Loop.

Sometimes, one of those hidden objects is central to the plot: a dropped gun, a torn-up receipt or bloodstained clothing. More often, the player is in search of a different currency: stars. If a player wishes to complete the next part of the story, he must replay the Base Layer multiple times to earn the stars needed to unlock the next forensic investigation. The Core Loop is "play hidden object levels to earn stars to progress the story to unlock new hidden object levels."

I focus on the relationship between the Base and the Retention Layer because I believe that the Core Loop needs to be more than just a repetitive action. When a service-game designer says that it is critical that you have a polished and designed Core Loop, they don't mean that you must have a Base Layer with AAA levels of polish. They mean that the inter-relationship between moment-to-moment action and long-term progression must be polished and clear to players. In a farming game like *Hay Day*, with no Base Layer to speak of, it means that the Core Loop is the larger goal for the player: planting crops to earn money to unlock new crops and machinery to make new food stuffs and to do all of this to level up and do it some more.

Note that the Core Loop may extend into the Superfan Layer. Players might participate in activities in the Base Layer to gain resources or progress

LAYERS NOT GAMES

When I first developed the Pyramid, I used the phrase Base Game, Retention Game and Superfan Game. (And other people used the terms Meta Game and Elder Game).

I avoid those terms now because *there is only one game*. When talking to my clients, I discovered that they assumed that the Base, Retention and Superfan Games were three distinct experiences that needed to be designed. Teams would triple the amount of work they were trying to do to design all three.

That is not the point. There is one game with multiple layers. The Retention Layer aims to drive people through the Base Layer, creating the Core Loop. The Superfan Layer gives players more reason to repeat the Core Loop to achieve their long-term goals.

You are building one game. Build it in layers.

in the Retention Layer, or they might be doing it for Superfan reasons: to progress in the elder game, to strengthen their clan or for social status. I will introduce the Superfan Layer in Chapter 7: The Superfan Layer.

There are three basic types of Core Loop:

- A *linear* Core Loop, common to narrative games

- A *strategic* Core Loop, where choices made in both the Base and Retention Layers matter, common to strategy games and some action games

- A *replayable* Core Loop, common to service games such as endless runners or collectible card games

A **linear Core Loop** consists of completing unique missions or levels to make progress through the narrative and to unlock new chapters. It can be seen in mission-based games like *Call of Duty* or *X-Wing* and in narrative games like *Uncharted*. The player has little or no agency in the Retention Layer. The design objective is to draw players through the levels, replaying difficult ones multiple times until they beat them. In this case, the Base Layer is rarely procedural or random. It is more likely to be scripted to deliver a specific experience. This approach is more often seen in product games than service games, largely because it is expensive to implement.

The **strategic Core Loop** gives players agency in the Base Layer, in the Retention Layer and in the resources or objectives that they bring between the two. The strategic map in *Total War* offers a different style of gameplay to the individual battles. A player can choose when, where and why they fight on the strategic layer. She can prepare huge armies to crush her foes in huge battles or use tactical skill to fight free of an ambush. She can choose to minimise fighting by focusing on trading, diplomacy and espionage. She can also influence the Retention Layer from within the Base Layer: destroying an army by chasing down its fleeing troops with light cavalry removes a threat from the strategic map.

In *XCom: Enemy Unknown*, the nerve-wracking Base Layer missions offer intense, focused gameplay. The Retention Layer is strategic: figuring out what rooms are needed in your base, prioritising research, and manufacturing new, powerful weapons. There are multiple links between the Base and Retention Layers. If the player fails in a mission, global panic levels can rise, and countries can pull out of XCom, withdrawing their funding. Although a Base Layer mission might have its own objectives set by the game (Kill all aliens; Rescue a VIP), the player might also have her own objectives: to capture an alien alive to be researched by the scientists or to recover a piece of alien technology. The link between the Base and Retention Layers is two-way and sophisticated.

A **replayable Core Loop** encourages the player to replay the Base Layer over and over again. In this case, the Base Layer is often procedural, or involves interactions with another human player. In *Temple Run*, the player plays as an Indiana Jones/Lara Croft character, running at a constant speed along a path through an untamed jungle. He swipes left or right to make turns on the path, and up or down to jump over or duck under hazards. The Base Layer is not a scripted, crafted experience: it is procedurally generated and full of random turns, hazards, coins and power-ups. The player can replay it many times, earning coins to make progression through the Retention Layer of unlocking all the power-ups and characters.

The Base Layer in *CSR Racing* is a simple rhythm action game, where the player must time the changes of gears to get maximum speed. It is not procedurally generated; it is just repeated each time. But the player may have changed his or her experience by taking a different car into the Base Layer, or by choosing a high-stakes race to beat a boss character in the game. The Core Loop consists of repeating the identical Base Layer to earn resources that unlock or upgrade cars to repeat the cycle again.

Modern Combat Versus is a first-person shooter (FPS) on iOS and Android. Players take a squad of agents into four-on-four battles and return with rewards that include Experience Points (XP), Korpens and loot crates. Loot crates contain currency and may contain new agents. Korpens are used to buy new agents. The Core Loop for a player of *Modern Combat Versus* is "fight in the Base Layer to earn loot crates and Korpens to unlock new agents and upgrade existing agents in the Retention Layer to improve my chances and enjoyment in the Base Layer."

A successful Core Loop connects the Base and Retention Layers such that the two combined are greater than the sum of the parts. An example of this is Playrix's hit Match-3 game, *Gardenscapes*. The Base Layer is so-so: it is a perfectly good Match-3 game with nice touches, but it lacks the polish of *Candy Crush Saga* and its visual rewards for setting off special bombs and fireworks have little pizzazz. Its Retention Layer, on the other hand, is awesome (Figure 4.2).

The game is story-based. The player has inherited a house from a long-lost uncle. The house is in good shape, but butler Austin is sad to report the that garden is a complete mess. Can the player help him to clean it up? How? By playing a Match-3 level of course! Each completed level earns the player a star that can be spent to sweep up leaves, repair a treehouse or install new benches. The purpose of the Match-3 game is no longer just to get to have fun, to get to the next level or to make progress along a map. It is now to restore a faded garden to its former glory, planting trees, attracting wildlife and making the garden a delightful place to spend time in.

FIGURE 4.2 Stars earned in *Gardenscapes* let players bring a derelict garden back to bloom.

Playrix has used its Retention Layer to harness the desire for players to "play house," and in doing so, it has elevated an average Match-3 game into a consistent performer in the top-grossing charts.

THE GEARBOX

The Base and Retention Layers can be highly separate. In the first chapter, I told the story of a client who is developing the Retention Layer in-house and has commissioned a third-party developer, in another country, to develop the Base Layer. This delineation makes it clear that the Base Layer and the Retention Layer are separate parts of the game, with their own unique challenges and objectives. By the time a game ships, however, the two components need to be one seamless whole. Which means that you need to design a gearbox to transmit information and fun between the Base and Retention Layers.

This is not a technical issue. The game can transmit all sorts of information between a strategic map and a tactical mission without the player needing to know about it. But for the Core Loop to work effectively, players must see, experience and understand the connections between the Base and Retention Layers. Without that understanding, they will not feel fulfilled and rewarded by the game (Figure 4.3).

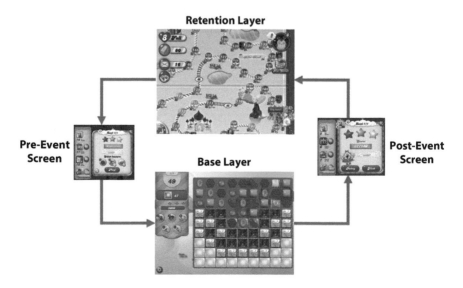

FIGURE 4.3   How the Pre- and Post-Event screens create the Core Loop.

THREE DESIGN RAZORS

In philosophy, a razor is a principle or rule of thumb that allows one to eliminate unlikely explanations for a phenomenon. The most famous is Occam's Razor, "among competing hypotheses, the one with the fewest assumptions should be selected," which can be paraphrased as "of all the competing possibilities, the simplest is often the most likely."[1]

These design razors are three principles to help the game designer understand if it is worth designing and launching a feature.

- Will the player *see* the feature you are designing?
- Will the player *understand* the feature you are designing?
- Will the player *value* the feature you are designing?

If not, you have more design work to do.

As a designer, you need to give the player the information that they need to enjoy the Base Layer. They must understand what they need to do in the Base Layer but also why it matters and what value you can get out of it. You can do this with a Pre-Event Screen and a Post-Event Screen. To my mind, these are the two most important screens in your game.

THE PRE-EVENT SCREEN

Figure 4.4 shows the pre-mission briefing from *XCom: Enemy Unknown*. From this screen, the player can choose which soldiers to take on the mission, arm them with fearsome alien technology and see that there is an

FIGURE 4.4   The pre-mission briefing in *XCom: Enemy Unknown*.

option to build an Officer Training School to enable larger squads (although this player is targeting the Army of Four achievement in the game by fighting with a reduced squad size). It is a sophisticated Pre-Mission Screen, conveying a lot of information to the player. It gives her tactical choices about what to take into the Base Layer as well as offering ideas for Retention Layer gameplay, such as which buildings to build, which weapons to manufacture and which technologies to research.

Figure 4.5 shows a simpler version of a Pre-Event Screen taken from *Candy Crush Saga*. There are fewer options in *Candy Crush Saga*. The player has no choice over which level to complete next. He has to do the next one. The only strategic choice he can make is whether to purchase consumable boosts to make the level easier. Nevertheless, *Candy Crush Saga* displays some Retention-Layer information on this screen, including the high scores of some (in this case, made-up) friends and my progression towards a free gift, as well as pointing out that it is possible to earn three stars in this level and that my target is to achieve a score of 10,000.

The purpose of the Pre-Event Screen is to provide a connection between the Retention Layer and the Base Layer. It allows players to understand their progress and, if appropriate, to show them how their achievement in the Retention Layer is making their Base Layer easier or has given them

FIGURE 4.5 The Pre-Event Screen in *Candy Crush Saga*.

more tactical choices. It can also set up new goals in the Base Layer, such as achieving three stars or completing a specific challenge.

Not all games have a Pre-Event Screen. In *Temple Run,* you are dropped straight into the action, fleeing from half a dozen skull-faced monkeys that moment that you press Play. In *Hearthstone*, the challenge comes from a human opponent, not from the game, so there is no need for such a complex screen. In *Words with Friends* or similar social games, the turns are short, and players do not want to be interrupted by a Pre-Event Screen every time they take their go.

THE POST-EVENT SCREEN

After the player has had fun, you need to show a Post-Event Screen.

This can be triggered by two different outcomes: the player can either succeed in his objective, or he can fail. In many service games, there is no direct failure, just the end of the game. As an example, take the Game Over screen shown in Figure 4.6. It is taken from *Harbour Master* from Imangi Games, a game released in 2009, in the early days of smartphone gaming. *Harbour Master* is a puzzle game where players dock and unload ships in a busy port. The ships come at an increasing pace, and players berth them as quickly as possible in the appropriate dock, wait for them to unload and navigate them back out to sea, all while avoiding other vessels and working out holding patterns to keep the ships safe while all the berths are full. When the player inevitably fails,

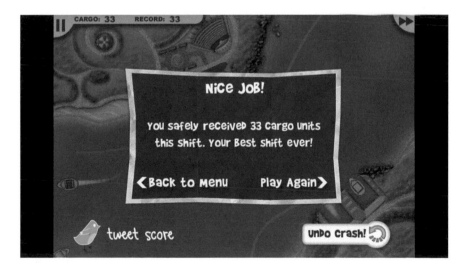

FIGURE 4.6 *Harbour Master's* Game Over screen.

FIGURE 4.7   Candy Crush Saga's Post-Event Screen.

Harbour Master does not say "Game Over." It offers a congratulatory, "Nice job! You safely received 33 cargo units this shift."

Harbour Master has a "Play again" option on its Post-Event Screen because it has no appreciable Retention Layer. Players can beat their previous high score, and unlock new maps, but the main retention technique is just that the Base Layer is really fun.

In *Candy Crush Saga,* the Post-Event Screen pictured in Figure 4.7 mirrors the Pre-Event Screen. I have been added at position 5 on the leaderboard. My three stars are now filled in. The animated character is jumping up and down with my performance. When I move on to the map, a little train moves from level 253 to level 254, giving a numerical and visual sense of progress.

Given that *XCom: Enemy Unknown* has a more sophisticated Retention Layer, it is unsurprising that the results screen has more information and feedback for the player. As well as a traditional stats screen, *XCom* tells players what they have recovered from the mission, as shown in Figure 4.8.

This player has unlocked new research and recovered a variety of different aliens for research or to sell. The Retention Layer encourages players to capture specimens of the different alien species they encounter. Doing so unlocks research which in turn unlocks new equipment and abilities.

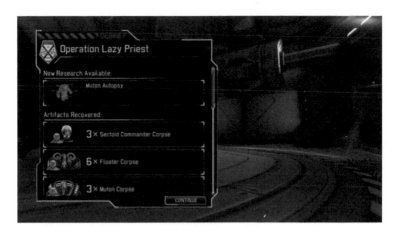

FIGURE 4.8   *XCom: Enemy Unknown* results screen.

THE SPECIAL WORLD

It is possible to think of the Pre- and Post-Event Screens as part of the Hero's Journey, the story-telling structure popularised by mythologist Joseph Campbell in *The Hero with a Thousand Faces*. Campbell identified the basic structure that underpins most stories. He explained how the hero must journey from the Ordinary World into the Special World, recruit allies and face ordeals, finally returning with the Elixir to be reborn back in the Ordinary World.[2]

Consider the Retention Layer as the Ordinary World. The player is safe, and decisions do not have immediate life-or-death consequences. At some point, the player desires to leave the Ordinary World to go on an adventure. The Base Layer is the Special World, a place full of danger and treachery but also replete with the rewards that the player needs in the Ordinary World. The Pre- and Post-Event Screens act as Thresholds and as the Road Back as players make the transition between the Ordinary and Special Worlds.

Seen through this lens, there is advantage in having a clear "crossing of the Threshold," together with symmetry between the Pre- and Post-Event Screens. In *Rodeo Stampede*, the player is fired out of a cannon away from the safety of the airborne zoo and into a herd of stampeding animals. In *Angry Birds: Transformers*, the player is delivered to the start of the level by Astrotrain and exits by boarding Astrotrain and flying to safety. The symmetry of the Pre-Event and Post-Event actions and screens help to close the Core Loop and evoke the transitions between the Ordinary and Special Worlds.

As always, there is no right and wrong. We've discussed that some games, like resource managers and idle clickers, have no Base Layer. Other games, particularly ones with replayable Core Loops, opt to get the player into the action as fast as possible. For those games where the Retention Layer is sophisticated, and the interaction between the Base and Retention Layers a source of fun and long-term engagement, building a Core Loop with strong, informative, emotionally engaging Pre- and Post-Event Screens is a route to building an enduring, popular game.

CHAPTER 5

The Session and the On-Ramp

THE PYRAMID IS A FRAMEWORK for the strategy of your game design. The Session is tactical. It forms the fundamental building block of service games. It addresses the questions: How will I get my players to open my game? How do I let them have fun? How do I signal that it might be time to go? How do I make sure that they come back?

Let's start from first principles. Each time a player starts playing your game, it is inevitable that they are going to stop. I don't mean eventually. I mean at the end of that session. Humans have other responsibilities and needs. They need to work, to eat, to sleep and to go to the bathroom. At some point, they need a break.

The successful game designer thinks about the four components of the Session, which are set out in Figure 5.1.

- The **On-Ramp** makes it easy for players to decide to fire up your game, rather than choosing something else from the plethora of alternative entertainment choices (including other games but, more dangerously, Facebook, Instagram and other social media experiences).

- **Playtime**, when the players have a fun, rewarding and enjoyable experience.

- The **Off-Ramp**, also known as "Time To Go," when we start signalling to players that they have had a good session (whether that be

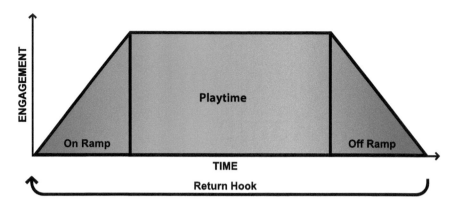

FIGURE 5.1   The anatomy of the Session.

measured by fun, achievement, progression, etc.) and hint that now might be a good time to leave.

- **A Return Hook**, which gives players a reason to come back at some point in the future, whether that be minutes, hours or days away.

These four elements, taken together, form the core of your game design. It is one of the most useful conceptual structures for understanding and designing better service games.

THE IMPORTANCE OF ATTENTION

The biggest challenge for any game designer is to make someone want to play their game.

This can be divided into two parts:

- **Acquisition**: How to make users buy or download a game and install it on their PC, phone or console.

- **Retention**: How to encourage users to open this game on a regular basis in the face of enormous competition for attention.

In the days before digital distribution and free-to-play (F2P) games, it was possible to focus only on getting the initial sale. Games were designed to have strong "box" appeal. They had to be easy to explain, easy to sell and easy to market. If you are making a service game, the big battle is not to get players to *buy* your game, it is to get them to *play* it.

In 1971, social scientist Herbert Simon made a profound prediction about the malaise that would come to consume our modern civilisation.

> "In an information-rich world, the wealth of information means a dearth of something else: a scarcity of whatever it is that information consumes. What information consumes is rather obvious: it consumes the attention of its recipients. Hence a wealth of information creates a poverty of attention."[1]

In the 21st century, Simon's predictions have come true. We live in an always-on, connected society where we receive demands on our attention at all waking hours (and some not-waking ones too). As Tim Wu has written in *The Attention Merchants*, we have chosen to admit advertisers and businesses into the innermost recesses of our lives: into our houses via television, into our pockets via our smartphones and even into our bedrooms. According to Deloitte's Global Mobile Consumer Survey, 40% of Americans look at their phone within five minutes of waking up, 30% look at it within five minutes before going to sleep and 50% check it in the middle of the night. On average, Americans look at their phones 47 times a day, rising to 82 times for 18- to 24-year-olds.[2]

Facebook is a global behemoth that has a market capitalisation of more than $500 billion based on harvesting our attention and selling it to advertisers. Instagram, Twitter, Snapchat, YouTube: these are all services that compete for our attention. The news industry has changed, becoming more lurid and driven by clickbait headlines in a desperate bid for what remains of our attention. Some of the most successful video-game companies in the world (Supercell, King, Electronic Arts) all desperately vie for our attention.

How on earth will the video game you are designing stand out in this cacophony?

The first thing to realise is that your competition is not just other games; it is anything that is vying for your player's attention. If you are making a service-based game on mobile, the biggest danger is social media. You are competing with the status-driven game of Facebook and Instagram or the outrage-driven platform of Twitter. If you are on PC, you are competing with social media, but also with Netflix, YouTube and paid games. On console, you are competing with some of the highest-budget entertainment products on the planet. Your job is to make it easy for the player to choose to play *your* game, not any of the other rival entertainment choices in the market.

About four years ago, I had two games on the go. On Steam, I was playing *Legend of Grimrock*, an action role-playing game (RPG) released in 2012 and a homage to the classic 1987 title *Dungeon Master*. On my iPad, I was playing *Pocket Planes*, Nimblebits' puzzle logistic game in which you attempt to deliver passengers and cargo around an 8-bit pixel art world using a collection of aeroplanes that varies from a tiny little Bearclaw to the enormous Skyliner.

My children were young, and I had just encouraged them to go to sleep after much wrangling. I came downstairs, looked at my PC in the corner and thought to myself, "I don't have time for *Grimrock*." I flopped down on the sofa, pulled out my iPad and started playing *Pocket Planes*. Two and a half hours later, I was still there.

The truth is that I had plenty of time for *Grimrock*. I just didn't want to make the commitment to the game. *Legend of Grimrock* is a core game. It demands your attention. You must memorise the map and solve spatial awareness puzzles. You must commit. *Pocket Planes*, in contrast, made it easy for me to go into the game and make small tweaks: collect some cargo in Delhi, send a plane off to Rio, deal with transfer passengers in Rome. Before long, I was involved in a spatial awareness puzzle as complex as the ones in *Grimrock*, but the game had eased me into it.

Note that this is not a criticism of *Legend of Grimrock*. It is a great paid game that has reviewed well, been popular and spawned a sequel. Instead, it is an illustration of how service games need to think differently about their priorities if they are to draw their audiences in and keep them playing.

This mental model applies outside the realm of games. Imagine that you are returning home from work after a hard day at work. You look at the television and notice that there is a good, worthy movie that you would like to see scheduled for this evening: perhaps *12 Years a Slave*, *Schindler's List* or *Amistad*. You decide that you haven't got time to watch that movie. Perhaps you'll watch it next time it is on or via on-demand at the weekend. In the meantime, you switch to *50 Best Advertising Jingles of the 1980s* or *The 30 Best Childhood Cartoons Ever!* You watch for a few moments, telling yourself that you might stop and do something else after this clip or the next ad break. Before you know it, you are approaching midnight and wondering where the evening went, even as you continue to wait to discover which childhood cartoon made it to number one. If you are younger than 40, the equivalent is failing to watch the worthy movie that you have

---

ONBOARDING versus **THE ON-RAMP**

The On-Ramp is not the same as onboarding. Most developers focus substantial effort on the onboarding process, getting players to understand the game, to enjoy the game and to get through the initial tutorial or First-Time User Experience (FTUE). They often spend less time on the On-Ramp.

The *onboarding* process is about getting players to engage with and understand your game the *first* time that they play.

The *On-Ramp* is about making it easy for players to choose your game *every* time they play it.

---

flagged in Netflix and watching an old *Star Trek* boxed set or video after video on YouTube instead.

The television show and YouTube autoplay videos capture your attention by making it easy to choose to start watching. You don't have to decide upfront to commit three hours of your time to it. It's broken up into bite-sized chunks that are not alarming. It is an easy On-Ramp.

The On-Ramp

The On-Ramp is important on all devices, but it is critical on mobile. In mobile game design, the question "do you have an easy On-Ramp?" has become popularised as "does your game pass the Starbucks test?" I first heard this phrase in a presentation given by Torsten Reil, CEO of NaturalMotion, the company behind *Clumsy Ninja*, *My Horse* and *CSR Racing* that was purchased by Zynga for $527 million in 2014. Reil's definition of the Starbucks test is "Have I got time for a meaningful interaction in the time it takes the barista to make my macchiato?"

This question is both profound and misleading. It has led to some fundamental misunderstandings of mobile gameplay and has allowed designers to ignore the value of the On-Ramp when making games for PC and console as well.

The Starbucks test is not a hard-and-fast rule, but it is a good discipline for all designers to consider. It can be broken down into two separate questions:

- Have I got time for this game right now?

- Will the game provide sufficient fun or progress for the time and effort I must invest to start playing?

These questions are very device specific because use case and player demand vary by device.

- My smartphone is generally in my pocket all the time. I am never far away from it. I therefore expect games to be rapidly accessible and rapidly meaningful. The On-Ramp must be quick.

- My tablet is not always with me. I prefer to get comfortable on a sofa to play games on it. I will forgive a game for a slower load time than I would with my smart phone.

- My Steam games are on my PC. My PC is often on and automatically updated, so I can get to Steam quickly.

- On console, I must boot the kids off the telly, switch from Apple TV or a terrestrial channel to my PlayStation, wait for a loading time and so on. Generally, I won't play a console game unless I know that I have an hour or two of uninterrupted game time to spare.

The On-Ramp is a technical issue AND a design issue. From a technical standpoint, you want to ensure that the game loads quickly with as few impediments as possible, an objective that is often in conflict with the ambitions of the art team. From a design standpoint, it is no good getting the player into the game if the player does not remember what they are trying to achieve or why. Console games can struggle with this if they are designed with the assumption that users will play for long sessions. The designers can forget that when the player next boots the game, after a week or more away from it, they need help to ease them back into the action. Mobile games, which often expect players to log in multiple times per day, excel at rewarding players for coming back and making it clear what they should do next.

CCP, developers of space combat MMO *EVE Online*, have a different way of describing the same problem. They talk about the *activation energy* of a game. A mobile idle game like *Nonstop Knight* has a different level of activation energy than *EVE: Valkyrie*, which is played in virtual reality on your PlayStation 4. This difference is vital and means that developers must be careful about which habits, designs or tropes they are taking from platform to platform and business model to business model. Not all design decisions work equally well on all platforms.

I want to devote some time to looking at "where" people play mobile games. If you ask a core gamer when mobile games are played, they are likely to respond, "they are snackable games for use on the bus or the train, or maybe the john, when people can't play proper games." This is not what the survey data suggests.

In 2013, comScore research showed that there were 20 million Monthly Active Users (MAUs) of mobile games in the United Kingdom, of which 6 million play every day.[3] Sixty-four per cent of those players play at home in the living room and 45% play at home in the bedroom compared with 33% who play while commuting and 27% who play at work. Playing while queuing is a minority activity, despite the popular perception amongst core gamers that this is the use case for mobile games (Figure 5.2).

Verto Analytics adds that most mobile gaming takes place in the evening, which paints a different picture to the popular perception of mobile gaming.[4] It is not something that people do when they can't access their PC or console; it is competing directly with those platforms, and with primetime television. (Although comScore also points out that 4 million British mobile gamers, or about 20%, play games while also watching television.)

This data puts the Starbucks test in context. The Starbucks test helps us to design games that people will choose to pick up and play *right now*. That is not because mobile games must be snackable so they can be played while queuing or on the loo. It is because being snackable improves the On-Ramp. If players get into your game and have fun or make progress quickly, it makes it easier for them to choose your game over other entertainment choices. Product games can still benefit from improving

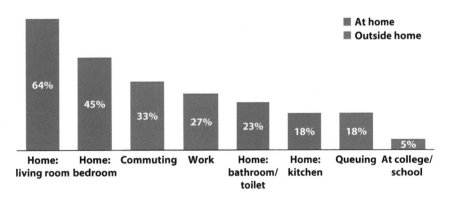

FIGURE 5.2   Location when playing mobile games.[5]

their ability to pass the Starbucks test because more players will choose to play their game if it is quick to get to the fun.

THE SESSION-LENGTH PARADOX

The Session-Length Paradox is the most surprising fact about the Starbucks Test and session length.

If you shorten the Session-length promise, the Session length may get longer.

The Session-length promise refers to the player's expectation of how long it will take from tapping or clicking on the game icon to having a meaningful experience in the game. That meaning might be fun gameplay or collecting a reward. It has to be enough to justify choosing to load the game now rather than later.

PopCap's *Bejeweled Blitz* is a fast Match-3 game based on its *Bejeweled* franchise. The twist is that the game is not endless. Players have just 60 seconds to score as many points as they can. Most people usually have one minute to spare: *Bejeweled Blitz* passes the Starbucks test, offers short-Session gameplay and creates an easy On-Ramp. At the height of its popularity, the average session length for *Bejeweled Blitz* was 43 minutes.[6]

Supercell's *Clash Royale* has a marvellous On-Ramp, yet in many ways it is so disconnected from the main game that it could be retrofitted to any game. Figure 5.3 shows the home screen from *Clash Royale*. The player has four chests, filling four available slots. Each chest takes three hours to unlock. For the highlighted chest, the countdown has already begun. In just over an hour, she will need to come back to the game to start the countdown for the next chest, or she is missing out. It is possible to get in to *Clash Royale*, open a chest and start a new one counting down in under 30 seconds. That is a very fast On-Ramp.

The player now has an empty chest slot. She can either go away and come back in three hours to claim another chest and start the countdown for the next one, or she can think, "Oh, I'm here now, I'll just have one game—they only take three minutes" and refill her chest slot. The Session-length promise is short: 30 seconds for to claim a chest and start a new countdown; three minutes to play a single match. The Session length can end up a lot longer if she chooses to play multiple matches.

This is not unique to service games. My favourite games have a heady mix of Base and Retention Layer gameplay. The *Total War* series is full of intense, tactical battles, overlaid with resource management, diplomacy and grand strategy. *Jagged Alliance 2* requires careful planning in its turn-based squad

FIGURE 5.3 *Clash Royale*'s home screen.

combat, combined with a strategic objective to retake a tropical island from a ruthless dictator, all while maintaining the morale, health and equipment of a rag-tag group of mercenaries.[7] The *X-Com* series is the granddaddy of this mix. As a student and in the early days of my career, I would start playing an *X-Com* game in the evening. I would complete a tense mission fighting a rear-guard action against the aliens invading Earth. I would return to my base with wounded soldiers to heal, alien technology to research and new weapons to build. After spending some time fiddling with my resource allocation, I would fast-forward time until a new mission came up. "Do I have time to do another battle?" I would ask myself, and far too often, I would answer myself in the affirmative, even as the sun came up on a new day.

Passing the Starbucks test doesn't mean that the only option is to play the game in short bursts. The most successful service games give players a choice. You can come in and do something meaningful soon after you arrive. You can choose to stay if you are having fun and it fits with the obligations of your life. The *Session promise* is short, but the Session length can be long. Paradoxically, in my work with clients, we have sometimes found that when we tackle Session-length issues, the Session length gets longer, but the all-important metric of whether players are coming back also goes up.

HOW TO PASS THE STARBUCKS TEST

Older players may remember that one of the selling points of Blizzard's massively multiplayer online role-playing game (MMORPG) *World of Warcraft* was its short sessions. In a review for *GameSpy* in 2004, Allen Rausch wrote, "The effect of the game's abbreviated time scale simply can't be underestimated.... Players with only a half-hour to play on a weeknight can actually log on and get something accomplished."[8] Compared with the prevailing MMORPGs of the time—of which *EverQuest* is perhaps the most remembered—this was accessible, short Session gameplay that enabled *World of Warcraft* to blow past the previous peak of success for subscription-based massively multiplayer online (MMO) games and reach 12 million monthly subscribers.

World of Warcraft does not pass the Starbucks test. Its Sessions are too long for that. It illustrates the deeper point that players need to believe they can have a great experience with a meaningful reward for the effort that they have invested in a time that feels appropriate to them given the device on which they are playing and their expectations of the game. Different players have different expectations or desires when playing a game, so there is not an absolute definition of what this balance of effort and reward looks like. The Starbucks test is a useful tool for developers as they seek the right balance.

Some of the most successful free-to-play games in the world fail to pass the Starbucks test. Other games could have done much better if they had tried to pay attention to it. The companies that fail the Starbucks test are usually those who have not designed their games with the use case and life patterns of their users in mind. (*Fallout Shelter* from Bethesda is a great example.) In Figure 5.4, I set out some ideas of what will help you pass the Starbucks test, and what will make it harder for you to do so.

"Good" and "bad" is not the same as "do" and "don't do." Video-game design is not about right and wrong. There is no "correct" design. Game design is about understanding the consequences of your decisions and choosing whether the trade-offs are worth the benefits. For example, *League of Legends* is one of the most successful free-to-play games on the planet, with over 140 million monthly active users and more than $1 billion in annual revenue. It requires online connectivity and matchmaking, it is player versus player (PvP) and it is complex. *League of Legends* fails the Starbucks test, but its gameplay, its community, its social pressures and its plain old fun mean that it can be successful without passing the Starbucks test.

GOOD	BAD
Short load times	Splash screens
Instant rewards	High-end 3D engines (Unity, Unreal)
Not "tidy your room"	PvP and matchmaking
"One more go" gameplay	Online connectivity
	Complexity (unless it is in layers)
	Interrupting menus
	No "suspend" behaviour

FIGURE 5.4   Development decisions that will impact the Starbucks test.

My favourite free-to-play game, *Hearthstone*, is successful, despite having many "bad" elements from the list in Figure 5.4. It is built on Unity. It requires an Internet connection. It needs players to commit to playing an online game for 10–15 minutes against another human. I won't play *Hearthstone* when my kids are in the bath because I am worried that if they need me and I must choose whether to go to their aid or abandon a tense ranked game, I might make the wrong decision. (Just kidding! Of course I'd make the right decision and rescue my kids. On the other hand, why put yourself in a position that may require a hard choice?) When my kids are in the bath, rather than playing *Hearthstone*, I will choose a game that I can quit at any time with no consequences like *Adventure Capitalist* or *Pocket Planes*, or one where the interactions are so short I can leave at short notice, like *Marvel Contest of Champions*.

Short load times are always better than long load times. Many games, particularly those with impressive graphics, will have long load times. It is always worth optimising load times, but sometimes it is a valid trade-off: "I believe that my players will enjoy my game more, and that marketing will be significantly easier, if I optimise for great-looking graphics over short load times." This is a valid position and may even be true. What it means is that you risk optimising for *cheaper customer downloads* at the expense of easier *long-term customer retention*. You will have to compensate for this by developing strong reasons for people to come back to the game.

In my experience, the push for higher-fidelity graphics is common amongst studios with a strong background in product-based games. Be careful with this decision. If it has a big impact on load times, you are likely to see the negative impact in long-term retention numbers and not in immediate downloads or critical reception.

Instant rewards are rewards for coming back to the game. When you log into Facebook, you immediately get to see what your friends are up to or how many interactions your most recent posts have received. It is rapid, satisfying feedback. Video games have an opportunity to give players immediate feedback, and mobile games are particularly good at doing this, partially because the competition with Facebook and other social media channels is so strong on mobile devices.

The objective of your retention strategy is to get me to return to your game frequently: every single day or multiple times per day on mobile or every week or multiple times per week on PC and console. Many games achieve this goal by luring me back with rewards and bonuses. More dubious methods threaten me with a stick by taking away bonuses or applying "decay" to my progress while I'm away. In all of this, it's easy to overlook the most important thing of all—how do I feel when I come back to your game?

Regardless of what platform it's on, clicking on a game icon should make me feel good. Games are about fun and escapism. When I come back to your game, my first feeling should be "ah, I'm glad I opened this game!" Yet all too often, games welcome their players back by throwing menial tasks at them— a list of everything that's gone wrong since you were away and a host of dull actions to take to fix it all. Take Playfish's now defunct *Restaurant City*, for example—each time you logged in to the game, your restaurant was full of litter and rubbish that you had to pick up and throw out. Your first feeling wasn't "I'm a world-famous restaurant tycoon!," it was, "Ugh, I'm a binman."

When I come back to your game, I want to feel like a god—like a returning emperor being welcomed back to a world where he rules supreme. Those first few seconds back in the game are your opportunity to thank me for returning and to remind me why I spend time with your game. The first thing you see when you log in to *Tiny Tower* each day is a shower of bonuses—a screen telling you how much money you've made since you last logged in, giving you bonus cash in the form of rent every 24 hours, and occasionally even giving you premium currency to celebrate a tower resident's birthday. Square Enix' iOS version of *The World Ends With You* is another great example; your powers level up even while you're offline, so the first screen you see when you come back is a host of new XP and powers racking up.

None of this is to say that your game can't have chores or repeating daily tasks of some description. Rather, it's a question of how and when you present those tasks. The first seconds after I log in aren't the right time; I want you to make me feel good about my decision to play your game again. I don't want to be told to *tidy my room*.

One more go gameplay is a powerful tool. It works well if the gameplay is short. *Bejeweled Blitz* is great fun to play in the Base Layer and has its "one minute" rule, so you always have time for one more go. *Flappy Bird, Crossy Road* and *Subway Surfers* are similar; the basic gameplay is so fun and short that you can always have one more go. The rule doesn't just apply to F2P games: fiendishly difficult indie game *Super Hexagon* has an addictive one-more-go feel, and each run is short. (I rarely survive longer than 10 seconds. My record is 14.) Matches in *Hearthstone, League of Legends* and *Team Fortress 2* have the same quality. In product games, Base Layers that fit this mould include missions in *X-Com*, football matches in *FIFA*, and playing a turn in *Civilisation* (even though a single turn in *Civilisation* can take a long time). The principle is to ensure that players know that there is a short activity that is enjoyable and rewarding enough to make it easy for them to fire up the game; that is so fun that they just keep playing; and that they leave the game remembering that they really enjoyed the experience.

The purpose of the "Good" side of Figure 5.4 is to focus your design efforts on making sure that your game is easy to get in to, that it passes the Starbucks test, and that it gets a positive answer to two critical questions in the minds of your players: have I got time for this game right now? Is the reward for getting into the game worth it, compared to the alternatives?

The "Bad" side is all about minimising the disruption to the On-Ramp. Sometimes, the trade-off is unavoidable. If the game needs high-fidelity graphics, it will be slower to load. But it is a trade-off, and there are consequences.

Splash screens and developer logos are an interruption that can slow down load times. It takes approximately eight seconds to load *Crossy Road* on my iPhone 7, and the Hipster Whale logo is visible for about five of them. It's possible, indeed probable, that the logo is covering up a loading time, but the impression that I get is that the developer puts advertising its name as a higher priority than getting me into the game fast. Although there is nothing is wrong with showcasing your company or logo, the critical objective is to make players feel that they are getting into the game fast, even if you are using tricks.

Supercell's farming simulation *Hay Day* is slow to load, partially because it requires a permanent online connection. Once the game is loaded, there is a five-second animation sequence where the clouds part and the camera zooms in on your farm. I suspect (but don't know) that this is a piece of theatre, designed to distract the player and make them think the game is ready to play, even as Supercell is continuing to initialise the game in the background. It's a smart trick.

At the opposite extreme, Bethesda's *Fallout Shelter* has one of the worst On-Ramps in modern F2P game design. The game takes two minutes to load on my iPad Air. There is a long splash screen. Halfway through the loading process, I am presented with a screen asking me which vault I wish to load. *I only have one!* There is then a further minute of loading time. I find myself visiting Facebook on my phone to pass time while I wait for *Fallout Shelter* to load. I enjoyed *Fallout Shelter* and made significant progress, but I churned from the game because the On-Ramp became sufficiently painful that I would always choose one of the dozens of other games on my iPad.

Bethesda is a company with a strong PC gaming legacy. It pushed the envelope with *Fallout Shelter*, both by increasing the graphical fidelity of resource management games on tablets and by its surprise launch tactics, announcing the game at trade show E3 in 2015 and making it available to download that same day. The game has been a critical and financial success. It is not a game that has had the longevity of other successful F2P games, though, and the On-Ramp problem is part of that.

I mention **high-end 3D engines** like Unity and Unreal in my list of bad points. Both engines are awesome and have democratised the process of making video games in a way that has been advantageous to the diversity of video-game genres. Both platforms enable developers to make good-looking games cost-effectively. They are also slower to load.

In Table 5.1, I list out the load times of some mobile games, all carried on my iPad Air.

The fast-loading games are older, have lower-fidelity graphics and may have been developed in Cocos 2D. Modern games are developed in Unity or Unreal. They are slower to load.

TABLE 5.1   Loading Times for Selected Mobile Titles.

Pocket Frogs	5 seconds
Pocket Trains	5 seconds
Disco Zoo	10 seconds
Temple Run	11 seconds
Crossy Road	17 seconds
Angry Birds Transformers	23 seconds
Angry Birds Go!	30 seconds
Candy Crush Saga	33 seconds
Clumsy Ninja	35 seconds
Hay Day	41 seconds
Hearthstone	45 seconds
Fallout Shelter	2 minutes, 1 second

My point is not that you should avoid engines like Unity or Unreal. Unity is awesome. It enables rapid development and there is a vast pool of game developers who know how to use it and can get up and running quickly. Unreal enables developers to push the graphical quality of their game. My point is that each decision you take has *consequences*. By choosing flashy graphics and either Unreal or Unity over pixel art and Cocos 2D, you are making the On-Ramp slower. You will need to compensate for this weakened On-Ramp by offering awesome gameplay, clever retention tricks or whatever it is that your game can offer to get players back into the game on a regular basis.

Over time, Unity and Unreal will improve the loading times of the engine, while designers and marketers will push ever more features into the game that slow down the loading time. Programmers will be stuck in the middle. There is no right answer to this conundrum. Just be aware that slow loading times will hurt your long-term retention.

Online connectivity and **PvP or matchmaking** are also bad for the On-Ramp. Requiring online connections for PvP games such as *Words with Friends* makes sense because the game does not function without a network connection. Many games that are single player, like *Hay Day*, or that offer significant offline gameplay, like *Marvel Contest of Champions*, require players to be online all the time.

With *Hay Day*, my thesis is that the game is designed to be fun but also to get players to the point of wanting to spend money. If the player is offline, they will not be able to access the shop and spend money. I believe that Supercell has decided to stop players having access to the game unless they are connected, so that the game does not succeed in creating desire such that the player attempts to visit the shop but fails in satisfying the desire—and earning money—because the player is offline. I suspect that *Marvel Contest of Champions* has a similar issue, but in its case, as well as being focused on purchases, the developers, Kabam, are keen to get players involved in alliances of other players, which is not possible if you are playing offline.

There are other advantages of requiring online connectivity. It makes hacking the game for advantage harder. The game relies on a server clock, not a local clock, which makes managing the experience easier and more consistent for developers. It means you can run dynamic updates in the background. It may be a sensible decision for developers, but it hurts the On-Ramp.

There is no excuse for **interrupting menus** like the ones I have described in *Fallout Shelter*.

Finally, I include **suspend behaviour**. If I shut my iPad during a game of *Candy Crush Saga*, I can return in a week and it will still be there. If I try to do the same on *Hearthstone*, the game logs me out. *Fallout Shelter* just crashes. If I am not certain that I have time for a lengthy gameplay session, I will pick games where I can drop out easily.

The Starbucks test seems to be very focused on mobile, and there is no doubt that it is a key determinant of success on that platform. It is also relevant to other platforms. Idle games like *Clicker Heroes* or *Adventure Capitalist* need to load fast. But even traditional console or PC games would benefit from thinking about how to get players into the game fast as they compete for attention with the rest of the digital world. It was a competitive advantage for *World of Warcraft* in 2004, and it has a role in the success of short-Session, modern, core games like *League of Legends*.

Many successful F2P games have bad On-Ramps. *Hearthstone*, *League of Legends* and *Team Fortress 2* are all successful games that fail many of my tests. As you design your game, there are some important questions you should ask yourself:

- What is the anticipated rhythm of player's interaction with your game? Is it multiple times a day for a short Session, like idle games or Supercell's titles? Is it once a week for a long Session, like *League of Legends* or *Crossfire*? The more often a player is expected to load the game, the more important an easy On-Ramp becomes.

- Can I mitigate the slow On-Ramp? Can I load assets in a different order? Do I need multiplayer? Can I use art or animation to disguise loading times and make the player feel as if they are getting into the game faster?

- How can I reward the player for coming back to the game in a way that feels fun and fitting with the genre?

- How can I get them back into the Core Loop with a clear understanding of what they are doing, and why?

It can be easier to distract the user than it is to deliver an engineering solution. This is fine, as long it helps you deliver an easy On-Ramp. A long time ago, I was an investment banker at Deutsche Bank and the firm had just built shiny new offices on London Wall. High-powered bankers complained that the new lifts were too slow. The response by building operations was masterful. They announced that there would be a major overhaul of the lifts. A crack team had been booked to renovate the lifts over the weekend. We would notice a substantial improvement on Monday. They shut down the lifts on Saturday and Sunday with workmen coming in and out. They confirmed there was an improvement on Monday, and the bankers reported that they were much happier with the lift speed. The lift speed had not changed. All the building management team had done was install mirrors in the lifts.

Sometimes sleight-of-hand is the answer.

Remember that you do not have to do everything on the good list or avoid everything on the bad list to make a successful game. They are trade-offs. Some features make no sense for your target platform or genre or audience. Each decision has consequences, and you either need to mitigate the consequences through some other design structure or accept the downsides of the decision in return for the upside that you believe that you will get.

The purpose of the On-Ramp is to get the player back into the game. A game with a good On-Ramp will tend to be more successful than one without because it has won the most important battle in the 21st century: the battle for attention. Now that you have got the attention, the next chapter will focus on what do with it.

CHAPTER 6

The Session: Playtime, the Off-Ramp and Return Hook

I N THE PREVIOUS CHAPTER, we introduced the concept of the Session and the all-important On-Ramp that makes it easy for players to decide that they have time to play your game right now and that it will be fun and rewarding to do so.

Now let's consider the rest of the Session: Playtime, the Off-Ramp and the Return Hook (Figure 6.1).

PLAYTIME

Playtime is what players do when they are playing the game. Whole books have been written on the topic.[1] I have covered much of what is important for Playtime in the chapter on the Base Layer. To summarise, it is critical that your players have fun (for some value of fun) or a meaningful experience (for some value of meaningful) during each session. If you fail here, all the retention techniques in the world are unlikely to keep players coming back.

THE OFF-RAMP

At some point during every single Session, your players will need to leave your game. As game makers, you have some agency over this process. You can kick them out, try to keep them in or give gentle signals that now

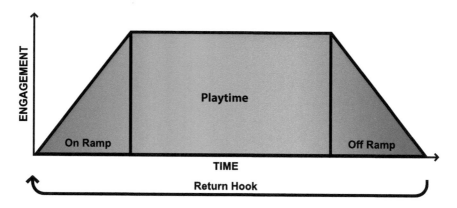

FIGURE 6.1   The Session: Playtime and the Off-Ramp.

would be a sensible time to go. There are examples of all three approaches amongst successful video games. My recommendation is that you:

- Signal that the main tasks are done.

- Let people stay if they want.

- Plant a hook to bring them back to begin the next session.

The Off-Ramp is the partner of the On-Ramp. It does not mean that you need to kick your players out. It means that you need to think about when there is a natural break in the game rhythm and how you can offer the players the choice of carrying on or leaving. It can have many different contexts, and it is not about hard-and-fast rules. It will vary from game to game, genre to genre and player to player. Here are some examples of potential moments to offer an Off-Ramp:

- When the player completes a level of a traditional console game such as *Dishonoured* or *Tomb Raider.*

- When a player has harvested his crops, planted new ones and set his machines running in *Hay Day.*

- Completing all the daily missions in *Marvel Strike Force.*

- Getting stuck on a difficult level of *Candy Crush Saga* and running out of lives.

- Running out of energy in *Marvel Contest of Champions.*

The Off-Ramp is part of the overall *promise of the Session length*. It promises the player that the game respects her time and that it will provide moments in the gameplay where it would be appropriate to put the game down and come back later. An anecdote might help make this clearer. The people I know who play *Candy Crush Saga* are often busy people, particularly the mothers of my children's friends. One of them told me that she would not play *Candy Crush Saga* if it did not have the life system. You lose a life whenever you fail to complete a level, players have five lives by default, and a life is regenerated every ten minutes. "I know that when I play *Candy Crush,* I will eventually run out of lives and have to stop. I don't have the willpower to make myself stop, so if it weren't for the lives, I would never play the game at all."[2]

The key message is that successful service games are not focused on extending the Session length for their players. They are trying to keep players playing for the long haul. Marathon gameplay Sessions—the type that teenage boys like to brag about—are not cool for the majority of the global audience of game players. They are not practical for most people. Jobs, family and other commitments take precedence. A game needs to make it easy for people to start playing a Session, and a vital component of that is making people believe that it will be easy for them to stop.

For many years, the Holy Grail for game designers was to make an addictive game. Not all games were focused on this, but many games—*Football Manager, Minecraft, Everquest*—were praised and recognised because they were so damned addictive. Service game designers still want players to come back to their games, but in a different way to product game designers. One metaphor I use to illustrate this is the *chocolate cake problem.*

If you give me a piece of chocolate cake, covered in icing and chocolate buttons, and I eat it, it will be lovely. If you give me another piece, and I eat it, it will be nice. If you give me the whole cake, and I eat the entire thing, I will feel sick, and all the chocolate cake, including the first, delicious slice, will now be horrible.[3]

Solving the chocolate cake problem is one of the key considerations that service-game designers must wrestle with if they want to keep their players engaged with the game over months or years. It is also why "energy" has proven to be such an enduring and popular mechanic amongst designers of free-to-play (F2P) games.

THE ROLE OF ENERGY

In the early days of free-to-play, energy was a ubiquitous mechanic. Every action in *Farmville* and similar *-ville* style games from Zynga, such as planting crops, harvesting crops or feeding your animals, depleted your energy from a finite pool. When the energy bar was empty, players had the choice of waiting for it to refill, paying for energy with real money or spamming their friends to ask for more.[4]

To critics of the F2P revolution, it looks as if this model was an aggressive monetisation strategy. As soon as a player starts to enjoy the game, they would be blocked and asked for money—a bait-and-switch. Leaving aside that this was the model that worked for arcade machines—the original core games—monetisation is not the primary purpose of this system. Energy is a retention mechanic, with potential side benefits of monetisation and social virality. As Owen Mahoney, CEO of Nexon, publisher of *MapleStory*, says, "The number one job is not to monetise. It's to keep the user coming back for years or months on end."[5]

Energy has become a staple of service games, particularly on mobile. It is a mechanic that I try not to use because it is inelegant and clunky. (See Figure 6.2 for a list of the pros and cons of energy.) Nevertheless, it delivers on many objectives that a service-game designer needs to achieve, and hence I often end up with it in the games I work on.

Energy comes in many forms. Sometimes it is overt, as in the energy resources that you use to plant crops in *Farmville* or to enter a battle in *Marvel Contest of Champions*. Sometimes it is rebranded, like fuel in *CSR Racing*. Sometimes it is a hidden constraint: in *Hay Day*, there is no energy, but the game parcels out the number of agricultural plots and industrial machines you can place in your farm. Once you have set all the machines running and crops growing, you are, in *Hay Day* terms, out of energy. *Candy Crush Saga* uses lives in the same role: you don't use up any "energy" when you complete a level, but if you fail a level, you lose one of your five lives. Lives recharge over time, but they behave like energy in other games.

On the positive side, energy is a useful tool for the designer. By allocating, say, 10 units of fuel to a racing game, the designer **controls the Session length** by determining that most players will complete only ten races before they end their session. This addresses the chocolate cake problem because it **signals the end of the Session** to the player.

Energy is evolving from being a Zynga-style hard stop ("Pay up or push off!") to a gentler signalling mechanic. When you have planted all your

PROS	CONS
Signals the end of the session	It's clunky
Controls session length	It may be a sign of "evil F2P"
Parcels out gameplay	It can prevent your biggest players from playing
Reduces player boredom	It is not generous
Can make choices matter more	
Can be monetised (side benefit)	

FIGURE 6.2 The pros and cons of energy.

crops in *Hay Day* and set your machines running, the game has signalled that you have done all that is "necessary." If you are a min-maxer, the type of player who wants to play the game as efficiently as possible, you can leave now, safe in the knowledge that you have used your time effectively to move forward in the game.[6] If you are enjoying just pottering about on your farm, you can stay. In *Candy Crush Saga*, the five-life limit kicks you out of the game before you get so frustrated with being stuck on a level that you rage-quit. The *Hearthstone* Challenge system discussed in Chapter 3's section, "Retention Layer 16, Challenges," is a nudge towards an Off-Ramp that players are free to ignore.

Some games choose to **parcel out gameplay**. The cynical interpretation of this is that if a game has boring mechanics and lets you repeat them until you get bored, you will play until you are bored and then never open the game again. By inserting energy into the mix, designers can prevent players from reaching their boredom threshold, or as the cynics might say, noticing the shallowness of the game play experience. Although this trick will work for a while, eventually, most players will see through it.

The positive interpretation of the same process is that energy solves the chocolate cake problem: I will enjoy chocolate cake more if it is spread out over time, and the same is true for gameplay. Parcelling it out over time increases by enjoyment of the game.

Energy can also make **choices matter more**. In *CSR Racing*, players need to race many times to grind out the currency to upgrade their cars. As a min-maxer, it would be easy for me to grind boring low-level races over and over again until I upgrade my car enough to be certain that I can beat the next boss. As I approach the end of my fuel and hence the end of my Session, I start looking at the next boss race and try to figure out if I can beat him yet. If it is possible, but not easy, I might well decide to use my last unit of fuel to take on the boss, so I can beat him in this Session, rather than racing another low-level and dull grind race against a weak opponent. The scarcity of the energy acts as risk-reward trade-off where I am deciding to take the risk of taking on a strong opponent to get the satisfaction of winning and having an exciting finish to my Session.

This delivers against the needs of Self-Determination Theory (SDT), which suggests that players need to be able to demonstrate competence. It also delivers *flow*, by encouraging players to engage with the game at the edge of their competence. Psychologist Mihaly Csikszentmihalyi developed the concept of flow, which he describes as "being completely involved in an activity for its own sake. The ego falls away. Time flies. Every action, movement, and thought follows inevitably from the previous one, like playing jazz. Your whole being is involved, and you're using your skills to the utmost."[7] Flow is only possible when there is a balance of challenge and skill. If the activity is too hard, it feels frustrating; too easy, and it feels boring.

Figure 6.3 shows the flow zone. If a player has no restriction on what they can do, they might choose to grind for resources in events that they can beat easily. It might be an efficient way to get resources, but it is boring. In this setup, with a repetitive Base Layer like the one in *CSR Racing*, energy acts as an encouragement to choose races and events that are challenging enough to avoid this boredom and will help to keep players retained for longer.

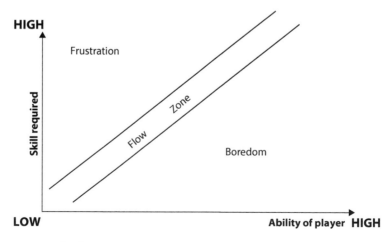

FIGURE 6.3 The flow zone exists where challenge and ability are well matched.

OPERANT CONDITIONING CHAMBERS, OR SKINNER BOXES

An Operant Conditioning Chamber, also known as a Skinner box, is a piece of laboratory equipment designed to study animal behaviour. It is named after B. F. Skinner, a US psychologist and proponent of behaviourism, the school of psychology that argues that behaviour is the consequence of reinforcement, and that by using external stimuli to reward or punish certain behaviours, it is possible to train, or condition, a creature to respond in predictable ways to those stimuli in the future.

Skinner trained pigeons to play table tennis. Initially he gave them rewards for looking at the ball or pecking it so that it moved. Eventually, he rewarded them only when they managed to get the ball past an opponent, and hey presto, pigeons playing ping pong.[8]

Video games are good at this type of reinforcement. If you are a gamer, odds are you can't walk your avatar past a crate or loot box in a video game without looking inside. The effect is stronger if the reward inside is not predictable but random. If there is a chance that the loot is rare or powerful, the compulsion to engage is hard to overcome.

Games have long given players rewards, often of variable amounts, in return for a carrying out specific actions, whether those actions involve skill, as in an arcade game, or simply turning up, as in a resource-management game. Service games (and social media) also harness these techniques to get players to return to the game frequently or to engage in particular actions that the designers value.

Finally, energy can be **monetised**. This is a side benefit, but it is also the most visible aspect of energy to non-developers. Few companies are happy to drop the monetisation aspect of energy because for a subset of players, energy can be an attractive item to buy and can deliver anything between 20% and 50% of a game's revenue. However, developers would be well advised to treat energy as a tool to use to enhance retention, and to consider the revenue potential as a secondary benefit.

On the negative side, energy risks being seen as a sign of **evil F2P**. It has become synonymous with the manipulative, Skinner-box approach to video-game design that has more in common with the gambling industry's desire to create addiction rather than the games industry's focus on entertainment. (There is overlap between the two industries.) It is a **clunky** tool that can leave the player feeling a lack of control. It can constrain the amount that your Superfans can play, which may be fine from a monetisation standpoint, but if these players do not suffer from the chocolate cake problem, then letting them engage with the game heavily might be a good thing.

Energy does not seem **generous**. Successful F2P is about giving players access to entertainment for free and allowing those who love what you to do to spend lots of money on things they really value. Energy constrains access to the game and limits your players' freedom to explore. This can hurt retention and monetisation. In the end, there are a variety of ways to achieve the positive objectives that an energy system delivers, and I would recommend searching for those first, before resorting to energy.

Sometimes, however, players want to keep playing. They have a whole evening with nothing ahead of them but rubbish television and are enjoying playing your game. How does a designer entertain that player? The answer is to let them potter.

POTTERING

The Oxford English Dictionary defines *to potter* as "work or occupy yourself in a desultory but pleasant manner." (It also points out that in the United States, the word is "putter.") I define it in these terms:

> "Imagine a middle-aged man passing the time in his own space. It might be a garage, or a garden, or a spare room. He might be gardening, tinkering with a car or doing a small piece of DIY. He may have a beer in his hand or a cup of tea. The important thing is that he is on his own, doing nothing in particular, in a way that is somehow satisfying and relaxing at the same time. That's pottering."

Video games are full of pottering. There are some games where pottering is the sole purpose, but more often, it is light relief. No one can absorb their entertainment at full intensity all the time. It is important to have ups and downs. Pottering in video games is the equivalent of the humorous sidekick in a Hollywood blockbuster who slows down the pace before the director ratchets it back up again.

Pottering is not a universal necessity. In narrative-driven games (and I'm thinking of the very narrative here, like Telltales' *The Walking Dead* or the *Mean Girls* storyline in *Episode*), the need to move the story forward is paramount. The writers build light relief into their "game-on-rails" structure, and there is no need for the free-form pottering that you find in other games.

Some games have pottering in spades. Most role-playing games (RPGs) have inventory management and load-out optimisation: prime examples of pottering. Any game with a crafting system is a pottering game. Research, technology trees, upgrade paths, the books of lore hidden through *Baldur's Gate* and the lengthy exposition in *Planescape Torment* are all forms of pottering. Deck-building card games offer a clear division between the intensity of playing a match and the gentle relaxation of building a deck, tweaking a card choice, or considering whether it is worth crafting a new legendary card.

As service games have evolved, so has the role of pottering. A simplistic timeline of pottering might trace the development of simple arcade games, which just wanted your money and had no place for pottering, through to home computer games which needed to offer hours of gameplay to justify the substantial upfront payment, to early free-to-play games, which used energy to kick players out to disguise their lack of substance, to more advanced service games, which have realised that they need to cater to many different constituencies. They need to cater to people who don't have much time right now, but want to come in and have a short burst of fun or progress, as well as to those for whom a couple of hours with the game would be great. They also need to let players experience different levels of intensity during a Session, from the intense concentration of a firefight in *XCom* or a match in *League of Legends* to the more relaxed planning of your research tree or configuring a Runebook.

One of the most successful games of recent times, *Minecraft*, is a pottering game. The player can choose their own goals. They can jump between building something functional and creating something beautiful. They can set out to find a rare ore, or they can wander the landscape, admiring the unexpected scenery that emerges from a procedural generator. *Minecraft* is chock-full of loops, with much of its gameplay delivering addictive joy through Skinner-box style nature of its resource drops. Yet it is also one of the most freeform games ever.

There are no fixed rules about how to develop a pottering system in your game, but here are some thoughts on the motivations of why people engage with pottering and how to deliver it.

Enjoyable Make-Work

Some people enjoy the endless tinkering of making their environment neater, more efficient or expressive, even if it has little direct, mechanical impact on the game.

- Arranging things just so, like the music-loving protagonist in Nick Hornby's novel *High Fidelity* who arranged his albums biographically to chart the highs and lows of his love life.

- Moving a factory or conveyor belt in *Factorio* to improve efficiency or to make the factory more beautiful (although, to be fair, the whole of *Factorio* is a pottering game.)

- Arranging items and resources in an inventory to be more efficient or just more visually pleasing. (I spend an alarming amount of time moving items around the fictional island of Arulco in *Jagged Alliance 2*.)

Discovering More about the World and Theory Crafting

I discussed previously that idle games appealed to min-maxing players who want the progression and levelling up of an RPG, but without narrative and lore getting in the world. There is a cohort of people for whom exactly the opposite is true, the Bartle Explorers who love exploring worlds and discovering the narrative detail that underpins the games that they love. It satisfies the needs of gamers who favour Immersion in Quantic Foundry's Motivation Model, seeking Fantasy and Story.[9]

It is the opposite trait to the people who like idle games that strip away the lore and narrative from a traditional RPG. These players will look for opportunities to inhabit the world. Min-maxers, meanwhile, will look for ways to play the game more "optimally":

- Exploring the different technology trees and research available in *Civilisation*.

- Reading every journal, book and item description in a Bioware RPG.

- Crafting new decks in a collectible card game like *Hearthstone* or *Duelyst*.

Self-Expression

Self-expression is at its strongest when it is seen by other players, as we will see in Chapter 8: What Will People Pay for? If you are trying to generate revenue from self-expression, it is hard, although not impossible, to do that in a single-player game. On the other hand, if what you are trying to do is to allow players to tinker and potter, that can be done in a variety of ways in a single-player game.

- Creating a visually pleasing farm in *Hay Day* is irrelevant to the game mechanics. The game does not care if your farm is beautiful. But you might, and other players might.

- Changing outfits in an RPG.

- In many games, this also leads to Time to Penis (TTP), the length of time it takes for someone to make a large phallic object using whatever resources the game offers. If you give players any form of self-expression in your game, TTP will be short.

The objective from a design perspective is to allow players to choose their length of Session: to let them decide if today they just want to come in, achieve something, and then get out again, or if they want to spend a longer Session. To make them believe that this can be a short Session, and then to choose whether to stay or to go once they are in and playing.

Then, once the player is going to leave, it is critical to plant a Return Hook.

THE RETURN HOOK

A successful service game keeps people playing for days, weeks, months and years.

There is no magic bullet to making this happen. It requires skill, art, craft, judgment and not a little luck. To complement the strategic design of the Retention Layer, designers employ tactical Return Hooks to bring players back to the next session. Many of these techniques use bribes, rewards of in-game currency, items or loot crates to bring players back. *A successful game builds its Return Hooks into the core experience, making players come back to the game because they want to, not because they were bribed.* The Return Hooks set out here are a mixture of praise, bribes and other techniques that need to be paired with a successful Retention Layer to work well.

Many of these Return Hooks can be retrofitted to the game after launch. I often recommend not implementing these features until at least soft launch, so that you can determine whether your game has a strong Retention Layer without the crutch of these techniques.

Return Hook 1: Welcome Back

As a designer, you want players to come back to your game. When players do what we want, we should make them feel great. Idle game *Adventure Capitalist* shows you a screen that tells you how much money you earned while you were away. In Figure 6.4, you can see that I earned $460 quinvigintillion in the six or so hours that I was away from the game.[10]

Return Hook 2: Rewards

A simple Return Hook is to tell players to come back in a fixed time to get a reward.

Marvel Contest of Champions gives players the opportunity to claim a free crystal, once every 4 hours and once every 24 hours.

- The four-hour crystal contains a random low-level reward such as a health potion or some of the many in-game currencies.

- The 24-hour crystal contains more valuable rewards, such as a playable character.

This system is designed to build a regular habit of returning to the game with a predictable cadence.

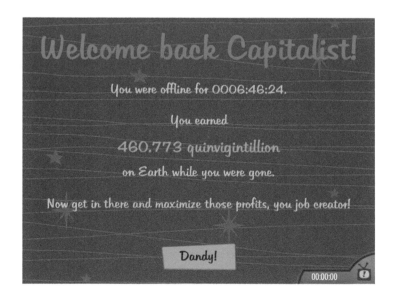

FIGURE 6.4 *Adventure Capitalist* rewards you for returning to the game by telling you how much you earned while you were away.

Return Hook 3: Accumulator Rewards

Accumulator rewards are a daily login bonus that rewards players for coming back multiple days in a row. Figure 6.5 shows the daily login screen for *Adventure Capitalist*. On day one, the player gets one gold, a premium currency. If the player logs in every day, the reward increases until the player earns a valuable premium item (in this case, a permanent ×3 profit multiplier), at which point the accumulator resets to day one. If the player misses a day, the accumulator resets without the large reward.

Bejeweled Blitz uses a slot-machine style generator to add a random element to its daily reward. In Figure 6.6, I have won 6,500 gold coins for returning and spinning my slot machine. The system shows complexity in layers; as an advanced player, I notice that I have gained a 100-gold bonus for this being my first day, which rises over time, as well as a bonus of 3,900 gold because 39 of my Facebook friends have installed the game, a small nudge to encourage me to invite more friends to play.[11]

Simpson's Tapped Out combines the two mechanics. Figure 6.7 shows that it has a five-day accumulator, earning in-game currency, at the end of which players earn a mystery box that can contain a variety of different rewards. The game is rewarding players for turning up five days in a row with a lottery ticket that offers the chance of winning a large in-game prize.

FIGURE 6.5   The daily login reward screen from *Adventure Capitalist*.

FIGURE 6.6 *Bejeweled Blitz* daily spin bonus.

Many of these games cap out their rewards after five or seven days. *The Simpsons* has a five-day accumulator, *Adventure Capitalist* had seven and most games seem to choose between three and seven days. My personal theory is that the choice of these durations is based on Loss Aversion. (See box on p. 54.)

Designers want players to come back to the game regularly. They want them to feel good about coming back. By coming back every day for a week, the player can feel good about the rewards he is earning. On the other hand, if he misses logging in for just a single day, he can lose a lot of accumulated progress. Designers must balance the increase in rewards with making sure that, if a player misses a day, he doesn't subsequently log in, see how much he has lost from at the accumulator and, because that loss feels so painful, choose never to log in again. Even if the response is not that extreme, the experience might weaken the On-Ramp, because when the player looks at the icon on their phone, he thinks, "That's the game that makes me feel bad when I load it."

This is only a theory. You can test out different accumulators in your games, and I'd be delighted if you shared the results of the tests with me via my website at www.gamesbrief.com if you do. You can also observe other games. Zynga experimented with open-ended accumulators that just kept going up with *Empires and Allies*, but it is not a model they have replicated recently. More recently, *Marvel Puzzle Quest* has an endless accumulator. One of my friends has clocked up 206 days of continuous logins to the game. I have been told that the accumulator is not actually cumulative: it's just a count of the days since you first logged in, but I don't

FIGURE 6.7 The daily accumulator from *Simpsons: Tapped Out.*

dare tell my friend this. I don't think he would forgive me when his login
streak dropped from 206 to 1 if my information proved to be erroneous.

Increasingly, we are seeing 30-day accumulators emerging, which were
first popularised in Asian markets. The model allows players to get a loyalty stamp for each day that they log in during the 30-day period. There
is no "return to zero" if players miss a day, unlike in the accumulators
explained previously. Instead, a player that misses a day is no longer on
track to get the biggest payout that month. If you design the accumulator
with large rewards for logging in for a total of, say, 5, 10, 20, and 27 days
per month, you can incentivise players to come back regularly to get their
next reward.

Login bonuses can be a powerful tool in your arsenal. However, they
are easy to design, well-known, and don't help you to learn whether the
core of your game has strong, natural retention. They are invaluable in a
live game but are unlikely to merit being in a soft launch candidate when
you are still trying to find the fun.

Return Hook 4: Appointment Mechanics

An Appointment Mechanic would ideally be a core part of the Retention
Layer as described in Chapter 3: The Retention Layer. If that is not possible, it is possible to retrofit an Appointment Mechanic onto most games.

Clash Royale's sessioning system, described on p. 80, is an elegant, external Appointment Mechanic. A player triggers a countdown to open one of
up to four chests that she earned by playing a match. At the end of the
countdown, which typically lasts three hours, she is motivated to return
to the game. She can choose to place a new chest in the unlock queue and
quit the game—a short Session with an easy On-Ramp—or she can think,

"I'm in the game now, I might as well have another match to earn a new chest." After the player has opened all four chests, she is encouraged to have a longer Session to refill the collection. It's an elegant mechanic to get players to revisit the game several times in the day and have a reason for a longer Session in the evening if they haven't already filled their chest collection that day—genuinely brilliant.

Return Hook 5: Decay

Michael Katkoff, writer of the excellent *Deconstructor of Fun*, describes a decay or wither system as "a mechanic that punishes a player for not returning to the game on time."[12] It has fallen out of favour with many developers because of the danger of feeling like a punishment if you do not return on time. Katkoff says, "What I see is a polarization of this mechanic: casual games such as *Hay Day* and *Farmville* have abandoned it while more [competitive] games such as *Boom Beach* and *Clash of Clans* have adopted this mechanic and taken it to extremes."[13]

Part of this is to do with the metaphor: when a crop withers, the player may feel that the designers are punishing him for not coming back; in a competitive game like *Clash of Clans*, being attacked by rivals is part of the core gameplay, and it makes sense that if you have not logged in for a while, your base has been looted.

An elegant Return Hook using decay will match the metaphor, genre and audience of the game, has a balance of punishment for not returning sooner and reward for returning at all and gives the player a sense of agency over the period within which they must return or risk being punished.

Return Hook 6: Live Events

Nearly all successful service games have a packed calendar of live events. These events drive player engagement and retention. It is easy to think of them as being core to your success.

This is not true.

Events are only valuable *once you have proven that your Core Loop works*. Applied too early, live events act as a Band-Aid, addressing the symptom—that you have poor retention—but not the cause—that you have not created a compelling Core Loop.

As I explain in Chapter 12: Production, there is a fundamental difference between development operations (that I call Development Agency, shortened to Dev Agency) and live operations (Live Agency). In Dev Agency, the design team is trying to "find the fun." Through the process of concepting, pre-production, production, soft-launch and hard launch, the team is experimenting to build the best, most-effective game that delivers on their creative vision while being fun and rewarding for the player and profitable for the organisation. That is Dev Agency. Once the game is live and functioning, a new set of priorities takes over. The game is now in Live Agency, when radical changes to gameplay and systems are hard to the point of impossibility. The objective now is to provide new updates and services that improve gameplay, retention and monetisation over time.

I recommend to my clients that they leave many obvious systems (like live events, daily login bonuses and even social features) from their game until after soft launch. The purpose of the soft launch is to demonstrate that you have found the fun in your game and the metrics are good enough to justify a marketed launch. Many of the obvious F2P tools are excellent for *amplifying* the fun that you have built into your Core Loop, but they are rarely the core of your experience. They are a distraction from your development priorities. Worse, they can make you believe that the beating heart of your game is stronger than it really is. That can kill games.

Live events can also be expensive to operate, requiring high levels of manual engagement. That is fine if your game is ticking over nicely and the live agents can work to maximise retention and revenue through a range of content drops and events. It is a problem if the game cannot be successful without this ongoing investment to sustain it.

Note that events *are* a powerful revenue generator once your game has found its mojo. They are one of the primary tools that live agents need to encourage existing players to spend more time and more money in the game. I am a massive supporter of events, but only once you are confident that you have found the fun in your Core Loop. If your Core Loop is not engaging in the first place, you are kidding yourself if you think events can save you. You should not use events as your primary Return Hook until you have proven that you can get high quality retention without them.

Return Hook 7: Social

Social Return Hooks can vary from the innate to the nagging. The same approach applies to social as applies to events. If the social design is central to your game experience, like the turn-taking in *Words with Friends* or *Draw Something* or the matchmaking in any player versus player (PvP) game, then it is important to include in your soft launch candidate, and you can adapt your system to function as a Return Hook as well.

If the design is external, nagging and could be retrofitted later with no harm to the game, like gifts in *Farmville* or soliciting for extra lives in *Candy Crush Saga*, it is best omitted until after soft launch.

Return Hook 8: Nudge

Repeat after me: local notifications are not a Return Hook. Sure, many successful games have them. I get pinged by *Marvel Contest of Champions* on a regular basis. It does get me back sometimes. It does sometimes work. But it feels like a needy boyfriend begging his girlfriend to spend time with him; the game has not earned my time, it has begged for it.

Many developers think that implementing a Return Hook is a simple coding question: hook up local notifications, Facebook alerts or an e-mail system, and ask the player to come back. The problem with this is that it is not systemic. It is, at best, a Band-Aid.

Let's think through some of the issues. The first is that you need to get permission for the game to give players local notifications or ask them to provide you with an e-mail address. For one of my clients (admittedly working on a branded game for a major advertiser), the opt-in rate for local notifications was less than 2%. Many local notifications add little value to the player, saying nothing more than, "Please come back to my game." Some games manage this better: *Hay Day* notifies players when the first of the crops are ready to be harvested, and again when all of them are harvested. This is useful to the player but only because it is paired with an appointment mechanic.

Secondly, a local notification is not, in its own right, something that a player wants. They might want to get the rewards from opening a chest in *Clash Royale*, they might want to take their turn in *Words with Friends* quickly so that they don't leave their friend waiting or they might want to log in to *Clash of Clans* because their shield has run out and they need to protect their base. In each of these cases, the local notifications are not the reason the player returns; they return because they are motivated by one of the other Return Hooks listed in this section. The notification nudged the return. It was not the cause of it.

Developers are improving their use of local notifications all the time. They wait until the player has started an action that has a timer and ask if they would like to be alerted when the countdown reaches zero. They explain why the notifications might be useful to the player, rather than just asking because they would be useful to the developer. They might pop up their own dialogue box to ask for permission first. If a player says no, they can ask again later, which is much harder if the player has denied permission at an operating-system level. These improvements mean that it is possible to get local notification acceptance rates up to a much higher rate, perhaps as high as 50%.

Local notifications are a useful tool to make your Return Hooks more powerful. They are not a Return Hook in their own right. You should make sure you have people returning to your game because of the mechanics you have built long before you bother to build local notifications.

We have now covered the core framework for designing a successful service game. We have explored the Base Layer and the Retention Layer and how the Core Loop connects them. We have considered the Session. We have investigated how to build a successful On-Ramp and make it easy for players to decide that they have time to play your game right now and that it will be fun and rewarding to do so. We have thought about offering an Off-Ramp by signalling to players that they have reached a point where it would be sensible for them to leave if they want to, while also making it possible for them to extend their Session by pottering. We have looked at different ways of planting Return Hooks and encouraging players to start the cycle over with the next Session.

The focus on retention is critical, but we also need to look at the subset of your players who generate most of the revenue. It is time to meet the Superfan.

CHAPTER 7

The Superfan Layer

S ERVICE GAMES NEED TO engage their Superfans.

There is a myth about free-to-play (F2P) games that because only a small percentage of your audience will pay anything at all in your game, you must have a vast audience to succeed. Like many myths, there is a kernel of truth hidden within it, but it can be dangerous to take it at face value.

In February 2014, mobile marketing firm Swrve published its first *Mobile Games Monetization* report.[1] The headline was shocking: "Swrve Finds that 0.15% of Mobile Gamers Contribute 50% of All In-Game Revenue." Swrve found that the vast majority of players spend no money in a game in a given month. In the month that Swrve studied, only 1.5% of players spent any money on mobile games. The mathematically agile amongst readers will note that means that 98.5% spent no money at all. Swrve broke the data down further, as shown in Figure 7.1.

Swrve charts every paying player in the month in deciles by total spend. As they say in their report, "in plain English, that means we show the bottom 10%—that is, the 10% of users who spent the least in total—on the left and move in 10% steps to the top 10% on the right." One way to think about this is that Swrve took all the users in a given month and ranked them by order of spend. They then grouped them into ten "buckets." The first bucket is the 10% of users who spent the least, the last group is the 10% who spent the most, with eight buckets in between.

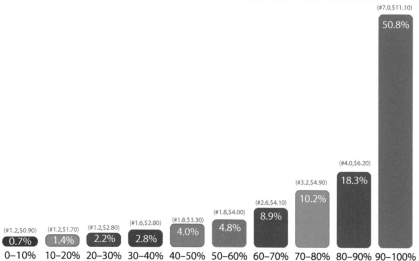

PERCENTAGE OF TOTAL REVENUE BY PLAYER SPEND CATEGORY

FIGURE 7.1 Swrve's analysis of spend in mobile games in January 2014. The numbers in parentheses show the average number of transactions and average spend in that month for each decile.

Swrve provided additional data, too. It showed, for example, that the bucket with the least spend, the bottom 10% of spenders, generated 0.7% of total revenue, with an average of 1.2 transactions in that month and an average purchase price of $0.90 per transaction. For the 50%–60% decile, those figures are 4.8% of the revenue with an average of 1.8 transactions and an average purchase price of $4.00.

By grouping users into buckets, we can start to get a mental model of how spend is spread. The picture that Swrve paints is one where a limited number of players are the core of the revenue. The top bucket, which is that 10% of users who spent the most, represented 50.8% of total spend. They completed an average of 7.0 transactions with an average transaction value of $11.10. The top 20% taken together represent 69.1% of revenue, and the top 30% make 79.3% of revenue. Remember, these figures are of *paying* players. Only 1.5% of players spent *any money at all* in this month, so the top decile represents 0.15% of the total playing audience. Looking at the top three deciles, or 30% of total spend, we see that nearly 80% of the revenue (79.3%) comes from just half a percent (0.45% of the audience.)

A WORD ABOUT AVERAGES

In service-based games, averages are misleading.

Humans tend to understand averages through the lens of physical properties. If I tell you that the height of an average male human is 5′9″ and ask you to guess the height of the next male human to walk through the door, 5′9″ would not only be a pretty good guess, you are unlikely to be more than 6 inches wrong in either direction.

Wealth, on the other hand, is not constrained by physical properties. The median wealth of a US household is $68,828.[2] The richest man in the world, Jeff Bezos, had a net worth of $91 billion in 2017.[3] Jeff Bezos is more than a million times richer than the median household.

In practical terms, this means that when you read an "average" figure about service games, you need to think hard about what it tells you. In the world of physical products, if a game generated retail revenue of $40 million and sold a million units, you could surmise not only that the average sale price was $40, but that most sales took place at around that value.

If a service game says it has a million players and $40 million in revenue, you have no idea whether that means that most players spend about $40, or one crazy rich tycoon is spending $40 million on the game and everyone else is playing for free.

For most games, the distribution is likely to look like the Swrve data shown in Figure 7.1. Most people spend nothing, then those who do follow a distribution that is closer to a power law than a Normal distribution. A useful test is to query your data for the mean spend, the median spend, and the modal spend. The closer they are together, the more your game generates revenue according to a Normal distribution. The further they are apart, the more your game follows a Power Law distribution (Figure 7.2).

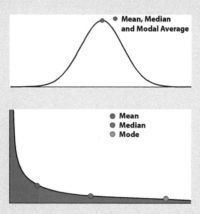

Figure 7.2   Illustrative graphs of a normal distribution (top) and a power law (bottom).

A successful service game has many users but, if it is free-to-play, many of those players are not spending. To generate sufficient revenue from those who do, you need to enable the Superfans. That means letting *the players who love your game spends lots of money on things they really value.* Let's break that down into its constituent parts.

> *The players who love your game*: It is hard to get people who are not enjoying your game to pay you anything at all, particularly when an alternative free game is easy to find on a mobile store or on the Internet. The focus on making people love what you do—the difference between hunting whales and nurturing Superfans—means that you are at less risk from "buyer's remorse." If your strategy is to trick a player into spending, they will figure that out, possibly after the first transaction. Because customer acquisition is expensive and difficult, it is a risky approach to hoodwink players into spending; it makes them less likely to come back for more. It is much easier to create fans, then Superfans, and to give them continued opportunities to spend.

> *Spend lots of money*: The Swrve data makes it clear how dependent the F2P industry is on a subset of users to generate the majority of revenue for its games. We are long past the days when we could say, "users spend an average of 99 cents on a game," and mean "most people spend 99 cents." To give a different example, if you imagine that your game has a conversion rate of 1%, then to generate the same revenue as you previously got from your customers all spending 99 cents, you now need 1% of your audience to spend $99. Your game design must enable players to spend lots of money.

> *On things they really value*: A single transaction is valuable, but repeat transactions are even more so. As the Swrve data in Figure 7.1 shows, the Superfans not only spend more per transaction ($11.10 average compared with $6.20 for the next decile), they have more transactions (7.0 transactions per month compared with 4.0 transactions). If you are selling the users snake oil or tricking them into spending using nothing but psychological techniques, they are unlikely to keep coming back.

Getting these three components right—making a game that users, or at least some of them, love, letting them spend lots of money and making sure that they get something that they value in return—is at the heart of a successful F2P game.

WORDS TO BAN #1: WHALES

I hate the term *whales*.

It is a word drawn from the gambling industry to describe their high rollers, the heavy spenders who gamble huge sums of money and often lose them.[4]

I hate the word *whales* because words have power. When you hear a phrase, it guides your thoughts. If I tell you not to think of a white bear, a mental image of a polar bear is likely to appear in your mind's eye.

Let's think about what the word *whales* implies. It associates high spenders with the majestic creatures that swim in pods across the vast expanse of the Earth's oceans. We (or at least some of us) track those creatures down in large, ocean-going, factory ships. We hunt them from fast, armed launches. We fire grenade harpoons deep into their flesh, where they explode.

To become part of this hunt, we abandon, temporarily, part of our humanity. We view these creatures not as majestic wonders but as fodder for our cannon, beasts whose role is to serve humankind. We hunt them for our own commercial purpose, and we need to get them fast for fear our rivals from Norway, Iceland or Japan will get there first.[5]

When we view our players as potential whales, we dehumanise them. We create a mind-set where players are dumb creatures too stupid to "outwit" our monetisation systems. Where predatory tactics are justified by "survival of the fittest" and where we must race to hunt down the whales in our games before a rival company snaffles them.

Contrast that with treating your most engaged players as Superfans. If you want to create fans of your game, you must create something that people love. You must nurture your players until they become fans. You must nurture those fans until they become Superfans.

A whale is not an aspirational noun. Few people aspire to be whales. Many people aspire to be fans. I want to make the kind of games where people are proud to say, "I'm a Superfan of that game."

I get accused of rebranding "whales" as "Superfans" because it has a better PR ring to it. It is true that Superfans sounds better in the press, but that is not the reason I try to ban the word with my clients. I ban it because if you focus on Superfans, it helps you, as game developers, have empathy with what you are trying to do to become a commercially successful service game: make games that people want to keep playing and offer them things that they value, that they can buy, and keep on buying, with no sense of buyer's remorse.

VARIABLE PRICING

The value of enabling the Superfans is that you are able to, in terms an economist would use, access the entire length of the demand curve. The demand curve depicts the relationship between the price of a certain commodity and the amount of it that your customers are willing and able to purchase at any given price. Figure 7.3 shows an illustrative demand curve.

In the old world of physical distribution, it was not practical to have hundreds of different price points for every game. If I walked into GameStop and picked up a copy of *Tomb Raider*, the sales assistant had no idea if I was Lara Croft's greatest fan or if I hated posh English explorers and everything they stand for. He didn't know if I would pay an enormous premium to be one of the first people to explore Lara's new adventures or if he would have to pay me to even try the game out. So he asks me for $40 and I can take it or leave it.

In economics, the demand curve is often paired with the supply curve to estimate the equilibrium price. The market clearing price is determined by figuring out where the demand curve (how much customers are willing to pay) and the supply curve (how much suppliers are willing to sell at) meet. The emergence of digital distribution, competition and piracy has led to the collapse of the market clearing price of much digital content. Album sales have collapsed and video games have seen a rush to free on mobile and to cheap on PC. Consumers now have an enormity of choice. There is so much high-quality content available, legally or illegally, that they can enjoy all the entertainment that they have time to consume in a

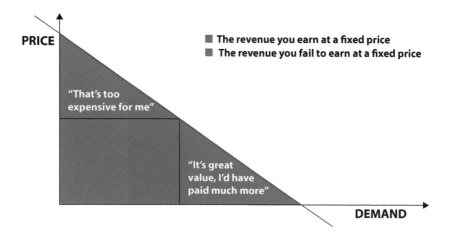

FIGURE 7.3 An illustrative demand curve.

dozen lifetimes without paying a cent. Developers creating a service game have significant competition outside their own game.

But they have none within it.

Within your own game, you are a monopoly supplier. You control access to the content, to the upgrades, to the currencies and to the packs of collectible content. You have built a world where players want to spend time and money, and no one else can put things into it. You have absolute control over what you sell, for how much, and to whom.

When you are the only supplier of a commodity, like the content, currency and other in-app purchases in your game, you no longer have to worry about the supply curve. The only thing that you need to do is to satisfy the demands of your players, whether they are freeloaders or Superfans. The objective of a service game designer is to create a place where players have the desire to spend time and money and then to fulfil those desires. In doing so, you are addressing the challenge of free not by suing your customers, or by complaining about the unfairness of changing business models and the elimination of the old lock on distribution exerted by a few powerful publishers. You are building a business that is dependent on finding Superfans, satisfying their needs and desires and enabling them to spend lots of money. Framed through that lens, building games for Superfans is empowering.

WHAT MAKES A SUCCESSFUL SUPERFAN LAYER?

This is a million-dollar question. Or in the case of Supercell, the developer of *Clash of Clans* and *Hay Day* that was acquired by Chinese Internet giant Tencent in 2016, a $10-billion-dollar question. There are many answers, and lots of different games deliver a different Superfan experience for their most committed players.

Another way to look at the Superfan Layer is to consider that Superfans are created when *your* game becomes *their* hobby. They have changed from being *gamers* who play lots of games to Superfans who mainly play your game. (I am a Superfan of *Hearthstone* and have been for three years, to the detriment of my playtime in other games.) Typically, the Superfans are a tiny proportion of your player base. They make a huge time commitment to the game, and, as we have seen, they can easily be half of your revenue.

Some of the best data on Superfans comes from Kongregate. Kongregate started life as a portal for Flash-based web games but has morphed over the past decade into a successful destination and publisher for F2P games. CEO and co-founder Emily Greer started her career in direct marketing for catalogue retailers. Kongregate is therefore in the unusual position of having both access to statistical data for hundreds of different games on its platform together with a CEO who loves to analyse and talk about the aggregate data gleaned from those games. Greer's Game Developers Conference (GDC) talks are a wealth of information, and I highly recommend them.[6]

Kongregate is dependent on Superfans. In her 2015 GDC talk, Greer explained that only 2.1% of all the players who have ever been active on Kongregate spent any money on virtual goods or currency in the Kongregate platform, and 75% of Kongregate's revenue comes from those virtual goods and currency.[7] Figure 7.4 shows how spending breaks down on Kongregate's platform.

The chart shows that 54% of spenders have spent less than $10 on Kongregate, but they represent only 1% of Kongregate's revenue. The 4% of players who have spent more than $500 represent 72% of Kongregate's revenue. Remember that only 2.1% of players spend anything at all, so 72% of Kongregate's revenue comes from 0.084% (4% × 2.1%) of its audience. Kongregate is a Superfan business. In her GDC talk, Greer also revealed that average lifetime spend amongst all players is $117, but the median is $10, demonstrating that, like most variable pricing businesses, there is a power law at work here.

In a different lecture at GDC in 2013, Greer identified characteristics that make a successful Superfan game. "Every high ARPU (average revenue per

SPENDERS BY SPENDER CATEGORY

■ $1–$10 ■ $10–$50 ■ $50–$100
■ $100–$500 ■ $500+

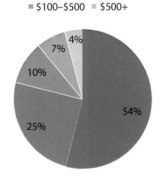

REVENUE BY SPENDER CATEGORY

■ $1–$10 ■ $10–$50 ■ $50–$100
■ $100–$500 ■ $500+

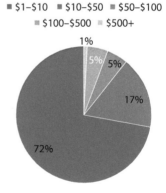

FIGURE 7.4 Breakdown of Kongregate's spenders and revenue. (Adapted from Emily Greer, "Don't Call Them Whales: F2P Spenders and Virtual Value", March 4, 2015. https://blog.kongregate.com/dont-call-themwhales-f2p-spenders -and-virtual-value/.)

user) and high revenue game on Kongregate has a strongly social and competitive endgame." Superfan Layers are often where the game changes and adapts for a smaller community of highly engaged players. The Superfan Layer is often competitive and collaborative, a social experience. It is me and my friends against you and your friends. A clash. Of clans.

The four key themes set out below emerge from Greer's analysis of games with successful Superfan Layers.

Guilds or Leagues

Guilds, leagues and alliances give Superfans purpose in the game. It engages Cialdini's Social Proof ("this is how people play") and can also trigger Commitment ("I've got to do this or I'll let the clan down") and Reciprocity ("They helped me, now I need to pay them back"). It can also help to drive monetisation. Although there is a stigma in some territories around pay-to-win, this is often lessened if the purpose of spending is "not to let your buddies down" or "spending to compensate for my lack of practice or skill." The creation of guilds and leagues creates strong positive *and* negative reinforcement to engage with the game because players have to keep their promises to other humans within the game, and if they let them down, they can be punished by being ostracised from the guild.

Guild Warfare or Leaderboards

There are a variety of ways to foster competition between groups of players in video games. Greer's point is that successful Superfan games have groups of players coming together and then offering those players a way to compete with other, similarly committed players, either directly or indirectly.

PvP (Either Synchronous or Asynchronous)

Player versus player (PvP) gameplay offers variety, unpredictability and, for some players, a desire to beat the opponent that is so strong, it can drive purchase behaviour. Although Bartle Killers are only about a quarter of the market, they are the easiest to monetise.[8] In some games, it can be critical to spend money on yourself or your guild to remain in the top echelons of the game. *Wired* interviewed Superfans of *Clash of Clans* who were spending $5,000 a month or more to remain competitive. A player who went by the name Metamorphaz told *Wired* that "he just wants to be a good teammate. He's not interested in topping the leaderboards, but loves the feeling of sending his highly-leveled troops to help out his fellow clan members."[9] These players are not spending money to get the things in the game, as much as to increase their social bonds or status within the game.

Visible Status and Character Progression

Alongside character progression is self-expression. Superfans not only want to do well, they want to be seen to do well. We will cover why people spend and on what in Chapter 8: What Will People Pay For?

DIFFERENT STRATEGIES FOR THE SUPERFAN LAYER

There is no "one-size-fits-all solution" for the Superfan layer. For some games, the Superfan Layer is mainly incentivising players to keep playing the Core Loop time and again. In *Crossy Road*, completionist players might want to collect all the different road-crossing avatars. This can take a long time to grind, or you can spend money to accelerate the process. In *Kingdom Rush*, where I have completed all the achievements in all three games, the Superfan Layer again appeals to completionists. Much of the game is about replaying levels over and over again to unlock specific achievements—some of which are hard enough that is worth considering spending money to upgrade your abilities or buy special powers. In *Candy Crush Saga*, the driver is to make progress along the map and to complete new levels, although player motivation can be driven by "desire to progress," by "competition with your friends" or both. I have spent money in *Candy Crush Saga* on durable upgrades such as increasing my available pool of lives from five to eight.

At the other extreme, we have strategy games where the Superfan Layer is almost a game in its own right. Players of mobile strategy titles like *Clash of Clans* or *Mobile Strike* participate in alliances that need commitment and time from the players. Successful players might need to spend thousands of dollars to stay at the very top of the leaderboard. In *Hearthstone*, I have spent more than £1,000 to have access to all the different cards that I want, although this has not enabled me to pay to win. I usually end a season in the top 10% of players and occasionally in the top 0.5% (but not yet Legend). I would class myself as a Superfan of *Hearthstone*.

An apocryphal story from *World of Tanks* can illustrate the unexpected nature of a Superfan Layer. *World of Tanks* is a popular tank-fighting game with a strong following in Central and Eastern Europe and the former Soviet Union. A Russian oligarch started playing the game and enjoyed it so much he spent lots of money to acquire lots of the best gear in the game. Unfortunately, all the gear and no idea of what to do with it is not a winning strategy in *World of Tanks* and the oligarch continued to lose.

So, he did what any self-respecting oligarch would do: he hired body-guards. He searched through *World of Tanks* looking for skilled players that he liked. He offered them the chance to quit their jobs and come to work for him. Their job: *World of Tanks* players. Their only responsibil-ity was that whenever the oligarch called, day or night, they had to drop whatever they were doing, log into the game and form a protective screen around the oligarch. He could then storm through the game, shooting whomever he fancied with a team of bodyguards to protect him from his own incompetence.[10]

The moral of this anecdote is that developers are not always in control of their Superfan Layer. At first, the Russian oligarch spent money in the way that the developers expected, by buying cool gear for himself. He then started to spend money in a way that they did not expect, and they could not track. He bankrolled an entire squad of players to form his own private army in the game. Players who love what you do will spend lots of money on things they truly value, whether you intend them to or not.

Perhaps the most famous *laissez-faire* game of all is *EVE Online*. Launched in 2003, *EVE Online* is a persistent, massively multiplayer online (MMO) game set in space where the only rule is that, other than hacking the code, anything goes. Players can mine, trade, craft, explore, or band together into guilds, known as corporations, and start galactic battles that can change the destiny of the single shared universe.

EVE Online was launched as a subscription MMO. After the initial trial, which at different times in *EVE*'s history has lasted between 14 and 30 days, it was not possible to play the game for free. That changed in November 2016, when *EVE* went free-to-play, enabling players to play the game for free forever, although certain skills and ships are only available to Omega players.[11] Becoming an Omega player, however, is not only a matter of spending money.

In 2008, *EVE Online* introduced Plex, a virtual currency, at a time when real money in a video game was a new concept. Plex is not a traditional virtual currency. It is an in-game item that represents 30 days of subscrip-tion to *EVE Online*. Until recently, it was an item in the in-game inventory that could be stolen by other players or destroyed. It can be purchased with ISK, an in-game currency that players earn by mining, crafting, trading or raiding. Some players play the game entirely for free by earning so much money in game they can buy the Plex they need to pay for the subscrip-tion (in the old business model) or upgrade their clone to Omega state (in the new business model) from players who don't have so much free time. Those players buy Plex from CCP, the game developers, and sell it for ISK in the game, enabling them to buy the things that they want or need within the game. The system enables variable pricing within a subscription game without breaking the economy or the player experience.

The Superfan Layer in *EVE Online* is complex. Major corporations in *EVE* have all the trappings of real-world corporations. They have CEOs and boards of directors. They have HR managers with complex spreadsheets of who does what and when. They have manufacturing teams making the items the corporation needs, logistics teams getting the items to where they are needed, and finance teams to make sure the corporation has the working capital to pay for it all.

They also have spies.

One of the most famous players in the *EVE* universe is known as the Mittani. His real name is Alexander Gianturco and his background is corporate law, but he became famous through his role as spymaster for an Alliance called GoonSwarm. In 2009, the most powerful Alliance in the *EVE Online* universe was called Band of Brothers, a collection of corporations (*EVE*'s version of guilds) that controlled vast swathes of space. Band of Brothers owned, or was building, many of *EVE*'s biggest capital ships, Titans, whose real-world value is estimated at about $6,000 each.

A disgruntled senior member of Band of Brothers, with the in-game name of Haargoth Agamar, contacted the Mittani offering his services. Gianturco realised that he had a fabulous opportunity. Agamar had the appropriate permissions to disband the Band of Brothers alliance, to eliminate its sovereignty and to shut down its defences across vast swathes of the online galaxy. When he did so, the Mittani would be able to re-register the corporation's name and identity and prevent Band of Brothers ever reforming.

The BBC reported on the story like this:

> "The chief executive of the world's biggest corporation gets a phone call in the middle of the night. Thanks to industrial espionage, the company has been bankrupted, assets stripped, bank accounts emptied. When trading starts the next day, even the company name will be gone."[12]

In the space of 24 hours, Band of Brother's domination of the world of *EVE Online* was ended. Although it would take the GoonSwarm and its allies some time to move in and mop up the remnants of the corporation, Band of Brothers was gone. The Mittani took to the Internet, via forums, press interviews and YouTube videos to explain what had happened and his role at the centre of it.

The Mittani is a construct, a character played by a real-life human. For Alexander Gianturco, there is more to *EVE Online* than flying a spaceship in the fictional universe of New Eden. His conversations with the character known as Haargoth Agamar took place outside the confines of the game, and the Mittani has become known as the most important *EVE Online* player who never logs into the game.

The Superfan Layer of *EVE Online* takes place within the game but also outside it. (This is a true metagame. See What Is the Metagame?) For many *EVE Online* players, *EVE* is the only game they play. It takes as many hours a week as a full-time job. It is a true commitment. Those players have become Superfans.

I'd like to give as a final example a game that I have worked on since 2008. *Stronghold Kingdoms* is the massively multiplayer online version of *Stronghold*, the castle-building strategy game first released in 2001 by Firefly Studios. Firefly has taken its loyal audience and created for them a persistent, medieval world where players build villages, protect them with castles and engage in diplomacy, scouting and warfare to control parishes, shires and even entire countries.

The most important screen for Superfans in *Stronghold Kingdoms* is shown in Figure 7.5. It is the Glory race. The highest-level factions in the game compete to see who will be the first to reach Glory Rank 1. When a faction reaches that exalted position, the race is declared over. It is time for a new age on that world and the race starts again. It can take months for a Glory race to be completed, and factions strive hard to win it. However, many players are not aware of its existence. Like the ordinary people in *Game of Thrones*, they try to get on with their gaming lives, building villages and castles and expanding their influence while factions vie above their heads—and occasionally sweep by, destroying everything in their path. As you can see from the screenshot, the Glory race is not a high-fidelity experience. It is experienced outside the game in the players' heads, in their forums and communications channels. It was enabled by Firefly, but it is not visible to every single player at all times. It is a game for Superfans.

The Pyramid Is Not One-Size-Fits-All

Throughout this section, I've talked about the Base Layer, the Retention Layer and the Superfan Layer as three parts of the whole—the segments

WHAT IS THE METAGAME?

I have avoided using the term *metagame* in this book. Metagame has many different definitions in current usage in the games industry. For some companies, it is everything that is not the Base Layer. The Retention Layer, the Superfan Layer and everything outside the game is the metagame. Bungie called the campaign scoring in *Halo 3* the metagame, for example.

For some designers, the end game, or the elder game, is the metagame. This is often the stage when players band together to make a big impact on the game or is just very advanced, single-player game play. It doesn't seem very meta to me.

Richard Garfield, designer of *Magic the Gathering*, is often credited with inventing the term in a talk at GDC in 2000.

> "My definition of the metagame is broad. It is how a game interfaces with life. A particular game, played with the exact same rules will mean different things to differ people, and those differences are the metagame. The rule of poker may not change between a casino game, a neighbourhood nickel-dime-quarter game, and a game played for matchsticks but the player experience in those games will certainly change. The experience of roleplaying with a group of story-oriented players and playing with some goal-oriented power partners is completely different, even though the underlying rules being played with may be the same."[13]

Chris Bateman, philosopher and game designer, defines metagame design as "player experience design at the level of the community."[14] I agree. I find the use of *metagame* to mean "everything other than the Base Layer" unhelpful to designers and foolish in its assumption that the Base Layer is the "proper" game and everything else is external to the experience.

As a result, I use the word rarely. I use metagame, in an etymologically precise way, to mean everything outside the game. It means the changing card decks in *Hearthstone* or the changing team compositions in *League of Legends*. I use it for Alliance politics in *EVE Online*. The metagame can be defined as "external aspects of the game that have an influence over the game itself."

Everything else falls into the Base Layer, the Retention Layer or the Superfan Layer.

FIGURE 7.5 *Stronghold Kingdoms'* Glory.

of a successful, profitable, enjoyable game. I've drawn the Pyramid with a triangular shape, with each layer sitting neatly above the next.

The reality is not so neat. Many games have different-shaped pyramids. An accessible game that is easy to pick up and play that you can replay again and again is mostly a Base Layer game. For endless runners like *Minion Rush* or *Sonic Dash*, or any game based on classic arcade gameplay, the success of the game depends more on the joy of playing the Base Layer than the long-term, strategic enjoyment of the Retention Layer. The Pyramid for a game like this might have a wide base, a narrow Retention Layer and very little for the Superfans. This is a game for the mass market, where the potential for Superfans to spend thousands of dollars on things they really value is limited.

A resource management game like *Hay Day* or an idle game like *Adventure Capitalist* is a Retention Layer game. Its Base Layer barely exists. The joy for a player is found in the optimisation and efficiency of making progress through a game that is less about fail-states and more about medium and long-term goals. These games may or may not have a Superfan Layer, but they typically have a tiny Base Layer.

Some games are much more about the Superfan Layer. *Mobile Strike* focuses lots of effort in the early experience to get players to join alliances.

I do not have specific insight into their strategy, but my hypothesis is that *Mobile Strike* is a Superfan-centric game. If players are not in alliances, they are unlikely ever to engage with the deep, social (and, for developer Machine Zone, profitable) gameplay that exists in the social, collaborative and competitive Superfan Layer.

As for *EVE Online*, it is sufficiently complicated that almost everyone who plays it is a Superfan.

In designing for Superfans, game developers must think broadly about what their players want, what they will value, and what they can sensibly sell them without breaking the game. At the heart of this is answering the question: what will people pay for?

CHAPTER 8

What Will People Pay For?

T HE SALE OF VIRTUAL goods has long confused observers who do not participate in video games. Journalists seem to find the idea particularly hard. In 2009, Claire Cain Miller and Brad Stone wrote in the *New York Times*, "Silicon Valley may have discovered the perfect business: charging real money for products that do not exist." In September 2011, Nick Wingfield wrote in the *Wall Street Journal*, "To understand why Zynga, Inc. is among the tech industry's hottest companies, consider how it gets people to buy things that don't exist." "Marketing Fanciful Items in the Land of Make Believe" was the headline above an article in the *New York Times*.[1]

That smart journalists can show so little understanding of the world around them still surprises me.

Let's start with the basics. When you buy a newspaper, do you buy some dead trees mashed into pulp and squashed into flat sheets? Or are you buying the ideas and thoughts, news and analysis, opinion and entertainment that those pages contain? When you buy a movie, are you buying a shiny disc or are you buying the ability to be transported to another time and place for the next two hours? When you buy an album, are you buying the physical product, or the ability for music to make you feel, to make your heart soar and your emotions flow?

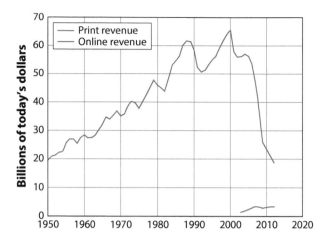

FIGURE 8.1   Advertising revenue for US newspapers.[2]

Of course, in the 21st century, hardly anyone buys newspapers or CDs. We long ago separated the value of content from its distribution method. For decades, newspaper magnates thought that they were in the business of selling news. They are not.

Figure 8.1 shows advertising revenue for US newspapers, as published by the Newspaper Association of America in 2012. It grew from $20 billion in 1950 to more than $60 billion in 2000, before falling precipitously in barely a decade back to the 1950 level. Online advertising revenue for the newspaper industry did grow during the decade of decline, but not by anywhere near enough to replace the revenue lost from print.

It is no coincidence that newspaper revenue peaked in 2000, the height of the dotcom boom when new Internet companies could raise money cheaply to try to disrupt exist businesses. Many failed, but many of the most iconic businesses of the present day succeeded: Amazon went public in 1997, eBay in 1998 and Google, a relative latecomer to the search business, in 2004.

The technology of the Internet decimated newspapers. It did so by exposing the great lie of the newspaper industry: that newspapers sell news. What newspapers sell is *distribution*.

Distribution in the pre-digital era was hard. Every day, newspaper businesses had to discover the news, write it down, edit it, typeset it, print it and distribute it across the whole country to be read by millions of people over breakfast. Newspaper proprietors realised that they had solved the difficult problem of getting these sheets of paper in front of people. They also realised that people wanted more than just news.

They wanted sports and puzzles, the weather and financial reports, television listings and opinion columns. They also realised that advertisers wanted to reach those audiences.

In 1833, a young businessman named Benjamin Day started a new business. He launched a newspaper, the *New York Sun*, at a price of one cent, a massive discount to the more usual price of six cents. Day lost money on every single copy. His insight was that by selling cheaply, he could build a large audience that would make him more attractive to advertisers. Day was one of the first of the "attention merchants," a phrase coined by Tim Wu, a professor at Columbia University in his book of the same name.[3]

By the end of the 20th century, the model was clear. Sell newspapers at a loss, or even give them away for free. Make up the shortfall, and perhaps a profit, by charging advertisers to reach the audience you had created. Then the Internet came along and changed everything.

The Internet is an unparalleled tool for distributing information. It has enabled business to exist that could not have existed in the pre-digital age. I run a website called *GAMESbrief*, a site dedicated to people who are interested in the business of games. In the pre-digital era, this would have been a magazine, and it would have been difficult to run profitably. I would have needed journalists, typesetters, printers and workers in vans delivering papers to retailers. I would have needed an advertising sales force to sell the ads required to subsidise the existence of the magazine.

Now, I can build it myself. I set up the website. I wrote blog posts and analysis articles to see if there was an audience. I built a consultancy on the back of the website. At times, I have had expert help from skilled freelancers to move the site forward, and at times, I have had none.[4] In a good month, I get 10,000 readers, for a site that I can run and maintain on my own. From my living room. In my underpants. I don't, but I could. (I apologise for this mental image.)

The classified ads left the newspapers first. Why scour through page after page of hardcopy when a searchable database is so much better? Job listings. Property. Cars. Then areas of content that were valuable to certain advertisers: Finance. Personal Finance. Sport. Even the weather. The newspapers were left with news and opinion, which few people valued enough to pay for.

It turns out that newspapers did not sell what they thought they did. They thought they sold news when they actually sold distribution—the ability to reach readers—to third parties who can now, thanks to the Internet, access that distribution cheaply for themselves. There is still enormous social value to quality news reporting. In both the United States and the United Kingdom, we are seeing the negative consequences of reduced budgets for traditional news reporting. This is exacerbated by the growth in click-bait journalism, driven by a business need that values page impressions and shareability over accuracy and balance. Unfortunately, the social value of news is not matched by the preparedness of readers to pay for it.

The same phenomenon is at work in the entertainment industries. We used to think that we sold books, movies or games. To take the example of a book, we are now selling two products that used to be indivisible. A book is both a collection of dead organic matter—the distribution mechanism—and the ideas and facts and stories contained within—the content. For 500 years, from Gutenberg until the invention of the Internet, the separation was a philosophical construct. You could not have the book without the paper. The Internet, and subsequent technologies such as the e-book, the e-reader and the tablet, made the philosophical distinction real.

The consequence is that book publishers have had to think differently about their product. Some readers value the physical books: I buy all my business and game design books in physical format because they are more useful to me that way. I can scribble in them. I can find the argument I want by flicking through the pages. When I want to remember an argument, I turn my head to my bookshelf and see Chris Anderson's *Free* or Raph Koster's *A Theory of Fun* and all their ideas come flooding back to me. Books are, for me, additional memory, an external hard drive I can access when I need to.

For other people, they are physical objects that are joyful in their own right. They might be things they can gift or share. They might be status symbols (more of that later).

On the other hand, some books I choose not to buy physically. Trashy action thrillers. Genre fiction. Disposable entertainment. They do not merit taking up room in my home. (I live in London. Space is scarce.) Those books I keep on my Kindle. One explanation for the sudden success of E. L. James erotic novel, *50 Shades of Grey* was the rise of the e-reader. According to Amazon, it sold four times as many copies digitally as physically.[5] Some things you don't want to display to other people.

These trends are showing a broader theme: the separation of content from distribution. In the pre-Internet era, publishers could protect the value of content because they were members of an elite few—an oligopoly—that controlled access to distribution. It was not possible to get a record made, a book published or a video game into stores without a publisher. The publisher was financier and gatekeeper, and it could extract what economists call "economic rent" from its control of the means of distribution.

The Internet has destroyed that era, and the rise of F2P games is a direct and successful response to this situation. To understand that, we need to look at the early days of the App Store.

At Macworld in January 2008, Steve Jobs introduced the idea of the App Store, a retail experience that would suit on top of the revolutionary iPhone. The App Store offered developers a better commercial deal: they would keep 70% of the revenue they generated, and Apple would keep 30%. The real heart of the announcement was not the revenue share, though. It was how Apple was going to handle a price point that was to change the way consumers viewed content on their phones:

> "We talk about the 70/30 revenue split, but the developer gets to pick the price, and you know what price a lot of developers will pick? Free. So when a developer wants to distribute an app for free, there is no charge for free apps. There is no charge to the user and there is no charge to the developer. We're going to pay for everything to get those apps out there for free. The developer and us have the exact same interest which is to get as many apps out in front of as many iPhone users as possible."[6]

Despite "free" being the main price point, the App Store generates a lot of revenue. Developers have earned more than $60 billion since the App Store launched in 2008. They made $20 billion in 2016 alone. They made $240 million on a single day: New Year's Day 2017.[7] They are making that revenue largely from games that are priced at free but played on a phone that costs hundreds of dollars. How did that happen?

It wasn't always going to be that way. Back in 2008, the going price for a game was $9.99. Games on feature phones sold for prices ranging from $3 for a simple puzzle game up to $7 for branded tie-ins like *Assassin's Creed* or a game based on the latest blockbuster movie. Charging a premium for games on the iPhone seemed sensible, especially when those games compared favourably with titles on platforms like the Nintendo DS, whose customers were used to spending $20 or more on a single game. Publishers like Sega and Electronic Arts released games such as *Super Monkey Ball*, *Bejeweled 2* and *Tetris* at very high prices.[8] As Justin Davis, editor of *IGN Wireless*, put it:

"When the App Store launched, companies like Gameloft thought they could get away with charging $3.99 or more for simple solitaire, chess and Sudoku apps. The companies didn't even consider the free competition that would result in these categories, either from budding programmers cutting their teeth on these uncomplicated genres or from companies releasing a free product to advertise their other paid titles."[9]

One of the main discovery mechanisms on the App Store was the top download charts. It didn't matter if your product sold for 99 cents or $9.99, Apple counted only the number of downloads. As Davis says:

"It became a painful choice for studios. Although in the end it ended up not being much of a choice at all. You could sell your title for $4.99, the price it likely deserved, and never sell enough copies to chart. Your game would be invisible to most iPhone owners. Or you could sell it for $0.99 and hope to sell five times as many copies by cracking the top twenty-five. The race to the bottom had begun."[10]

One of the great ironies of the App Store is that the top-grossing charts, charts that for the past decade have been dominated by F2P games, were introduced to help increase visibility of paid games.[11] Because they measured revenue, they helped titles with high price points and lower numbers of downloads to stand out against those with more downloads at lower price points.

The switch to free came later. Companies realised that paying *any money at all* up front was a barrier to entry. They reasoned that to make money, you need customers. To get customers, you don't want to charge them to enter the store. Steve Jobs had promised that Apple would absorb all the download and distribution costs of a free game. It reduced the marginal cost to zero. Many companies embraced this by making their games free, and after Apple enabled in-app purchases in free apps, figuring out what people would pay for inside the game later.[12]

COMPETITION NOT PIRACY

The initial response for any incumbent faced with a disruptive change is to resort to litigation. The music industry sued many fans, and in 2008, the games industry did the same. Publishers Codemasters and Atari appointed a law firm to serve notice on 25,000 UK residents, threatening to take them to court unless they coughed up £300 each for using file-sharing networks to distribute games. This was to mistake the heart of the problem. The issue was not people pirating your paid-for content on file-sharing networks. The much bigger threat was new entrants—companies like Supercell, Machine Zone, Riot Games and Smilegate—choosing to give away *Clash of Clans* and *Mobile Strike* and *League of Legends* and *Crossfire* for free. These are not poor-quality games. A free game must be *better* than a paid game to make any money because it can't extract cash from gamers before they have played the game. These are good games where the developers are choosing—of their own accord—to give the game away for free because they believe that they can make more money that way. The legacy industry was busy trying to use the courts to sue customers and to convince politicians that their livelihood was at stake because of all these—predominantly young—people "stealing" their content. Then new upstarts came along and said, "We think free is fine. Let them have it for free."

The threat that easy distribution has delivered is not piracy. It is competition.

We have already seen some casualties. Mid-tier publishers and developers have gone. Publishers like THQ and developers like Blitz Games Studios and Eurocom were not structured to compete in this digital age. Narrative games have struggled because narrative is too expensive to thrive in a service game. With the mid-tier market all but gone, narrative games have largely been confined to blockbusters like *Uncharted* and *Tomb Raider* and to indie titles like *Dear Esther* or *The Stanley Parable*, although titles like *Episode* and *Choices: Stories You Play* are experimenting on mobile.

When I talk to clients about service games, the biggest challenge that they have is coming to terms with the idea that they are not selling content anymore. They are giving content away for free. What they are selling now is emotion. How are going to make people pay for that?

WHAT BIOLOGY CAN TEACH US ABOUT SPENDING

The bower bird is a strange creature whose habits have confused biologists for years.

It flies across the outback of Australia building a structure that biologists have dubbed a bower. It has no practical purpose. It does not protect the bower bird from the elements. It has no defensive properties. It is not a nest. (The female bowerbird builds her own nest after the mating ritual is complete. The male bowerbird is a rubbish father.)

During the mating ritual, male bowerbirds build their bower to be as impressive as they can. Females visit to inspect the nest and the male performs a little dance. Eventually, the female selects a male, mates with him and the ritual is complete. Biologists were bemused about why the bowerbird spent so much effort on something that seemed so pointless.

In 1975, a biologist named Amotz Zahavi argued that Darwinian sexual selection (as opposed to natural selection, the "survival of the fittest" or most suited) was about selecting a high-quality mate to pass on high-quality genes to the next generation. One measure of quality is how much surplus energy a creature has. How do you determine how much surplus energy a creature has to squander? You make them squander it.

To Zahavi, the bowerbird's bower and dance were a demonstration of surplus energy. The bowerbird was saying to a prospective mate: "Look at me. I've built this totally pointless thing while flying across the outback and wasting my energy. I haven't been eaten yet and I still have the energy to do this silly little dance. Wouldn't you rather pass my genes on to the next generation than those of that bowerbird with a tiny bower over there?"

In modern human society, we don't build bowers. Instead, we demonstrate that we have energy to squander by spending time and money on "unnecessary" pursuits, such as seeking knowledge and learning, or in "conspicuous consumption," a term coined by Thorstein Veblen in his 1899 classic *The Theory of the Leisure Classes*. Marketers have subsequently embraced this approach, convincing us that we need expensive brands of cars, cosmetics, clothing or alcohol to appeal to the opposite sex. Evolutionary psychologist Geoffrey Miller has developed the idea further, arguing that those elements of the human mind that seem unhelpful for finding food and escaping predators—art, literature, altruism, creativity and so on—can be best understood as being about sexual selection.[13]

Over generations, this process has become embedded within our society. We don't buy things or do things simply to impress a potential mate. We do them as part of who we are, within the context of social groups. We dress in a particular way, own a particular brand of car, drink a particular beer, whisky or soda, watch a particular television show or read a particular book as part of a complex mix of who we are, who our friends and colleagues are and how we wish to be perceived by society.

This has always been so. It's just that in the past we had to do these things physically. I could display my sense of self in the clothes I wore when I went out. I could display it in the books (history, politics and literary fiction) that are on show in my living room versus the books (*Star Wars*, science fiction and fantasy) that I keep hidden away upstairs. This physical limitation went away with the emergence of Facebook.

SOCIAL NETWORKS AS ENABLERS OF VIRTUAL GOODS

In June 2017, Mark Zuckerberg announced that Facebook had 2 billion monthly users. Two billion separate individuals logged into Facebook that month. That's more than a quarter of the entire planet.

Humans are social animals. I argued above that we choose to spend time, money and effort on self-expression, originally because of the imperative of sexual selection and now, after generations of human evolution, as part of our social structures. This tends to be more important in social situations, in other words when we are out and about with other people, not when we are at home on our own.

Facebook has changed all that.[14] Two billion people are connected to other people via Facebook every month. Those people have an average of 150 friends. 150 people is also Dunbar's number, a number proposed by anthropologist Robin Dunbar as the number of people that a normal human can keep within their circle of friends and acquaintances. It is the size of a tribe, of a functioning unit in most armies and of a startup before it becomes too big to be managed like a startup and must be managed like a corporate.

Now that our friendships and relationships can exist in digital space as well as in physical space, so can our status displays. The ability to demonstrate our sense of self, to project profligacy and power, to display our altruism or our skill or our knowledge has now migrated into social networks, virtual worlds and digital games. If you are designing a game that has in-app purchases or downloadable items, you are no longer selling content. Players increasingly expect to get that for free. You now sell emotion: how you make people feel, amplified by social context.

One of my clients built an avatar system for their game. Players could choose to dress their character in clothing, armour and equipment. Avatar decoration has worked for many games, so much so that a frequent cry for how to monetise a F2P game is "Sell hats!" In this case, it wasn't working. No one was buying hats. Or anything else.

I sat down in front of the game. I customised my avatar. I turned to the developer and said, "OK, I've customised my character. How do I see yours?"

He looked at me blankly. I tried again. "How can I see your avatar?"

"You can't," he said. "We thought you would just want to make yourself look great."

"Let me ask you this," I asked. "When you are on your own, and no-one else is looking, do you slob out in jeans and a T-shirt, or do you dress in your finest clothes?"[15]

The client had built an avatar system that relied on social display to motivate players to spend money, but had failed to make a social system to support it. In fact, the game is very social. It is a competitive game with a sophisticated Superfan Layer where players spend significant time and money. They can see the progress that their guildmates and opponents are making. They choose to spend money in the Superfan Layer. They don't spend money on hats.

There are many reasons for *Fortnite*'s success, but one that is often overlooked by copycat developers is the spectator mode. Once you die in *Fortnite*, you get to watch your killer going about their business. When

---

DISPLAY, AGENCY, PERMANENCE

A successful virtual good system must consider three attributes:

- **Display**: Can other players see the virtual good? Hats sell much better in multiplayer games than in single player.
- **Agency**: Does the virtual good either have agency (i.e., a better gun) or is it displayed on a character that has agency (i.e., hats on the player avatar)?
- **Permanence**: Is there an opportunity to display their purchase forever? This doesn't mean that consumables can't sell, but that it is harder if the purchase does not contribute to some permanent marker of success.

As always, there are trade-offs. A game can encourage players to purchase consumable items to reach the top of a competitive leaderboard where the top 1% of players are rewarded with a permanent item. An item can be purely aesthetic with no gameplay benefits, but that can make it harder to sell.

your killer gets killed, you get to watch their killer and so on until you end up following the ultimate winner. So when you kill someone, you *know* that your victim's screen is now displaying your funky hat or groovy dance move. Epic addressed a key problem with selling self-expression items in shooting games, which is that to be successful, it is often better not to be seen. In *Fortnite*, players are made conspicuous to people they have just killed. This has all the advantages of self-expression without making the player vulnerable. Whether intentional or not, it was a smart move by Epic which enabled them to sell more than $250 million of cosmetic items in a single month.

The trading system in *Hay Day* is another great example. When a player wants to purchase something in *Hay Day*, he opens up a menu designed to resemble a classified advertising magazine. (Yes, really. In the 21st century.) He swipes through the pages looking for the planks or apples that he wants. He taps the item and is transported to the farm of the player who is selling it. It is likely that the item he wants has already been purchased, leaving the player disappointed.

Every programmer thinks they could make a better trading system. They could make an efficient market that lists all the commodities that are being bought and sold, create a market clearing price and deliver an efficient market. They have misunderstood the point: *Hay Day's* trading system is optimised for social, not for trade.

When a player tries to buy something, he is taken *to another person's farm*. He can see her activities and progress, shown by how many animals, fruit trees and farm machines she owns. Developer Supercell hides a red lockbox on most farms, containing premium currency or other valuable rewards. The player is incentivised to explore the whole of the trader's farm looking for the lockbox and along the way gets to see how good the farm is and how well decorated it is. He realises that, whenever he sells things, other players are coming to visit *his* farm, and perhaps he better spruce it up a bit.

As he explores the farm, he notices that some of the trees have withered. The trees have little exclamation marks above them. If he taps a tree, it comes back to life. Next time the trading player logs into *Hay Day*, she will see the visiting player's Facebook image hovering above the tree. She taps on his face, an acknowledgment of the gift, and the tree bursts into glorious fruit again. She is given the option of sending a thank-you card, which creates further interaction loops.

The whole structure of the *Hay Day* trading system exists to amplify the social connections between friends and strangers, to create a social awareness that you are visiting other people's homes and that they are visiting yours, and to create a welcoming environment that amplifies human desires to display progress, prowess, style or sense of self.

WHAT WILL PEOPLE PAY FOR IN VIDEO GAMES?

In 2007, Ian Livingstone, author of the *Fighting Fantasy* game books and former life president of video game maker Eidos, visited South Korea. On his return to the United Kingdom, he started talking about a new business model that was becoming amazingly successful there. The prime example was *Kartrider*, a game so popular that, within the first year, 12 million Koreans, one quarter of the population, had played it.[16] The game involves racing cartoon-like virtual cars around a virtual racetrack against other, real players. The game is free to play, but in the run-up to Christmas 2007, the company behind *Kartrider*, Nexon, decided to allow its users to buy Santa hats to wear while racing. They put them on sale for $1, and according to Livingstone, they sold a million hats within a week.

Game developers in the Western world were amazed. A Santa hat probably cost an afternoon of an artist's time to make. Yet, here it was generating $1 million in a week. It looked like a licence to print money. The developers were missing one important fact: the players were not paying for the game in the first place. They were not paying for the expensive game engine that managed the steering, the collision detection, the animation and the graphics that formed their entertainment experience. They were not paying for the design of the tracks. They were not paying for the work that went into balancing the performance of the different cars, the artwork of the characters, the points system or anything else. They were not paying for content. They were only paying for hats.

The precursor to *Kartrider* was *Quiz Quiz* (now *Q-play*). Nexon didn't plan on a virtual goods business model. In 2001, when the trial period of free membership ended, and they announced they would shortly start charging fees, membership plummeted by 90%. Nexon made membership free again and experimented with creating wigs, hats and shirts to decorate the avatars representing players in the quiz. The cosmetic items soon generated more than $150,000 per month.

If you think that spending $1 on a Santa hat is foolish, consider this: do you spend more than $1 every year on holiday celebrations or decorations. If you say no, you are either a curmudgeon, a hermit or a liar. I think that spending $1 on a Santa Hat as part of a social celebration in a place (albeit a virtual one) where I am surrounded by my friends seems cheap, and a

> **CURRENCIES, CONSUMABLES AND DURABLES**
>
> Service games sell many different things. These are some of the most common:
>
> - **Soft currency**, often known as dollars, gold or credits. Generally, this currency is used as a way of limiting progress in a game. Players have to earn soft currency to buy or unlock new things that they want, such as characters, buildings, upgrades or research.
> - **Hard, or premium, currency**, often known as gems. This is rarer and more valuable. It can be used for valuable upgrades, to skip time or to buy premium items in the store.
> - **Consumables** are items with a one-off use, such as boosts that give you an advantage in *Candy Crush Saga* levels. Currencies can also be thought of as consumables.
> - **Durables** are items that have permanent value. The Coin Doubler in *Jetpack Joyride*, the builder in *Clash of Clans* and additional queue slots for your machines in *Hay Day* are examples of durables.

darn site cheaper and better for the environment than buying a pair of novelty reindeer antlers for the office Christmas party.

The first person who bought a Santa hat in *Kartrider* might have thought, "Look at me, I'm the first person to have a Santa hat. Aren't I cool?" The next buyers might have wanted to be early trend setters. Then players will have started to think, "Everyone else has a Santa hat, I'd better buy one." The Santa hat satisfies different urges: the desire to celebrate, to be first, to stand out, to fit in, to share an experience with friends and acquaintances and to have fun. Not bad for only $1.

As you think about what players might want to pay for in your game, you have many vectors to consider. Here are just a few:

Self-Expression

Many people refer to this category of items as vanity. I think that is a mistake. You should offer products in your game that let people express themselves, not just demonstrate their vanity. If you use the word *vanity*, your brain is likely to go down certain pre-determined paths (hats!). If you think more broadly about the tools, items and elements with which players might express themselves, you are likely to come up with a range of potential things to sell. If they are cheap to make, you may be better off putting some items out there even if you aren't sure that they will sell. You might be surprised.

> ## WORDS TO BAN #2 VANITY ITEMS
>
> When creating items for players to purchase, developers sometimes refer to vanity items. These are typically cosmetic changes to the player's character or personal space in the game that have no impact on gameplay. *Team Fortress 2*'s hats are the iconic example.
>
> Vanity is not a positive word. Nobody likes to be thought of as vain. The developers are belittling the players who purchase these items by the use of words.
>
> Pick another term. Many people use *cosmetics*. I prefer *self-expression items* because the purpose of the variety of items that you offer is to allow your players to express themselves in your game.
>
> Stop calling your players vain.

Conspicuous Consumption

In 2008, developer Armin Heinrich published *I am Rich* on the App Store with a price point of $999.99 (see Figure 8.2). It had no functionality beyond displaying a red ruby and the following mantra: "I am rich. I deserv [*sic*] it. I am good, healthy & successful."[17] Heinrich described *I am Rich* as a work of art and was disappointed that Apple took the app down after only 24 hours. In which time, nine copies had been purchased (two of which were subsequently refunded).[18]

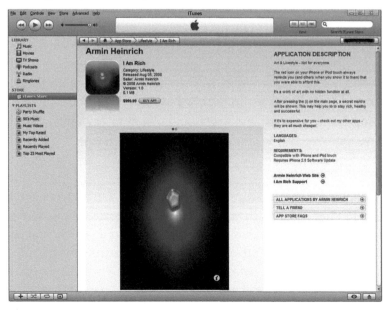

FIGURE 8.2   The App Store description for *I am Rich*.

In *Hearthstone*, there are gold versions of every card that cost four times as much to craft as normal versions. They make no difference to the gameplay but have more impressive animations. Some players covet the gold cards and will spend lots of money to get them.

Power

Some players just want to spend money to win. Handling pay-to-win is tricky for many game developers. On the one hand, if a player can just spend their way to victory, those who don't spend cry foul. On the other, if a virtual good has no impact on the game, is it worth buying?

If you are going to make a virtual good affect gameplay, which I recommend, it is safer for it to affect the Retention Layer (i.e., faster experience points gain and more currency rewards) than the Base Layer (improved damage and more hit points). Players are more accepting of items that affect the Retention Layer than the Base. For many gamers, particularly core gamers, the Base Layer is where "true" gameplay lives. It is the twitch-based, skilful test of player prowess. Giving one player a meaningful advantage in the Base Layer seems unfair to those players. The Retention Layer, on the other hand, is much more about trading time for money. If I buy an item that grants me additional experience or earns me more gold from every trip around the Core Loop into the Base Layer and back, I am making progress through the game faster, but in my head-to-head battles, I am at no advantage.

In *Hearthstone*, I can spend real money to acquire every single legendary card. Until I know how to use those cards, I will still lose every match I play. In *World of Tanks*, a new player who spends lots of money getting all the best gear will have his butt handed to him over and over again. A game feels fairer if in the moment-to-moment gameplay, one player cannot buy advantage over another.

The second element is that the genre of the game matters. It also matters to which Bartle types your game is likely to appeal. (See Bartle Types on p. 28.) The exact genre is less important than the nature of the game. If it is competitive, allowing players to buy competitive advantage is hard to do without alienating your players. Sometimes the competitive advantage is about knowledge rather than possession. In both *Hearthstone* and *League of Legends*, I am a better player if I know the strengths and weaknesses of all the heroes and champions. The quickest way of getting to know a character's weaknesses is to play as that character. You will soon learn how other people beat you. That often means spending real-world money to acquire the full range of cards or champions so that you can learn how to play against them.

For some players, *all* in-game purchases that affect any of the layers are pay-to-win. *You can't convince those players otherwise.* If they are not happy with *League of Legends*, *Hearthstone*, *Team Fortress 2* or dozens of other games, so be it. They are not your audience. Let them go and buy pay-once games. Focus your efforts on keeping your committed audience happy.

Relationships

I've argued that virtual goods are a social phenomenon. Being social is about having relationships with people: acquaintances, friends and more. Your virtual goods should have the potential to demonstrate this kind of emotion.

When I give my wife flowers, I am not saying, "Have some dead plants." I'm saying, "I love you," "I'm sorry" or "I saw these and thought of you." The value of the gift lies as much in the thought as in the raw value of the plants. (That said, the quality of the gift matters. When I was born, my father arrived at the hospital carrying a bedraggled bunch of daffodils he had grabbed at a petrol station on the way in. My mother considered that the pain and effort she had just been through merited more than a measly bunch of daffodils. She never forgave my father and never let daffodils into the house again.)

At the extreme, we have male players pretending to be female in MMOs in the hope that they will be given more free stuff. More broadly, think about how your audiences might act in a social way. Many successful F2P games harness this by making players care about the "good of the guild": they will spend money to help a guild mate, or so that their lack of skill does not let the clan down. These games turn the selfish purchase of items so that "I can win" into altruistic "I'm spending money for the good of the tribe."

Video series *Extra Credits* gives the example of a Money Bomb in an un-named Korean MMO.

> "When you used it, it exploded into goodies like a popping piñata. The buyer of the Money Bomb couldn't pick up any of the goodies that popped out, but everyone else around you could. People loved buying these things, because someone would walk into town and throw one of these babies down and it would turn into a party. The person who bought the Bomb would get tons of love from everyone around them, and often other people would announce that they were going to buy one too. Soon the town square turned into an impromptu online festival."[19]

As Extra Credits says, "build your game around finding joy for the human beings playing your game."

Content

It is still possible to sell content. There is still a viable, albeit competitive, opportunity to sell indie games on Steam. Downloadable content (DLC) adds significant value to many games. Publisher Paradox is a master at this strategy. The DLC for each of Paradox's most popular games, *Crusader Kings II* and *Europa Universalis IV*, tops out at more than $250.

Many developers, particularly those in free-to-play, have concluded that they are no longer selling content. They are selling emotion. They are selling how their players feel, in a social context, amplified by social networks. A successful game lets players spend money on things that matter to them in the context of strangers, acquaintances, friends and clan mates. It doesn't focus on selling access to content because content is better used as a tool for retention than for monetisation. It focuses on what will be important to players in the game and offers them the opportunity to spend money—lots of money—on that.

WHAT IF PEOPLE WON'T SPEND?: THE ADVERTISING OPTION

An increasing part of the free-to-play ecosystem is advertising revenue. Although paid games have embraced microtransactions, they are not adopting advertisements in their titles, and the backlash from consumers is likely to be high if they do.

Free games, as we've seen, have a high proportion of freeloaders. With often fewer than 3% of users every month choosing to spend money, that means 97% of users are not. These freeloaders have value, as the boxout on p. 146 shows. They provide liquidity and social context, as well as being potential converts in the future and helping to reduce marketing cost through telling their friends and helping keep a game in the charts. With the growing sophistication of the mobile advertising market, they are also a source of revenue themselves.

Mobile advertising is the fastest-growing segment of the advertising market, as consumers switch their time and attention to smartphones and tablets and away from newspapers, magazines and the desktop Internet. Media measurement company Zenith estimated that global ad spending on mobile grew by 34% in 2017, adding an astonishing $27 billion to reach $107 billion. Desktop advertising fell in the same period, dropping $2.9 billion, or 3%, to $96 billion. Figure 8.3 shows the winners and losers.

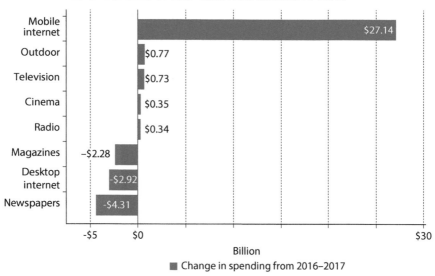

ESTIMATED GLOBAL AD SPEND CHANGE FROM 2016–2017

Mobile internet: $27.14
Outdoor: $0.77
Television: $0.73
Cinema: $0.35
Radio: $0.34
Magazines: −$2.28
Desktop internet: −$2.92
Newspapers: −$4.31

Billion
■ Change in spending from 2016–2017

FIGURE 8.3   Zenith's estimated global ad spend change 2016–2017.[20]

We have moved past the basic "play a level, then watch an ad" model of games design, although that system can still be seen in many games. We are increasingly seeing in-game advertising used in positive, thoughtful ways.

As an example, in *Angry Birds Transformers*, players collect coins and piggies in the Base Layer to user as resources in the Retention Layer. On a normal run through the Base Layer, a player might collect 500 coins and 30 pigs. On the Post-Event Screen, the game offers players the chance to watch a video ad to double the coins and pigs they earned on that run.

One day, my seven-year-old son came running into the room. "Daddy, Daddy, please can I watch an ad? Please!" We have a strict rule in our house that children are not allowed to watch adverts or click on in-app purchase buttons, but he had just completed a stellar run, earning something like 1,500 coins and 100 pigs. If he could double it, he would get about six times as much reward as usual. How many adverts get that response from a consumer? This is advertising as something that players *value*, given the clever design from the game makers.

(For the record, I said, "Yes" to my son's request. I wanted to reward him for following the rules. The game played a *Game of War* advert with an unnecessarily sexualised Kate Upton, which is one of the reasons we have the rule in the first place. Sometimes the games industry doesn't help itself.)

A similar model exists in *Rodeo Stampede*, where a player can choose to watch a video after a good run to double the rewards they get. This is advertising as *reward*, not advertising as an interrupting message that you must accept as your price of getting access to free content.

Disco Zoo takes the idea a step further. The Base Layer game in *Disco Zoo*, as you may remember, is a variant of *Battleships*. Players search a 5 × 5 grid for animals to rescue. They have a limited number of "shots" to find them. Players can get five additional shots by spending premium currency or by watching a video ad. The unusual element is that *Disco Zoo* limits the number of adverts that you can use in a session. I found myself playing the game until I *ran out of ads*. Ads became sufficiently valuable to me that I treated them as a resource, a source of energy that didn't kick me out of the game, but which gave me a reason to leave now and return later when my ads had recharged.

THE VALUE OF FREELOADERS

Freeloaders are valuable to your game. Embrace them; don't kick them out. Here is a list of just some of the value that they provide. You can find out more in other books I have written, including *The F2P Toolbox* and *The Curve*.

- *Liquidity*: They are the opponents in a game with matchmaking. They provide unpredictability in a multiplayer game. They are part of your content.
- *Future conversion*: You never know when someone will be in the right emotional or financial state to spend money. The longer they stay in your game and the more they enjoy it, the more opportunity you have to convert them to payers.
- *Marketing*: People who enjoy your game tell their friends. They improve the chart position of your game. They help you get new customers more cheaply.
- *Revenue*: F2P games generate an increasing proportion of their revenue from ads.
- *Social context*: Players enjoy games more when they offer relatedness, the component of Self-Determination Theory (SDT) that relates to connections with other humans. They also choose to spend time, money and effort on self-expression and demonstrating their prowess when other humans can see them. Freeloaders can make your game more fun AND more financially successful.[21]

In Match-3 game *Potion Pop*, a loading screen tip stated, "Spending money in the game will remove all adverts." This is an old-fashioned benefit. Although some games could benefit with fewer adverts (RockYou's reincarnation of *Gardens of Time* is almost unplayable because of the heavy advertising load), other games treat adverts as an opportunity to reward players or to give them agency over when to view them.[22] In this latter model, being told that you will lose access to advertisements might disincentivise you from spending money on in-app purchases at all.

Most advertisements shown in mobile games are for other mobile games. The big companies—Supercell, Machine Zone, Electronic Arts, King—are spending lots of money to acquire customers. They are subsidising upstart competitors with advertising dollars, while attempting to grab the upstarts' best players, the ones who are most likely to go on to spend money in their game. It is a strange pact but is currently working. There is a viable business feeding players into the games with a high lifetime value that sit at the top of the top-grossing charts.

I expect this situation to change. Facebook and Google have been the major beneficiaries of the migration of advertising from magazines, newspapers and the desktop Internet to mobile, but in the process, advertisers have become more comfortable with the medium. Video ads that players value are a powerful tool for brand advertising, and I expect increasing numbers of traditional advertisers from sectors like cars, clothing, travel and financial services to advertise in games. This will both increase the revenue potential of an ad-funded strategy as well as eliminating its biggest pitfall: that by selling ads in your game, you risk selling your best customers to your rivals.

The emergence of video advertising on mobile and tablet has made a new business model viable. Although most of my advice focuses on the high-end businesses that seek to generate high lifetime values through microtransactions, it is possible to make money from a large user base even if your users have a low propensity to spend. This is good news for the diversity of games and game makers in the industry.

Game design is rarely neat or elegant. Designers around the world have found different ways to solve the same problems of keeping players having fun in their game and choosing to spend money on their game, whatever business model they choose. The Pyramid is a framework that I have found exceptionally useful to diagnose the challenges facing the games I work on, to communicate with other developers about where I feel the problems lie and to ensure that we allocate resources efficiently between moment-to-moment gameplay, long-term goals and elder gameplay that appeals to Superfans, both in terms of time and money.

As always, there is no right answer, but I hope that this section has given you a new set of frameworks and tools to make better, more profitable and more enjoyable games.

CHAPTER 9

Production-Centric versus Design-Centric

T HE VIDEO-GAME INDUSTRY GREENLIGHT process is inefficient for service games. Although different organisations have different green-light systems, they all have the same objective: to reduce risk. This is an important consideration when the greenlight committee is being asked to commit tens of millions of dollars to developing a game and the same again to market and manufacture it. In these circumstances, reducing risk is a key role of the publisher.

A common element to the greenlight is the "vertical slice" that I first discussed in Chapter 1. The vertical slice is a whole piece of gameplay that showcases what the game will be like to a high degree of polish. It might be a crowded city in *Assassin's Creed*, a level in *LEGO® Star Wars* or a portal to Hell in a reboot of *Doom*. The greenlight committee spends a few minutes, possibly as much as an hour, playing—or watching a demonstrator playing—the game while they decide whether this game is worth bringing to market.

Once the vertical slice is approved, the development studio is tasked with creating a further 19 vertical slices, stringing them together with a narrative and hey presto, 20 levels and perhaps 20 hours of gameplay, which is enough to justify the $60 asking price.

I simplify. Greenlight processes are often more expensive and more exhaustive than this. Many games cannot be broken down into replicable vertical slices as easily as I described. Professional game publishers are keen to make the best choices to bring the most successful, most profitable and most enjoyable games to market. As development costs skyrocket, with studios having to make fewer and bigger bets, the importance of making the correct greenlight decision is growing. Even gigantic corporations, with significant processes, can get it wrong. In 2012, Square Enix cancelled the officially unannounced *Legacy of Kain: Dead Sun* after spending £7 million on development. It expected this to rise to £30 million including marketing costs. *Eurogamer* reports a Square Enix source saying, "I really want to like this game, but I'm worried it's not going to get there, and I don't want to spend £30 million to find out."[1]

This process is extremely dangerous for a service game. The reasons why include how product games are marketed, how they generate revenue and how they are made.

Let's start with the sales process. The sales-forecasting process for a product game is both simple and incredibly hard. It involves estimating how popular your game is going to be, by looking at similarly popular games and making a forecast—some would call it a guess—of how many units you are going to sell. There aren't that many variables. The price point for most AAA games is fixed at around the $60 mark. The number of units sold correlates well with aggregated Metacritic results, which is why publishers have started including bonuses in their development contracts if games hit an aggregated score threshold. In the contract for *Fallout: New Vegas*, publisher Bethesda promised developer Obsidian a bonus if the game achieved a Metacritic score of 85. It scored 84. The failure to hit the target cost Obsidian a million bucks.[2]

A publisher can use its experience combined with publicly available sales data to estimate how many units it is going to sell and at what price point. Multiply the two together, and it has a sales forecast. It is more complicated than that, but you get the idea. Let's now attempt to apply the same process to forecasting the revenue of a service game. This is based on a genuine conversation I had with the sales director of a major publisher who called me when I was on holiday to help him estimate how much money they would make from a new Asian massively multiplayer online (MMO) game that they were publishing in Europe.

Sales director: We forecast 1 million downloads in the first month.

Me (sipping gin and tonic): That's not a forecastable number. That's a choice. Without a strong Western brand, you will have to buy lots of downloads. There is no point in getting lots of users until we know that retention, conversion and average spend numbers are all looking good. I would halve that number.

Sales director: OK, from those million users, we estimate a conversion rate of 10%, so 10% of users will spend money that month.

Me (spitting gin and tonic out in surprise): That's a pretty aggressive figure. I've seen 10% in some PC games, but generally after optimisation and experimentation. Few games achieve that out of the gate.

Sales director: It's what they are getting in Asia.

Me: After four years of continuous optimisation and tweaking. The audience is different in Europe to Asia. They value different things. They respond to different messages. You may be able to get to 10%, but you are unlikely to get there in the first month. I would halve that number, and I still think that's optimistic.

Sales director: And we've put our average spend in at $25 per payer.

Me (spilling the last of my drink on the terrace): $25? That's high. Achievable, but high.

Sales director (defensively): That's what they achieve in Asia.

Me: Again, after they've honed and tweaked and tested and optimised for their market. You are very unlikely to achieve that when you start. I would halve that number.

If you've been paying attention, you will notice that I just halved his monthly audience, halved his conversion rate and halved his spend, which means that I reduced his sales forecast by 87.5%. And I still think I was optimistic.

A free-to-play (F2P) game with a million players can generate very little, or even zero, revenue. Developer RocketCat launched *Punch Quest*, a free-to-play endless runner/fighter, which the Verge described as a "mashup of *Jetpack Joyride* and *Streetfighter.*" *Punch Quest* had an average Metacritic rating in the 90s, and clocked up 630,000 downloads in the first week.

It made just over $10,000 in that week.[3]

For a critically acclaimed, popular game to make so little money shows the challenges of the F2P business model. It is not enough to make a game that people love. Developers have to make it easy for players to give them money, in a world where they are not demanding money upfront. Reviewers noted that *Punch Quest* was not aggressive in its monetisation. Jared Nelson of *Touch Arcade* wrote, "we felt somewhat guilty getting so much for free and were worried the developers might not see very much profit at all since the game's freemium structure was so hands-off. I mean, it was difficult to *even find* where the button was that let you buy in-game coins through IAP, which didn't bode well for *Punch Quest.*"[4] Reviewer Eli Hodapp said, "*Punch Quest* takes an insanely hands-off approach to directing players to buying the in-game currency. It's almost worrying in a way, as there is absolutely no reason to buy any additional Punchos [the game's premium currency]."[5]

The *Punch Quest* developers made a free, generous game that failed to signpost the mechanisms that enabled players to give the developers money. By mid-November, they abandoned the free-to-play model and made their game a paid title with a price of $0.99.[6]

In the old world of boxed product, it was hard to imagine having that many customers and making so little money. Sure, there were failed games, but they tended to fail because they did not get the customers they needed, or they did get the customers, but development costs had spiralled so far out of control that there was no possibility of ever breaking even. The North American video-game crash of 1983 had many causes, but a component was Atari's hubris in agreeing to pay a royalty of $25 million to Stephen Spielberg for the rights to make a home console version of his movie, *E.T., the Extra Terrestrial.* There were several problems, most notably that the game was commissioned in July 1982 and had to be in shops in time for Christmas that same year, which left only six weeks for development. To justify the enormous advance, Atari manufactured five million cartridges. Following hot on the heels of a poor port of *Pacman* earlier that year, when Atari had manufactured 12 million copies, even though its own research suggested that only 10 million people owned and used its console, the video game version of *E.T.* flopped. Atari dumped millions of cartridges in a landfill in the New Mexico desert.[7]

Thirty-five years later, and we have other examples for boxed products that destroyed whole companies. Ion Storm, founded by Jon Romero, one of the creators of *Doom* in 1996, took four years and $25 million of Eidos's money to launch *Daikatana,* a game that received a Metacritic rating of only 53.[8] Ion Storm was shut down in 2001.

Another example is Atari's *Enter the Matrix.* Here is the post I wrote about it on *GAMESbrief* when compiling a list of "Top Turkeys of the Noughties."

> Can a game that sold five million units really be a turkey?
> If it still doesn't make money, it can.
>
> *Enter the Matrix* was designed to integrate with *The Matrix Reloaded*, the second movie in the *Matrix* trilogy. Both game and movie suffered from a disjointed plotline that required viewers/ players to participate in both to make sense of the story.

Reviews weren't great (Metacritic: 62) and despite *Enter the Matrix*'s sales figures, Atari still reported a thumping great loss of $38.6 million in the financial year to March 31, 2004 (or a profit of $766,000 if you include a one-off dividend the company received).

Tellingly, Atari did not renew its option to make two further games based on the *Matrix* franchise. While it's possible that Atari simply didn't have the cash resources to make further AAA titles, it's also possible that the licence terms were so onerous that the company didn't make a profit even on a title that sold five million units. And given the critical battering that the films and the game received, perhaps it was a wise decision.

Either way, Atari founder Bruno Bonnell was forced out as CEO in November 2004. Atari has been in almost-permanent restructuring ever since, with five chief executives in the last five years.

And while *Enter the Matrix* is not entirely to blame, it is symptomatic of the whole sorry saga.[9]

I am not pretending that free-to-play or service games are an easy solution. Microsoft shut down *Fable Legends* after four years and $75 million in development cost without releasing it to the public.[10] *Nosgoth*, a competitive multiplayer online game born out of the cancelled *Legacy of Kain: Dead Sun*, was released into Early Access on Steam by publisher Square Enix and developer Psyonix in early 2015. It was shut down, while still in Early Access, in April 2016.[11] Scopely, a US publisher of mobile games, shut down *Breaking Bad: Empire Business* in June 2017, 19 months after it first soft-launched.[12]

The risks are high, and many projects fail. Against that background, what is the best way to launch the game?

CONTROL WHAT YOU CAN

In the world of physical distribution, few companies have the financial wherewithal to launch a game. *Call of Duty: Modern Warfare 2* cost $40–$50 million to develop. Add in marketing expenses and the cost of producing and distributing discs and the launch budget exceeded $200 million.[13] *Shadow of the Tomb Raider* cost $75–$100 million to develop, with an additional $35 million in marketing on top.[14] We are seeing fewer, larger titles fighting for the attention of core gamers, and those games cost a lot of money.

For publishers with a background in physical distribution, the game plan is known. Hard to execute, but known. First you need a decent game, preferably with a high Metacritic score because the correlation to sales is strong. Then you need to have great relationships with the primary distribution channels—retailers like GameStop and online stores like Steam. Thirdly, you need marketing muscle, lots of it. You need to be able to host giant booths at E3, spend money on television ads like it was going out of fashion and have an army of marketing personnel to connect with the press, YouTubers, vloggers, streamers and influencers that will raise awareness of your game.

If you have all these competitive advantages, you can then take a bet that your next title will justify its upfront expenditure. Sometimes that bet feels safe, like the next *Call of Duty*, and sometimes it is a bigger gamble, such as when you are trying to kickstart a franchise like *Destiny*. Either way, you are tapping into known distribution and marketing channels, asking consumers to pay up front, and then you take your bet.

Service games, particularly free-to-play ones, take a different approach.

The poster child for free-to-play success is Supercell. The company was founded in 2010 by a group of Finnish developers who had previously worked at mobile developer Sumea. CEO Ilkka Pannanen has described the culture of the company as being collections of people making games—cells—gathered into one larger organisation, the supercell. In the seven years since it was founded, Supercell has launched four blockbuster games: *Clash of Clans*, *Hay Day*, *Boom Beach* and *Clash Royale*. In 2016, Supercell generated revenue of €2.1 billion from its four games, and generated Earnings before Interest, Tax, Depreciation and Amortisation (EBITDA) of €917 million, a margin of 44%. In June 2016, TenCent acquired an 84.3% stake in Supercell for about €8.6 billion, valuing the whole of Supercell at more than $10 billion.

Supercell has not just had hit after hit. It has had many failures along the way. Its first game, *Gunshine*, was a real-time, massively multiplayer online role-playing game (MMORPG) targeted at the Facebook platform that failed to take off. Supercell pivoted in a decision to "bet the entire company on a strategy we would call 'tablet first'" before finding its first hit, *Hay Day*.

Supercell sets out its organisational vision on its company website.

"We've found that the best quality work comes from small teams in which every single member is passionate about what they do.

Oftentimes when teams become bigger, processes, bureaucracy and even politics emerge, and the work just isn't fun anymore. That's why we wanted to create an organizational model made up of very small teams, or 'cells' as we call them. Supercell is a collection of these cells. Each game comes from a cell, and they all operate extremely independently and have complete control over their own roadmap. Our organizational model is optimized for speed and passion, not for control."[15]

Supercell learned early that "it's usually better to kill games earlier rather than later. If it starts to feel like the game isn't going to work or isn't fun enough, it's usually a sign that you should have already killed it." The time line on the website lists a number of games that the company has killed: *Pets versus Orcs, Tower, Battle Buddies*. Two other titles, *Smash Land* and *Spooky Pop*, were killed during soft launch. Supercell has killed more than 14 titles versus the 5 that it has launched.

As Supercell says on its website:

"We'd like to think that every failure is a unique opportunity to learn, and every lesson will ultimately make us better at what we do. That's why we have a tradition of celebrating these lessons by drinking champagne every time we screw up."

Supercell gives enormous freedom to its teams. The kill decision is usually made by the teams themselves. Game lead Timur Haussila described two different outcomes in a conference presentation at the Montreal International Game Summit.[16] "*Boom Beach* was funny, but systems were confusing and some wanted to kill the game. The team believed in the title and kept working on it. *Smash Land*, by contrast, was killed after the team honestly decided if they wanted to keep working on the game for the next two years."[17]

Supercell does however have another backstop; its teams know that a game will not leave soft launch and be given a global, marketed launch unless it achieves certain financial and operational targets, known as Key Performance Indicators (KPIs) in the industry. This is a powerful combination. CEO Pannanen and the rest of the management team set the goals, enable the teams and get out of the way. The teams know that there is a fixed goal to shoot for: to make a fun, enjoyable game that hits the performance targets. If they don't believe they can do that, if they believe that the game is not going to be fun, or it is not going to hit its targets, or they just don't want to work on it for another two years, they can kill it. Supercell has a stated objective of staying small, and it particularly wants to keep its cells small, so that it can afford the inevitable failures that come as part of this strategy.

The Supercell strategy is, in many ways, a honed and polished variant of the Lean Startup strategy as espoused by Eric Ries. This is such an important point that I am going to devote the whole next section to it.

THE LEAN STARTUP

There is an unhelpful stereotype of the startup. It is three guys (and in the stereotype, it is usually guys) in a garage in California, living off noodles and staying up night after night to create a piece of software or hardware that will change the world. It is not helpful because, although this startup type exists, it is not the only form—far from it.

The core distinction that you need to make is whether you are a "corporate" business or whether you are a "startup" business. Most businesses are both, and your most important management skill is choosing when to use the skills and toolset of a corporate and when to use those of a startup.

A corporate knows what its business is. It knows how to do it. Its challenge is to keep doing it again and again, a little better than last time, and with no loss of quality. The main role of a manager in a corporate is to do what they did the previous year, but 5% better.

The archetypal corporate is, of course, your local one-man-band plumber. I use this example because it surprises people. But a plumber is running a business that his dad could have done or his dad's dad. He must find customers, using word-of-mouth and telephone directories, or their modern equivalent on the Internet. He charges by the hour to fix sinks and install bathtubs. He can run his business for 40 years without fundamental change to the business model.

A startup, in contrast, doesn't know what it is doing. It is trying to figure that out. Eric Ries, author of *The Lean Startup* and one of the most visible leaders of the Lean movement defines a startup as *a human organisation creating a product or service under conditions of extreme uncertainty.*[18] If we break that into its component parts, we see that a startup is a *human organisation*, a group of people. It is not a technology, an idea or a philosophy, or even a company. It is a collection of people creating *a product or service*, in other words, making something. They are doing it under *conditions of extreme uncertainty*. That sounds like the whole games industry.

Ries's mentor, a Stanford professor and writer called Steve Blank, has a slightly different definition. He defines a startup as *a temporary organisation designed to search for a repeatable and scalable business model*.[19] It is temporary because its purpose is to discover a way of making money, which usually means making a product or service that people want, that is not just a flash-in-the-pan, but can turn into a long-term business that can grow. The key point is that the purpose of a startup is to stop being a startup. To become a corporate that knows what it is doing, how to do it and that is concentrating on doing what it does better than it did it the previous year.

My third and final definition of a startup comes from Dave McClure, the potty-mouthed investor behind incubator 500 Startups. "A startup is an organisation that is confused about what its product is, who its customers are and how to make money. As soon as it figures out all three things, it ceases to be a startup and then becomes a real business. Most startups never do so."[20]

The principle that unites all three definitions is that the purpose of a startup is to figure stuff out. To eliminate uncertainty. To discover a business model that can be repeated and is still profitable as it grows. How to find out who its customers are, give them something that they want, and then figure out how to charge them for it.

The video-game industry, like all cultural industries, has long had to deal with uncertainty. If your industry is hit-driven, it is, by definition, uncertain. In his seminal work on Hollywood in the 1970s and 1980s, *Adventures in the Screen Trade*, Oscar-winning screenwriter William Goldman attempted to discover the secret of Hollywood's success. He interviewed directors, producers, movie executives, journalists and more to discover if they could predict what was going to be successful, and if so, how. His conclusion: Nobody could predict which movies were going to succeed and which movies were going to flop. "Nobody knows anything."[21]

In 1977, Twentieth Century Fox was convinced that it had a science-fiction hit on its hands. It had a great story, a strong cast, and a huge budget. They had two science-fiction movies planned for that year, one in which they had little confidence called *Star Wars* and their big-budget extravaganza, *Damnation Alley*. I'm guessing that you know which one of the two performed better at the box office.

The uncertainty in a hit-driven industry used to extend only to whether an audience would like a work, not how they would pay for it. In a pre-Internet era, you knew that if listeners liked your album, many of them would buy it. If reviews for your film were good, audiences would flock to the cinema. If you made a good game, gamers would buy it from their local game store.

The nature of the problem has changed for service, and particularly free-to-play, games. You are no longer just trying to build a great game. You are seeking a monopoly. What I mean by that is that competition for your game, and hence your pricing power, is a combination of the quality or desirability of your game together with the quality or desirability of rival choices. When your game is available on Steam or the App Store, players have the choice of all the other games on that store to choose from. That's thousands in the case of Steam and millions in the case of mobile stores.

On the other hand, if a player has engaged in your game and is enjoying it, the rival games on digital stores are irrelevant. If you allow a player to buy a hat, or virtual currency, or a piece of content within your game, you are the only company that can provide it. You are no longer competing on price with other entertainment options. You have created your own monopoly.

Being a monopoly doesn't mean that there are no checks and balances on your behaviour. If you behave like an asshole, your players will leave. If you gouge your players, they will leave. If you fail to keep delighting and exciting your players, they will leave. There are some sleazy psychological tricks that some companies have used, and we will discuss the ethics of those in Chapter 16, but in the long run, sleazy monopolies lose their customers because a game is only a monopoly *as long as players want to play it*. When you alienate your customers, there are literally a million alternatives that are easy for them to find and play for free.

The potential to create a monopoly is one way of explaining why F2P game design is so much more like a startup than a corporate. Every time you launch a game, you are launching a new *business* to a new audience and trying to figure out how to make money. You are not shipping a hit-driven creative product into a known marketing and distribution channel; even once you have acquired players through Steam, Google Play or the App Store, you are still figuring out what, in your game, players will value enough to pay for. You are continually learning.

My client who developed an avatar system that no one could see had not figured out what its product was.[22] The backlash against the virtual items in *EVE Online*, most famously over a monocle that cost $70 but could hardly be seen by other players, is part of the same problem.[23]

These are both examples of building a game (which in McClure's terms is finding your customers) but still not figuring out what the product is or how to make money. The job of a game developer in startup land—and all new F2P games are in startup land—is to discover what its audience will value and be happy to pay for. That is a classic startup challenge, and it means that we have many tools to address the challenge, starting with the core of the Lean methodology: validated learning.

VALIDATED LEARNING

The purpose of a startup is to learn fast. In a traditional startup, you know how fast you need to run. You know how much money you have in the bank, you know how much money is draining out each month, and some quick arithmetic will tell you how many months you have until you have to shut the doors and go back to the dreary corporate job you quit 18 months ago.

In the corporate world, you are a startup without that visibility. You may think that you have the backing of a large organisation with all the money it needs, so you are not in the same boat as a startup. You actually have it much worse.

In a corporate setting, the new department or project has *political capital*, not financial capital. It has the indefinable, unmeasurable support of the organisation. The problem with political capital is that you don't know how much you have. You don't know how fast it is draining away. You don't know what will suddenly make it change: the departure of a key supporter from the leadership team; struggles in a department unrelated to yours; or pressure from shareholders to focus on profitability, instead of growth. You do know that you need to keep topping up the political capital, but it can be hard to know how.

Our industry is littered with political capital draining away. British studio Lionhead, the brainchild of Peter Molyneux, developed *Black and White* and the *Fable* franchise and was bought by Microsoft in 2006.[24] Lionhead's political capital drained away during the extended, four-year development of *Fable Legends*. After the departure of Microsoft executive, Phil Harrison, who had been one of the key supporters within Microsoft of experiments in service and F2P games, perhaps it was inevitable that the project got canned.[25] As CEO of Electronic Arts (EA), John Riccitiello masterminded the acquisition of Playfish for $400 million in 2009, left EA in March 2013, and his successor shut Playfish down the following month. NCSoft lost patience with developer Richard Garriott following the disappointing performance of *Auto Assault* and *Tabula Rasa* and forced him out in 2008, leading to a costly lawsuit.[26]

The response of companies like Supercell, an exemplar of the new breed of game developer, is to treat developing a game the way a successful startup treats building a new business. It doesn't develop a three-year plan, stay locked away in a building somewhere for three years and then launch with a giant fanfare, only to discover that not only has the world changed around them, but no one likes their product anyway. Successful startups, to use Stanford professor Steve Blank's phrase, "get out of the building." They engage with their customers early and often. They test and they learn because the objective of a startup is to learn before it runs out of money or political capital. They become the masters of the Build–Measure–Learn cycle that enables successful products to emerge again and again.

Games companies have always prototyped and experimented to find the fun. In service-game design, the pace of experimentation and the feedback cycle are accelerated. A service game aims to launch much earlier than a product game would. It has a smaller feature set because players, developers and executives assume that significant features will be added after launch. It gets high quality data back from the tests so the team can make better decisions. The team has live player data to add to their design instincts and user testing as inputs into the design process. The team needs to be skilled at interpreting and responding to the data to make good, timely decisions.

The changing focus is leading to a change in production methods and schedules. Prototyping and pre-production phases are longer, and it is not unusual to see pre-production lasting for longer than production on mobile games. Games are being tested by being soft-launched at an earlier state of readiness than in the old days of Beta testing. Companies are getting better at responding to data and iterating.

Now that we have established the differences between product and service games, let's look at the different techniques needed to develop a service game.

CHAPTER 10

How to Develop
a Service Game

T HERE ARE MANY WAYS to develop games. I am not planning on covering them all here. I will propose one approach based on my experience in service games and working with startups, both in the games industry and outside it, where I have observed and analysed the benefits and pitfalls of a validated learning approach. There is not a single "right" way to approach validated learning, any more than there is a "right" way to do Agile development. Instead, I offer frameworks and principles to get you to the happy place where you have developed a game that audiences love and where you have identified whatever it is that players are willing to pay for over and over again.

FIRST PRINCIPLES

The first principle is that nobody knows anything. Our job as designers and developers is to have a vision or idea of the game that we want to make and to learn, as fast as possible, whether what we are making is going to be fun, profitable or, ideally, both.

Note that this is not a recommendation to carry out oodles of market research, focus testing or market segment analysis. That is corporate behaviour. If you are corporate, with a strong grasp of your marketing and distribution channels and you are simply trying to identify the next hit in a hit-driven industry, they have their place. But if you are trying to solve for Dave McClure's problems of not knowing what your product is, who your customers are or how to make money, they can be very distracting. As David Ogilvy, ad man extraordinaire, said, "consumers don't think how they feel. They don't say what they think and they don't do what they say."[1]

The quickest way to find out how they feel and what they think is to get your game into the hands of real players. This leads to the much-quoted and frequently misunderstood minimum viable product (MVP). In *The Lean Startup*, Eric Ries gives a great story about how he first realised the power of the Minimum Viable Product.[2] In 2004, Ries was the Chief Technology Officer of a startup called IMVU. Today, IMVU is as a 3D chat room aimed at young adults that boasts 50 million registered users and 3 million Monthly Active Users (MAUs), making its money from the sale of virtual items that visitors add to their avatars or use to decorate their homepages and private rooms. Back in 2004, that was not the vision. The team believed that the switching cost between Instant Messaging (IM) services was too high for them to attract users to their platform. They set out to build a 3D avatar system that could sit on top of existing IM clients like AOL Instant Messenger and Yahoo Instant Messenger. Ries assembled a team and he and his co-founders set themselves a target of 180 days to launch the product and attract their first paying customers.

As launch date approached, Ries found himself tempted to delay. He knew that, in his own words, "the first version was terrible … I was worried that the low quality of the product would tarnish my reputation as an engineer…. We all envisioned the damning newspaper headlines: 'Inept Entrepreneurs Build Dreadful Product.'"[3] As launch date approached, Ries's fears escalated, but he fought the impulse to delay further because he was "more afraid of another, even worse outcome than shipping a bad product: building something that nobody wants." The IMVU team pressed the button to launch the product.

And nothing happened.

Ries's marketing colleagues created a website where users could download IMVU. People came to the website, but nobody downloaded the 3D avatar code. Eventually, after bringing a variety of users into the office and watching them use it, they came to the startling realisation that their fundamental assumption was wrong. They assumed that nobody wanted to use multiple Instant Messaging services, so they had spent months building IMVU to work with ten different IM platforms. In practice, they found the opposite, many IM users, particularly teenage girls, used five, even ten different clients. What they would not do is download something like IMVU to share with their friends until they knew whether it was cool, which was hard to do with the initial product, nor would they (quite rightly) give their screen names on their favourite IM clients to strangers they had met through IMVU.

Ries and his fellow entrepreneurs pivoted IMVU to become a successful 3D Instant Messaging business, but Ries was unhappy. He was a devotee of Agile development, an approach to software that promised to help drive waste out of product development. Despite that, he had just "committed the biggest waste of all: building a product that [his] customers refused to use. That was really depressing."[4]

Ries had written most of the code that allowed IMVU to interoperate with a dozen different networks, code that was thrown away when the company pivoted to running its own platform. He asked himself the despairing question: "In the light of the fact that my work turned out to be a waste of time and energy, would the company have been just as well off if I had spent the last six months on a beach sipping umbrella drinks? Had I really been needed? Would it have been better if I had not done any work at all?"[5]

At first, Ries consoled himself with the argument that he had needed to build the flawed product to learn what his customers wanted. Ries soon identified the flaw in this thinking: *he had not set out to learn.* He had set out to build what he assumed people had wanted, and he was wrong. He ended up answering the question, "Would people download a 3D chatroom to work with their other IM clients?" by spending six months building a 3D chatroom, a couple of days building a website for them to download, and then discovering that no one downloaded it.

He could have learned that same fact in a couple of days by building the website, *not building the software at all* and seeing if anyone would download it. It would have been a faster, more efficient way of *learning what he needed to learn*, the principle of validated learning that has become the heart of the Lean Startup movement.[6]

I have learned from Ries's example. In August 2011, I ran a banner ad on my website, *GAMESbrief.* At the time, I had about 20,000 monthly visitors to a site that focused on the business of games. The leaderboard of 728 × 90 pixels showed a caricature of me and the title "*52 Game Idea Bombs*, by Nicholas Lovell."

Users who clicked on the banner landed on a page with the following message:

> Thank you for your interest in *52 Game Idea Bombs.*
>
> In November 2011, I'm going to launch a book covering 52 short, sharp, punchy ways to make your online game acquire customers, retain them AND make more money from them.
>
> By landing on this page, you've helped determine what the final product will look like. You may have clicked on a banner (where I am testing colours), or a text ad (where I am testing the title) or another test that I hadn't thought of when I wrote this post.
>
> So, thank you for your interest. If you want to support the project and be told when the book is released, just give me your email address in the form below.

I set myself an internal target of getting 100 e-mail addresses. I got 150 addresses in the first month, giving me the market test that there was sufficient demand to justify writing the thing. The Minimum Viable Product, for me, was a banner advertisement on a webpage. (*52 Game Idea Bombs* was delayed because Penguin commissioned me to write *The Curve* and morphed, after much testing, into *The F2P Toolbox,* which I self-published in 2014.)

The idea of testing using an ad is not new. In 1984, Ocean Software was a fledgling British publisher, making games for home computers such as the ZX Spectrum, VIC-20 and BBC Micro. Founder David Ward says

> "There was no research at all, nothing on how many of each machine had been sold, the demographic of those buying the machines and what they were being used for." Ocean's founders did some research and concluded that the predominant magazine at the time was *Your Computer.* "So, we took a punt," says Ward, "and bought the magazine's back page for six months to advertise four games… We created a tiny graph on the advert where the customer had to tick whether they had a VIC-20, a Spectrum or whatever and which of the four games they liked the look of. And sure enough, on Monday morning, we got all these envelopes in the post, and we opened them up. They had five-pound postal orders in them. We began to do a chart of the portion of users who had this machine or that machine and which game they wanted.

And this was on the ridiculously naïve assumption that we could get the game done and delivered within 28 days, otherwise you were outside the protocol of the Mail Order Association."[7]

Ocean commissioned and delivered three games for two platforms, the Spectrum and the VIC-20, and posted them to those who ordered. They sent the postal orders back to those they couldn't deliver to within the required 28 days.

These are extreme examples of a Minimum Viable Product. My audience expects me to be running business tests and letting my readers see that they are on the receiving end of an A/B test is something that fits with my brand expectations. Ocean Software was working at a time when a skilled programmer could create a finished product in just a few weeks. The Oliver twins, founders of Blitz Games Studios and Radiant Worlds, and at one point responsible for five of the Top 10 bestselling games in the United Kingdom, delivered their game *Fast Food* in a single weekend.[8]

Modern games don't have this luxury. AAA games can't be produced in a year. Few indie games can either. In the early days of the iPhone, developer Ethan Nicholas had a full-time job at Sun Microsystems and coded his hit game, *iShoot*, in his spare time. "I was working eighteen-hour days during *iShoot*'s development, [but despite that] it only took six weeks from start to finish—and that includes learning Objective C, Cocoa and OpenGL."[9] He grossed $600,000 in the first month with a game that looks amateurish compared to modern efforts, which is perhaps not surprising, given that it is nearly ten years old.[10] One hit wonder *Flappy Bird* took just a few days to code.[11]

Consumer expectations have risen. The bar for minimum in the MVP has risen. It is much harder for a scrappy game with good gameplay to break through when global giants like Supercell, King (now part of Activision) and Machine Zone release polished, high-quality, free games into the crowded marketplace.

That does not mean that the right response is to increase the complexity and cost of your product just to hit the minimum bar. Your commercial objective (which may not be the same as your artistic objective) is to figure out whether your players like your game, what they want from it to keep coming back to it and what they will pay for. You still need to focus on validated learning. The costs of learning have gone up from the early days of the browser and the smartphone, but the principles have not changed.

A key distinction here is how the startup thinks about risk versus how the corporate thinks about risk. (If you think inanimate constructs like companies can't think, you are wrong. The culture and nature of an organisation constrains how the organisation behaves and guides its actions, even if the individuals involved don't recognise this fact. I was once hired by the CEO of the Western arm of an Asian developer to be a "free-to-play virus, spreading through the organisation and infecting it with the new way of thinking." The individuals were welcoming, but the organisation fought back. Before long, I was up against the antibodies of corporate thinking: structure, process and even plain old habits. I lasted nearly a year of regular visits before I had to concede that, on this occasion, the corporate antibodies were too strong.)

Risk can be divided into two main types: operational risk and financial risk. (There are dozens of other risks, ranging from strategic to environmental to criminal, but these are the two types that most people deal with all the time.) Most practitioners, in their day-to-day lives, make decisions about how comfortable they are, or their organisation is, with accepting operational risk or whether they should spend more money and hence increase financial risk to reduce that operational risk.

Let me give you a fictional example. An aspiring author is keen to write the next piece of world-changing fan fiction or erotica, the next *Twilight* or *50 Shades of Grey*. She toils away on her word processor until her masterwork is complete. She uploads the manuscript to Amazon and her forefinger hovers over the publish button.

And falls away. She remembers that she was terrible at spelling at school and that her grammar sucks. She worries that if prospective readers see her atrocious punctuation in the first few pages, they will be put off her book, leave negative reviews and spell the end to her dreams of global stardom. So she finds a copy editor and spends $1,000 of her hard-earned savings to get the book proofread by a professional. Her operational risk—that no one will read her story because the spelling, punctuation and grammar is so bad—has been reduced, but her financial risk has ballooned to $1,000 because up until now, all she had invested in the project was her sweat, toil, tears and time.

When the manuscript is ready for submission again, she uploads it and her forefinger hovers over publish for a second time. This time she pauses to look at the cover art that she knocked up in five minutes in Microsoft Paint. That is going to hurt sales, she reasons, so it's back to the internet to search for a professional artist and another $1,000 coughed up.

For the third time, her forefinger hovers over publish. And now she is filled with doubts. Should she have a better marketing plan? Maybe she needs a physical distribution option to satisfy demand. Perhaps an ISBN would make people believe she was more serious about her writing. Her book is delayed and her costs go up and up and up.

Maybe she is right. Maybe she should spend all that money. Or maybe she should just publish and move on to her next book, and her next and her next. Self-published phenomenon Amanda Hocking had written 50 short stories and a novel by the time she was 17. By the time she was 27, she had 17 manuscripts, mainly in the genre of young adult paranormal and romantic fiction. She had also collected dozens, perhaps hundreds, of rejection letters. In April 2010, Hocking started selling her manuscripts as e-books in order to fund a trip to Chicago to see an exhibition of Jim Henson's the Muppets. In the first six months that she self-published her books, she made $20,000 selling 150,000 copies and by January 2012, she had sold 1.5 million copies and earned $2.5 million.[12]

At the point of publication, Hocking had nothing to lose. Her books had been rejected by every single publisher she had sent them to. She didn't have enough money to pay for the gas from her hometown of Austin, Minnesota, to Chicago, Illinois. Hocking had no choice but to take the operational risk because she didn't have access to money.

Compare that to a publishing executive at a book publisher or a game publisher. Think a little about the risks that those people face to their career or their livelihood. If they decide that a book or a game needs a new cover from a famous artist, they go to their boss to make the case for extracting additional funds from the company's budget. That is not their own money. If they spend more, the company's profits might be down, which might hurt the share price, which will upset the CEO or the shareholders, but it is far removed from the executive's livelihood.[13] They will authorise or demand additional budget for better copyediting, better art, better marketing, more consultants and experts and so on, all to reduce the operational risk that the product for which they are responsible fails.

The reason for this is easy to see. All creative endeavours are risky. Companies, however, are risk averse. If a creative project fails, and many will, the executives involved will need to be able to cover their asses. If someone says, "That game failed because it didn't have multiplayer," they can say, "You're wrong, it did have multiplayer." Hence, we have the phenomenon of multiplayer gameplay being squeezed into a single-player experiences like *Tomb Raider*. Or the game has to be multiplatform or multilingual, or—like *Star Citizen*, the crowd-funded space combat game that has raised more than $150 million without releasing anything yet— have the voice talents of Mark Hamill, Gary Oldman, Gillian Anderson,

John Rhys Davies and Andy Serkis.[14] Each one of these decisions decreases the operational risk that the game will fail by ticking more boxes on the marketing or product checklist, but each one increases the financial risk of the project and raises the break-even point needed to deliver a profitable product. It may raise the break-even point so high that there is no longer any possibility of a positive financial return. (And yes, I think *Star Citizen* is perilously close to this position.)

The Law of Conversation of Energy states that energy can neither be created nor destroyed, rather it transforms from one form to another. Risk is not exactly like energy: it can be created or destroyed. For our purposes, however, it is more often transformed. In the examples given, well-meaning executives have sought to reduce the operational risk that the project fails. In the process, they have increased the financial resources invested in the product and hence the financial risk. Whenever you invest time or effort to reduce risk, you may reduce *operational* risk but you increase *financial* risk. Operational risks can hurt your career; financial risks can destroy your studio. Finding the right balance is key to success.

A startup may decide to put a product out early because it is incapable of sustaining financial risk, since it has no money. Launching an unpolished product may be the lesser risk than going bankrupt. A corporate can continue to invest in a struggling product rather than killing it early and switching resources and effort to a different product or experiment. Its culture is focused on reducing operational risk, and so it struggles to solve the problem of a failing product by choosing not to make it. One of the biggest mistakes I have seen big studios making when engaging with free-to-play (F2P) or service-based gaming is mixing up these two forms of risk. They assume that their experience in AAA or boxed product development is going to be a bonus in this new segment. They apply all the techniques that they have learned to reduce operational risk when making games in the physical distribution era. They invest far too much time and money in a product, usually by focusing on polish and high-fidelity graphics to "show those upstart mobile studios how proper developers make games."[15] They increase their financial risk, by spending lots of money to eliminate operational risk, but without testing whether they can find and keep their audience and make money from them. Then their game flops.

Validated learning is a way to avoid these twin issues. It is focused on testing and iterating in a cycle that Ries calls Build–Measure–Learn. It involves identifying what you need to learn next and figuring out the most cost-effective way of learning it in a way that also protects your brand

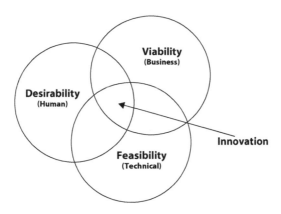

FIGURE 10.1   IDEO's Design Thinking.[16]

or reputation. One of the more useful ways of thinking about the different ways of experimenting to find what people want from your product comes from design agency IDEO. Their approach combines the wants of people, the needs of business and the capabilities of technology. They call it "Design Thinking." See Figure 10.1.

Feasibility encompasses whether your team has the ability to build whatever it is that you can imagine. Viability means that when you have built it, will enough people pay for it? And is it worth continuing to ramp the costs of developing the product, to add more polish or content or expensive voice actors, given that every time you increase the costs, you push the bar for viability ever higher? Desirability is the human element. Can we market it? Will they play it? Will they keep playing it?

In my work, I try to combine the approach of IDEO towards Design Thinking with Ries's Lean Startup approach of business management. My objective is to spend the least amount of time and money to figure out if the thing that I, or my clients, want to make is desirable for players, will make money for the business and is within the capabilities of the team.

This three-way pull is important. It leaves lots of room for creativity and innovation, because we are making games for players—for humans—who want to be excited, awed, impressed or engaged. Design thinking leaves plenty of room for that most elusive of qualities in video games: enduring fun. It also constrains the ambitions of the designers into making a product that will make a financial return. It encourages them to think about the constraints of the business and the technology and to make smart decisions about which elements of desirability are must-have, and which are just pandering to their whims and their egos. For game makers, I therefore focus not just on Minimum Viable Product, but also Minimum Feasible Product and Minimum Desirable Product. Combine the three and you get something that you can release to large numbers of real players: the Minimum Awesome Product.

MINIMUM FEASIBLE PRODUCT

The Minimum Feasible Product is what we can technically deliver. It is a traditional prototype. We ask, "We've had this idea. Can we make it?" We then deliver a prototype to answer these questions. We are focused on learning whether we have the *ability* to make a thing.

In the early days of computer games, many great experiences were developed by smart designers and programmers figuring out how to do things that had not been done before. David Braben and Ian Bell figured out how to encode the information for 256 planets into just 6 bytes when they coded space exploration game *Elite* for a home computer that had only 32 kilobytes of memory.[17] John Carmack was an expert at squeezing performance out of processors, performance that enabled him to deliver the revolutionary 3D environments of *Doom*.[18] In more modern times, Niantic harnessed the power of a variety of technologies, including databases, geolocation and smartphone cameras, to create *Ingress*, before supercharging the experience with the *Pokémon* brand to launch *Pokémon Go*.

Software problems have become easier to solve as the industry matures and Moore's Law, that processing power doubles every two years, continues to hold true. Problems that were impossibly hard to solve three decades ago can now be overcome with raw computing power. *Elite* would fit three times over in a blank Microsoft Word document. As that has happened, the danger is that we continue to ask the question, "Can we do it?" The question we should be asking is, "Should we do it?"

I see this time and again with teams that I work with. Someone comes up with an idea. The designers and coders start working through how they would implement it, the dependencies for other elements of the design or codebase, the consequences of turning this idea into reality. They can have lengthy discussions about the "how" before anyone has even asked if the idea is worth pursuing at all.

Three years ago, I raised a small amount of seed investment to make a game I am passionate about: an accessible, free-to-play, cars-with-guns game. I hadn't worked with the programmer before, but we both agreed that we were focused on prototypes. Six weeks into the project, our professional relationship had broken down, and we returned the money to the investors. The heart of the difference was in the definition of "prototype." I was aiming for desirability, trying to figure out what would make a game that players would want. The programmer was aiming for feasibility: he assumed that I had the design all worked out and the only question was how we were going to implement the ideas.

There is still a critical role for technical prototypes. There are still some things that are either brand new, or more usually, something that the team has never done before. I worked with the team at Firefly Studios while they prepared to launch *Stronghold Kingdoms* on mobile, and we were aware they had never released a mobile game before. We took a game we had thrown together in a game jam, *Wonky Tower*, and released it to the market with a tiny bit of polish not because we thought it would be a commercial success, but because we wanted to go through the process of submitting, launching, marketing (albeit with almost no budget) and trying to make money from a mobile app before we took our major intellectual property down the same route. The purpose of this launch was, as it should be, to learn.

In Chapter 13: Managing Creativity, I will discuss a variety of techniques to generate more creative ideas and how to evaluate them for the game-design process. For now, let's just say that the purpose of the Minimum Feasible Product is to determine if the team has the skills and knowledge to make the product that you want. However, the much bigger question is not whether you, the developers, can make it but whether they, the players, want it. A Minimum Feasible Product is a technical answer to a technical question. You need to ask questions about commercial issues (viability) and marketing potential (desirability) to make a successful, profitable game.

MINIMUM VIABLE PRODUCT

The Minimum Viable Product is the smallest thing that people will pay for. It is the test for whether the product can be a commercial success. There is, as you will no doubt be fed up of hearing by now, no right answer for what the MVP might be.

Let's take, for example, a pre-order campaign for a new video game. If the video game is the fifth game in a successful series from a proven developer, the number of pre-orders is not a great guide to whether the product will be a success. This game will likely sell oodles of copies, and its success is more dependent on execution and Metacritic review scores than it is on whether there is customer demand for the product. When you already have four games in the series showing you that there is demand for the product, making a fifth is not a great leap of faith.

On the other hand, if you are a developer who is famous for making gritty, open-world, anything-goes, crime-centric games on consoles and you want to make a game about a niche sport, maybe the pre-orders would tell you something. (Don't believe studios do this? Rockstar launched *Rockstar Games Presents Table Tennis*, a table tennis simulator, in 2006, to the surprise of gamers and the industry.) If you were working on the assumption that your core audience would move with you across genres, you might be very much mistaken. It would be good to know this earlier rather than later. It doesn't mean that you must can the project, but it might mean that you should scale down the ambition, and hence the cost, to remain commercially viable.

Kickstarter has become a useful tool for the Minimum Viable Product. As well as being a source of funding, Kickstarter has become a way of validating whether there is demand for a product. Some of the poster children of success on Kickstarter have been video games. Chris Roberts, the developer behind the *Wing Commander* series, raised $2.1 million from Kickstarter, but has gone on to raise more than $150 million directly from future consumers for *Star Citizen*.[19] Richard Garriott, creator of *Ultima*, raised just less than $2 million on Kickstarter and approximately another $10 million on his own website for *Shroud of the Avatar: Forsaken Virtues*.[20] In 2012, Tim Schafer famously set out to raise $400,000 to make a game he called *Double Fine Adventure* that subsequently turned into *Broken Age*. He blew through that target on the first day and raised $3.3 million on Kickstarter during the 30-day campaign. Other games include *Shenmue III, Torment: Tides of Numenera, Wasteland 2, Pillars of Eternity, BattleTech and Elite Dangerous*.[21]

Not all campaigns were so successful. The Oliver twins attempted to run a Kickstarter campaign to bring back their 8-bit hero *Dizzy*, a platforming egg-shaped character who starred in a dozen games between 1987 and 1992. In November 2012, the Oliver twins announced a Kickstarter titled *Dizzy Returns*, the first official sequel in more than 20 years. The Olivers sought $350,000 from fans to make the game; when the campaign ended on December 21, 2012, only $25,620 had been pledged. The Olivers were pragmatic about the failure of the campaign. In their update towards the end of the campaign they said

> "As sad as it is to see that the campaign will unlikely be successful, the *Dizzy Returns* Kickstarter has done part of what it set out to do – gauge interest in the idea of a new *Dizzy* game… There's certainly nothing to be ashamed or embarrassed about not being successfully funded; on the contrary, we're glad to have had this experience, and have learnt a great deal along the way."[22]

The Olivers set out to learn something with their Kickstarter campaign. When the campaign was announced, *Eurogamer's* Wesley Yin-Poole asked them why they didn't fund the game themselves. "As with any project we undertake, there are financial risks involved in making a game. Funding this project through Kickstarter means we get to test the water without that high-level risk. If there's not enough interest, whilst that would be very sad, the game won't be made, simple as that."[23] (They also needed the money. Few independent game developers are rich enough to support whole development teams on their own.)

Although the Olivers may not have opened the champagne to celebrate the demise of the Kickstarter, the failure of *Dizzy* was, in its own way, a success. Raising the money would have been best. But discovering that there was no demand for the return of *Dizzy* before spending $350,000 was a success in its own way, too.

Dreamquest Games took the same view. In December 2012, their Kickstarter for *Alpha Colony*, an exploration, trading and building simulator, failed to reach its $50,000 target by a heart-breaking $28. Just three more backers at the basic tier, and the game would have reached its target. However, lead developer Christopher Williamson thought that failure of the campaign might end up being a good thing. "Although many of you considered us falling $28 short really unfair, in the end, it is perhaps for the best. To be committed to deliver our dream game underfunded, understaffed, and leaving us all broke would have been even more heart-breaking than not funding at all."[24]

Kickstarter is not the only way of testing a game. In mobile gaming, we have the soft launch and in PC development we have long had the beta test. Games have been cancelled at this phase of development. Supercell killed *Smash Land* and *Spooky Pop* during soft launch. Rovio experimented with different genres for its *Angry Birds* franchise and has cancelled several in soft launch or shortly afterwards, including *Angry Birds Football, Angry Birds Ace Fighters* and *Angry Birds Goal*.[25] We've already seen that Scopely shut down *Breaking Bad: Empire Business* after 19 months in soft launch and Square Enix cancelled *Legacy of Kain* spinoff *Nosgoth* in Early Access.[26] It seems likely that poor key performance indicators (KPIs) were a factor in the decision, although there may often be other factors.

The two approaches that I have set out, while seeking the same goal, approach the problem from opposite directions. The marketing-led MVP strategy relies on announcing the product and allowing people, by their actions, to demonstrate their desire for the product. My advertisement for *The F2P Toolbox*, as described on p. 164, follows this strategy. As does crowdfunding a game that has not yet been made. Soft launch and extended beta tests take the opposite approach: the game has already been created and the developers control access to the product to test whether the game has the right characteristics to justify a global, marketed launch. They are trying to achieve the same objective—to figure out if the game can be a commercial success—from two different angles.

There are risks to both strategies. In the case of announcing a product before it exists, the company could gain a reputation for vapourware, products that are never going to see the light of day, which can damage its credibility and revenues. It might also suffer from the Osborne effect, hurting sales of a current product by announcing a new one too early, a term coined after the Osborne Computer Company announced a new product, took more than a year to release it, ran out of cash and went bankrupt in 1985.

There is, of course, significant risk to *not* following either of these approaches. That is the risk that you develop a product that no one wants, don't realise that no one wants it and go ahead and launch and market the turkey anyway. That is the kind of hubris that led Atari to bury millions of cartridges of *E.T., the Extra-Terrestrial* in the New Mexico desert, that led Eidos to spend $25 million on *Daikatana* and that led Scottish developer RealTime Worlds to spend $100 million on the over-ambitious title *APB* that flopped, destroying the company.[27]

The Minimum Viable Product is a tool that developers can use to focus their minds on whether they can build a product that is commercially viable. But games are not just products. They are entertainment.

They are culture. They are art. For developers to know if their game will be successful, they need to know if they can satisfy human needs. That is where the Minimum Desirable Product comes in.

MINIMUM DESIRABLE PRODUCT

The Minimum Desirable Product (MDP) is the smallest thing that will make players go "Yes, I want to play that." It is similar to the MVP because the test is whether people want it. But desirability and viability are different. A viable product is something that a sharp-suited MBA cares about with his spreadsheets and his forecasts. (I don't have an MBA. I do have sharp suits and spreadsheets.) A desirable product is one that players will talk about, anticipate, get excited about, pre-order and fill the forums with chatter about how excited they are at the prospect of getting their hands on the game.

With my clients, I don't focus on a single action or deliverable to be the MDP. Concept art is part of this, as are teaser videos and marketing collateral. In the end, I think the most useful value of the MDP is to remind people, whether executives or creators, that a successful game satisfies all three requirements. It is *desired by its players*. It is *commercially viable*. It is *technically feasible*. Only then can you have the product that you can launch to the market.

MINIMUM AWESOME PRODUCT

My synthesis of all these features above is a "Can we make the Minimum Awesome Product?"

- *MVP—Minimum viable product (MVP)*: A business person's definition. "Is there a market for this?"

- *MFP—Minimum feasible product*: An engineer's definition. "Can we make this?"

- MDP—*Minimum desirable product (MDP)*: A marketer's definition. "Will people want this?"

- *MAP—Minimum AWESOME product (MAP)*: A game maker's definition. "What's the smallest thing I can make that delivers on my creative vision, makes player say, 'That's awesome!' and has the potential to earn enough money to sustain my business."[28]

The Minimum Awesome Product approach encourages you to cut scope. Eliminate features that bloat the game. Eliminate features that will be valuable in Live Agency but are not essential to discovering if you have found sustainable, profitable fun. Get to a limited launch as quickly possible while creating something that is fun, shareable, that gives its players joy, that keeps them playing and encourages them to spend money. If you can do all of that without you going broke or running out of political capital in the process, you have created a Minimum Awesome Product, the key step to service-gaming success.

CHAPTER 11

How to Prototype and When to Pivot

I N THE PREVIOUS CHAPTER, I discussed the importance of prototyping and the Lean principle of validated learning. In this chapter, we will focus on the practical questions of how to do it.

PROTOTYPING THE BASE LAYER

For core gamers, the Base Layer *is* the game. A multiplayer online battle arena (MOBA) is all about the level design and how combat handles; gamers don't define a MOBA by the progression of champions, their upgrade paths or how you unlock them. *Candy Crush Saga* is a Match-3 puzzle game, and the progression and unlocks seem secondary. For core gamers, *Total War* games are about the battles, not the strategy, whereas *FIFA* is about the matches, not the progression.

There is nothing wrong with thinking about this as a player. It is dangerous for a designer.

Most developers already know how to prototype the Base Layer, and you should do so. It is one of the first things that you can build and test to see if the core of your game is fun. It is easy to show to other people. It is what publishers and funders expect to see. If you are unclear how to prototype a Base Layer, I suggest attending a Game Jam or reading the books I have recommended throughout this book and in the bibliography.

There are significant dangers to prototyping the Base Layer. The most significant one is forgetting the purpose of a prototype; it is validated learning. If you are a commercial organisation, you are not trying to figure out if you are capable of making this game. You know that you are. You are trying to figure out whether it is commercially sensible to make it. (If you are making games as a hobby, do whatever you like; if you are making games as art, that is also fine, but remember that being commercially viable means giving you the freedom to experiment. You can be commercially viable without making games in the style of VC-backed, megabucks-earning, mobile titles.)

A Base Layer prototype can gain a life and a momentum of its own. Developers start polishing the prototype. Executives give feedback like, "the controls aren't quite right" or, "it would look better with some particle effects and lens flare." Play testers say they like but it would be more awesome if it had x or y feature. These bits of feedback are valid, constructive and useful, but you must be cautious about whether they need to be implemented or whether they would best be added to a backlog for later. For now, you should be turning your attention to prototyping the Retention Layer.

HOW TO PROTOTYPE THE RETENTION LAYER

The purpose of the Retention Layer prototype is to experiment. Identify what you believe you need to build a compelling game that will keep players playing for days and weeks and months and years. Build a prototype to test this assumption. It is not guaranteed to give all the answers that you need, but it should set you on the way.

I discussed in Chapter 2: The Base Layer, that a simple way to think of the distinction between the two layers is to consider a soccer game. *FIFA*, where you control players who kick the ball around the pitch and try to score goals, is focused on the Base Layer. *Football Manager*, where you recruit players, manage finance and set tactics, is a Retention Layer game that does not let the player take control during the Base Layer. *Football Manager* has often been derided as a spreadsheet game, which makes it a perfect candidate for prototyping the Retention Layer. It should be possible to prototype a Retention Layer in Excel.

The Excel spreadsheet in Figure 11.1 is the Retention Layer prototype of a cars-with-guns games with the working title of *Car Runners*, and was put together by Andrew Roper of Spilt Milk Studios. The game is a puzzle

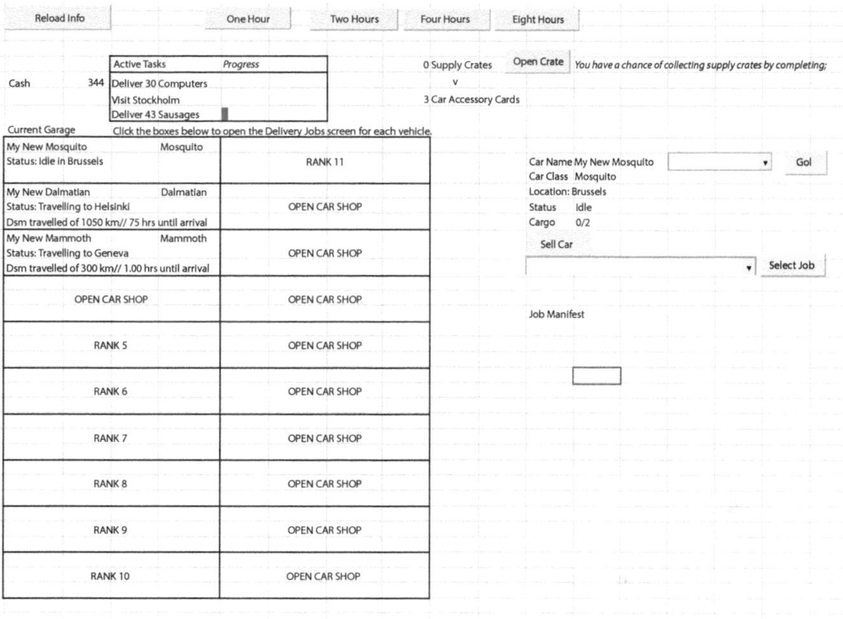

Reload Info		One Hour	Two Hours	Four Hours	Eight Hours	

	Active Tasks	Progress	0 Supply Crates	Open Crate — *You have a chance of collecting supply crates by completing;*
Cash 344	Deliver 30 Computers		v	
	Visit Stockholm		3 Car Accessory Cards	
	Deliver 43 Sausages			
Current Garage	Click the boxes below to open the Delivery Jobs screen for each vehicle.			

My New Mosquito   Mosquito
Status: Idle in Brussels   RANK 11

My New Dalmatian   Dalmatian
Status: Travelling to Helsinki   OPEN CAR SHOP
Dsm travelled of 1050 km// 75 hrs until arrival

My New Mammoth   Mammoth
Status: Travelling to Geneva   OPEN CAR SHOP
Dsm travelled of 300 km// 1.00 hrs until arrival

OPEN CAR SHOP   OPEN CAR SHOP

RANK 5   OPEN CAR SHOP

RANK 6   OPEN CAR SHOP

RANK 7   OPEN CAR SHOP

RANK 8   OPEN CAR SHOP

RANK 9   OPEN CAR SHOP

RANK 10   OPEN CAR SHOP

Car Name My New Mosquito   ▾   Go!
Car Class Mosquito
Location: Brussels
Status   Idle
Cargo   0/2

Sell Car

▾   Select Job

Job Manifest

FIGURE 11.1   The Retention Layer prototype of *Car Runners* (working title).

logistics game where players transport cargo to rebuild a world destroyed by a terrible plague, while fighting bandits and crazed survivors. We had already developed a Base Layer prototype on paper and were ready to create it in Unity. Before we progressed further, we built this prototype of the Retention Layer in Excel using Visual Basic.

In the prototype, I am trying to fill my garage with 20 cars, while also completing the active tasks to, for example, "Visit Stockholm" and "Deliver 43 Sausages." When I went to take a screengrab of the prototype to use in this book, I lost 10 minutes while I sent my Dalmatian to Helsinki to be nearer to Stockholm, made progress on the "Deliver Sausages" task and earned enough money to buy a Mammoth, the largest vehicle in the prototype. The prototype is working.

Making a retention prototype is not easy. It varies from game to game. Figure 11.2 reminds you of the key steps. You will be testing whether you can take your players from the Retention Layer to the Base Layer and back again, probably through a Pre-Event Screen and a Post-Event Screen. Here are some of the tips that I give my clients when explaining how to do it.

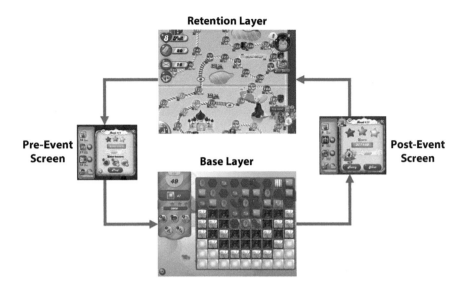

FIGURE 11.2   The key steps of the Core Loop.

Know Your Base Layer

When you make a Retention Layer, it is important that you know what your Base Layer is going to be, or to know that you are not going to have one, as in the case of a resource management game. You are going to simulate the Core Loop, the process of going into the Base Layer, making progress and earning rewards, which players will see or spend in the Retention Layer. It is hard to make this conceptual leap if whoever is testing the game does not know what the Base Layer will be.

It is possible to create a Retention Layer that could be added to any game. The map and progression structure from *Candy Crush Saga* has been used in many subsequent games from King. The chest system from *Clash Royale* has been lifted wholesale and used in other titles like Playdemic's *Golf Clash*. The narrative upgrade path in *Gardenscapes* is the Retention Layer of Playrix's next hit, *Homescapes*. These are all examples of Retention Layers that have little connection with their Base Layers.

Start with "Play"

The starting point of a Retention Layer prototype is the Play button (Figure 11.3). Make it clickable. Now make time pass. You could show

FIGURE 11.3   The start of a Retention Layer Prototype.

this with a bar sliding down or a timer that counts down for, perhaps, 10 seconds. While it goes down, you, or your testers, need to imagine that you are playing the Base Layer. You should avoid the temptation to reduce the delay to zero. You need testers to be forced to imagine playing the Base Layer.

Create a Post-Event Screen

After time has passed, during which the tester can imagine she is playing the Base Layer, have a Post-Event Screen that contains the outcome of the Base Layer. The information that appears on your results screen will vary by game: Did the player earn gold? Did she lose health? Did she gain experience points (XP)? Did she catch any items or bonuses or boosts? Show these on the screen, together with a big "Well Done!"[1] Show them their achievements in the Base Layer (Figure 11.4).

FIGURE 11.4   A Post-Event Screen in a Retention Layer prototype.

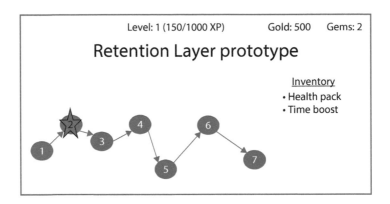

FIGURE 11.5   A Retention Layer homepage in a Retention Layer prototype.

Design the Retention Layer Homepage

Next, think about which elements of this progress need to be recorded. You may have an XP bar or a permanent statistic showing how much gold the player has. You may need to develop an inventory of power-ups or a technology tree showing the player the upgrades she has found. You may have a map, a level system or a star system. Start looking at how to show these on the Retention Layer homepage (Figure 11.5).

Go Back through the Core Loop

Press Play again. Let time pass. Earn more stuff and capture it in the permanent record. Start looking inside yourself to see what you might want to spend your hard-earned cash on. Do you care about progress across a map? The XP gains and levels? An achievement system like the tasks in the *Car Runners* prototype? A leaderboard? These are all possible next steps to be added to the prototype. I can't take you through every permutation. What I can say is that the purpose of the prototype is "validated learning." Make sure you know what you are trying to learn, and try to learn it. Every prototype is different.

When I worked on *Angry Birds Transformers*, game director Nick Harper built an early prototype of the Retention Layer in Flash. On the left in Figure 11.6 is Nick's original map. On the right is the map that appeared in the final game.

The briefing that appeared before each mission, the mission result screen and the way in which players unlocked new Autobots and Decepticons

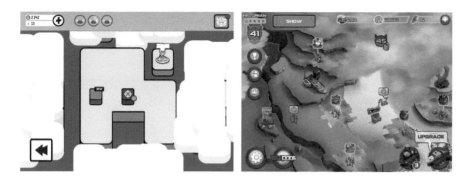

FIGURE 11.6   *Angry Birds Transformers* prototype and the final map.

were all fleshed out in Flash long before they made it to the final game. Not everything made it into the final game. Figure 11.7 shows some experiments with upgrade paths that were rejected or adapted before the game was released.

There is no fixed way of prototyping. There is one rule I can give you though, and it's not mine. It comes from Daniel Cook, creative director at Spryfox and designer of *Triple Town* and *Alphabears*. "Never let an artist anywhere near a prototype." A great artist can make a crappy game seem impressive and as if it will be fun and enjoyable, even if the mechanics and systems will not support enjoyment over time. Cook is an artist by background. He says in his Game Developers Conference (GDC) talk in 2013 that he thinks visually. His notebook is full of ideas that are sketched out in detail. He does not omit art from his prototypes because he thinks art is unimportant. Quite the opposite. "Art provides emotional investment at a time when that is *the last thing you need*." If you are prototyping with high-quality art, you will find it harder to throw away bad ideas or ideas that are not working at a system level, because you become emotionally involved. Art also usually wins over code because, as Cook says, "When art and code butt heads, the art almost always wins, because it is easy to understand."[2]

Cook's argument is, "If it's fun when it's crude, it will be doubly fun when we add graphics and emotional hooks." I agree. This is, however, one of the weaknesses of prototyping the Retention Layer. Only some people will be able to test your game. You can't put it in front of random strangers in the street. You can't pull your dad, your gran or your little brother and

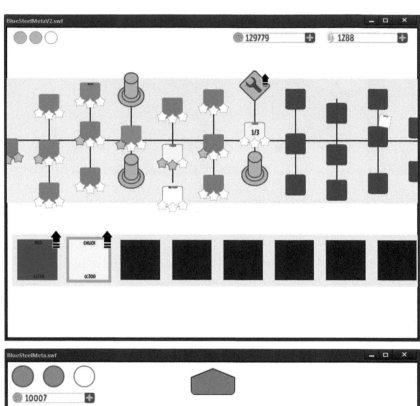

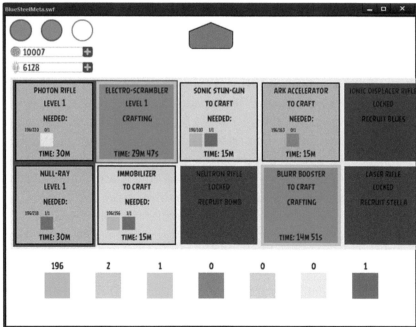

FIGURE 11.7   Dead ends in the *Angry Birds Transformers* prototyping process.

ask them to play it and expect to get valuable answers. The senior executive who will only spend three minutes with your prototype and needs to be wowed with "shiny" will not grok your prototype. The Retention Layer prototype is a tool for systems thinkers to explore whether the game will engage players for the long term.

This simplification does not mean that you don't have to worry about the User Experience (UX). Cook adds,

> "a point that I try to make, which is often lost, is that the interface you are prototyping still needs to be functional from a basic UX perspective. That means buttons should be recognizable as buttons. You should have text labels. If you have icons, use recognizable images like emoticons that help convey function. 'No art' does not mean 'unlabelled squares and circles'. Nor does it mean 'indecipherable programmer art'. Remove the polished, emotionally evocative art that sells your game. But still make your prototype functional. Otherwise, even people who understand prototypes will struggle to test what you've built."

Remember that the purpose of your prototype is to continue the process of validated learning. To make progress towards one or all of the Minimum Feasible Product (MFP), the Minimum Viable Product (MVP) or the Minimum Desirable Product (MDP). Poor UX and simple coder art may be sufficient if you are creating an MFP, a technical test to prove that you can solve a technology problem. It does nothing to prove out the fun (MDP) or your ability to create desire for your game or products within it (MVP). If you use the three lenses of the minimum product to evaluate your prototype, you can determine what the prototype needs to demonstrate the task you have set for it. That is the basis of successful, cost-effective prototyping.

The next step is to think about how the Base and Retention Layers interact and to build the Gearbox that you will need to create a strong Core Loop. Your primary tools are the Pre- and Post-Event Screens, where you can experiment with the information that you pass between the layers and that you expose to the player. Test whether the Core Loop is working: Do players want to engage again and again in the (imagined) Base Layer to earn resources that are valuable in the Retention Layer? Experiment and iterate for as long as you are still learning what you need to learn. Eventually, you will need to combine the Base and Retention Layers into a single build.

One of the most important production decisions to make in the prototyping and pre-production phase is when to slam the two prototypes together. The Retention Layer is usually not the game itself, unless you are making a resource-management game. It is a tool that enhances players' enjoyment of the Base Layer. It must interact with and give meaning to the Base Layer. Players must feel that by going through the Core Loop multiple times they are making understandable, enjoyable progress. It can be hard to tell if this is happening until the two prototypes co-exist in a single build. If you leave the slamming together of the two prototypes for too long, you may end up with two different games that do not work together well. Unpicking those design decisions can be a drag on your development schedule.

On the other hand, slamming the prototypes together has pitfalls. The most challenging problem is that your speed of iteration on the Retention Layer prototype has just slowed from a sprint to a shuffle. The feedback you receive will suddenly focus on camera positioning or user interface issues in the Base Layer. Any change to the Retention Layer will be queried for whether it has knock-on effects for the development of the Base Layer. You might get new builds once a week, rather than once an hour.

In one large project on which I am currently working, the team has decided to keep the Retention Layer and Base Layer prototypes separate until the last six months of development. The game has been in development for a year, from a brand that has, up until now, been console-based, paid games. The brand owner knows that they are product-centric and they are keen to force themselves to learn the challenges of F2P service games. Their solution is to build a Base Layer that can go through their normal user-testing and feedback channels, while also building a Retention Layer prototype that simulates the results of the Base Layer for release to hundreds of internal players. It is a good decision. It will encourage the team to build a Retention Layer that is fun and engaging rather than relying on the Base Layer to drive success. This, in turn, makes it much less likely that they get huge numbers of initial downloads because of the compelling visuals and Base Layer gameplay, but suffer from poor retention throughout the first month and beyond because of Retention Layer weaknesses.

The most extreme example I have seen is the example I gave in the opening chapter, when two different *studios* are working on the Base Layer and the Retention Layer. The brand-owning client is building a Retention Layer about progression, XP, upgrading and purchases at their head office.

An external developer, based in a different country, with specific expertise in the genre we are targeting, is building a separate Base Layer. I am seeing this approach more and more and think it is likely to become much more common in large-scale service games.

ASSETS versus SYSTEMS

When thinking about the different prototyping strategies, it is worth thinking about the different development philosophies of service-based, particularly free-to-play, games and product-based games. This is not about Agile versus Waterfall, given that most developers now believe that any project can be made with an Agile methodology. It is more about how we measure progress towards our design goals and how predictable they can be.

I've discussed the vertical slice, and how executives use it reduce operational, but not financial, risk. A service-game prototype aims to reduce financial risk, but that can be disconcerting to executives steeped in the old greenlight process.

"What's this?" asks the executive.

"A prototype to find the fun," replies the designer.

"Have you found it yet?"

"No," admits the designer.

"How much will it cost?"

"I only need me and a coder?" says the designer.

"How long will it take?" asks the executive.

"I don't know," says the designer.

Given the choice between operational risk and financial risk, many executives would rather spend $60 million on a known project that will be ready in two years than spend $100,000 on a prototyping process that may never lead to anything but may, as Supercell has shown, lead to repeatable, breakaway hits. I can't entirely blame the cautious executives. They have experience in managing the risks of large-scale, known projects. Their organisations are not set up for validated learning. In the terminology of Lean, they are corporates, not startups.

If you are going to make service games, particularly F2P ones, this approach is dangerous. If you are relying on the production of assets to be your Retention Layer, you are setting yourself up to have an expensive treadmill that will exhaust you financially just trying to keep up with your players. One truism of game development is that no matter how much content you launch with, players will exhaust it faster than you expected. If content is your mechanism of keeping players engaged, you will be on that treadmill within a week of launch. More dangerously, you are likely to be churning out content for a tiny subset of your players, the most engaged ones, rather than focusing your attention on the many players who dropped out of your game early on because it did not grab them. That way bankruptcy lies.

Product games have tended to rely on *assets* as their driver of retention. These are expensive but predictable. In that era, producers were paramount. They drove milestones and delivered retention by having level after level crafted by their teams. Service games tend to rely on *systems* to drive retention. They aim to make the art, audio and other assets amplify emotional engagement with the game, rather than acting as a primary driver of retention. In a service game, designers are the driver of retention, rather than producers. Producers retain a significant role, but the star of the designer is rising.

Designer is a complicated term in service games. Some studios believe their designers should focus on the Base Layer because they consider that to be pure gameplay. For these studios, the role of understanding progression and retention belongs to a product owner. Other studios consider the product owner to be the analyst who uses metrics to determine what should be fixed, before passing that over to the design team who cover both the Base and Retention Layers. I am making a different distinction here between someone whose job it is to get the right assets delivered on time and budget (a producer) and someone whose job is to deliver fun and retention through reusable systems (a designer). In the long term, I expect most successful games to have a single Game Director at the top, with a Design Director, who owns the creative vision, and a Product Owner, who owns the analytics, commercial strategy and Live Agency teams, reporting to him or her. As the game matures, there may no longer be a need for so many senior leaders. The Game Director and Design Director will move onto a new project that is in Development Agency phase, leaving the Product Owner as the person in charge for the remainder of the game's lifetime.

WHEN TO PIVOT

Pivot is the most overused word in business. It is mistakenly used to cover up mistakes or to justify expensive failures as learning experiences. This is only OK if the team had set out to learn that stuff. If not, it's a cock-up, not a pivot.

As Eric Ries said of his product failures in the early days of IMVU, "If the goal of those months was to learn important insights about customers, why did it take so long? Could we have learned those lessons earlier if I hadn't been so focused on making the product 'better' by adding features and fixing bugs?"[3]

Ries is right. Our objective is not to make a prototype better and better until we ship it. It is to learn what we need to learn from each prototype to inform our final design decisions. Sometimes, that will involve keeping the code base. Sometimes, that will involve throwing away the code that we have built once it has fulfilled its learning function. This is never easy. It is important. The purpose of a prototype is to learn. It is not to be the base of your product.

Designer Daniel Cook says, "the spirit of prototyping is one that is best suited to off-the-cuff hackers and geniuses. In mere hours, the prototype needs to be playable such that the feedback cycle can begin. Hackers, though deadly in the long run, will cobble a prototype together by hook or by crook. The code will stink, but it will work." He advises, and I agree, that you set strict limits on architectural work. If you think you might need a robust conversation system, hack it together, don't future-proof it. Odds are you will realise that this system is overkill for your hidden object game or first-person shooter, and you should throw it away. As Cook says, "The goal is to create a prototype that can be critiqued, trashed and thrown away. The goal is not to create a finished product. There is a time and a place for spending copious time on your architecture; the prototyping phase is not it…. Depending on the personality of your team, this can be one of your biggest project management challenges."[4]

This is particularly true for teams that are transitioning from work-for-hire and which are dominated by a production mentality, rather than a design mentality. Design-led teams risk never getting the game made, whereas production-led teams risk making a game that nobody likes. Throwing away code is something that programmers and producers find painful, but executives find even more painful, especially if their background is in work-for-hire studios that are used to charging out development capacity a person-rate of $x,000 per person-month. I once worked with a studio who spent far too much on a prototyping phase, for a total charge-out cost of $500,000. We concluded, eventually, that the prototype had demonstrated that this direction was not working. It was not fun and engaging. We prepared to dump it. Then a senior executive pointed out that we had spent half a million dollars on this feature. We were forced to keep it, even though everyone involved, *including the senior executive*, agreed that it was not fun.

USING THE SCIENTIFIC METHOD

The *Oxford English Dictionary* defines the scientific method as "A method of procedure that has characterized natural science since the 17th century, consisting of systematic observation, measurement, and experiment, and the formulation, testing, and modification of hypotheses."[5] At the heart of the scientific method are two principles: that experiments are designed to test predictions, and that criticism, particularly feedback from skilled practitioners and peer review, is critical to the advancement of knowledge.[6]

Video games are not science. They are art, craft and science, all rolled into one and combined with a healthy dose of luck. Zynga believed it had turned video-game making into a science and captured the rules in something it called the Zynga Playbook. It was so convinced that in 2009 it sued rival game developer Playdom for stealing the Playbook. In the lawsuit, Zynga stated,

> "The Zynga Playbook is literally the recipe book that contains Zynga's 'secret sauce'. [It] constitutes a collection in one document of many of the most material, non-public, commercially valuable, concepts, techniques, know-how and best practices for developing successful and distinctive social games. The Playbook is the result of years of testing, development, trial and error, analysing customer behaviour, game behaviour, optimizing past successful techniques, and collective know-how that Zynga has spent millions of dollars and more than tens of thousands of man hours developing and devising, and which could only be compiled by developing and deploying successful games over a period of years to millions of [players]."[7]

Zynga was wrong. The Playbook showed how to make a particular type of a game, for a particular type of audience. When that audience got bored of endless -*ville* games (*Farmville, CityVille, Castleville*), they left to other platforms. It wasn't only players who left. Chief Designer Brian Reynolds quit in 2013, along with many other talented game makers. Zynga's revenue fell from $1.3 billion in 2012 to $700 million in 2014. Making games according to a mythical "playbook" satisfies neither gamers, nor creators, nor, in the end, the money people.

Video games may not be science, but scientific principles are still useful. A video game is something that you can make, that people can enjoy and that hopefully can deliver a profit. These are all elements that can be tested. Eric Ries has shown that these principles can be extended, via validated learning, to creating new products and businesses. We can extend that to video games, through prototyping, through soft launch and through the pivot meeting.

THE PIVOT MEETING

The pivot meeting is one of my most useful tools in consulting, both to games companies and to non-game companies. The process is simple. *Fix a date* in the future for a "pivot meeting." If you are doing rapid prototyping, that meeting might be in a week, or a month. If you are doing a longer cycle of development, it might be three or six months. It should not be longer than that.

Next you need to *pose the question* for the pivot meeting. If you are a startup business, the question is simple: should we continue making and distributing our product in the same way, or do we need to change what we are doing?

A simple question often carries more complex questions beneath its surface. This one is no different. The pivot question for a game project might cover any or all of the following questions:

- Is our Base Layer working?

- Is our Retention Layer working?

- Do the Base Layer and the Retention Layer work well together?

- If not, should we throw one of them away? Which one? (In practice, it's nearly always the Retention Layer that gets changed because developers tend to get more invested, both financially and emotionally, in the Base Layer.)

- Have we got the business model right?

- What are people going to pay for? Will they pay enough to keep us in business?

- Will players keep playing?

- How will we reach new players cost-effectively? Should we redesign the game to be more friendly for streamers, or to have more viral hooks?

The list of possible pivot questions is endless. The top-level question is always: Should we carry on, or should we change course? Make sure you know the specific questions you are trying to answer through the validated learning process. *Everything that you are doing from now until the pivot meeting should be laser-focused on getting the information that you need to answer the pivot questions.* You are not trying to polish your product. You are not trying to turn your prototype into a better prototype. You are trying to learn, as fast and as cheaply as possible, if you are on the right track. If you are not, it is better to know sooner rather than later. As the mantra goes in Silicon Valley, "fail fast and fail often." My interpretation of that phrase is that if you learned something quickly and cheaply and were able to pivot away from it before it cost the company too much time and money, that was not a failure. It was an experiment that did its job.

This is one reason why Supercell's success seems to be more replicable than Zynga's. The Zynga Playbook was a set of rules for making a subset of video games that harnessed the viral nature of social networks and that targeted a new audience that had not had significant previous exposure to video games. Supercell's approach is more akin to the scientific method. It is a *process of discovery*, with a series of cheap experiments, rather than a *fixed ruleset* that struggles to adapt to changing market conditions. Supercell has had four hits in a row.[8] It has also killed at least a dozen games before a worldwide launch, and many more in the concepting or prototyping phases. We can't be certain that Supercell will continue to rake in the revenues, but it has demonstrated that it can repeat success on mobile over and over again, a feat that has proven impossible for many challengers.

The pivot meeting strategy has several advantages. The first is that it focuses people's minds. The team knows that their job is not just to "make this prototype," but to answer the question, "should we make this game?" They should feel empowered to do so. It is critical that the pivot meeting does not feel like a greenlight. The objective is not to sneak your pet project past the executives through a combination of vertical slice, office politics and, if necessary, some underhand trickery. It is to make the best possible decision for your game.

The second is that it makes it clear to the team what the objective for the next few weeks or months is going to be. It is not to polish the prototype. It is to ask the questions to which they need answers to inform their decision. These might be technical, commercial or focused on finding the fun.

Thirdly, a pivot meeting stops the endless arguments that go round and round in circles in the corridors, the water cooler and the pub. You know the ones. "I think we should move our game from space to the Wild West." "Maybe we should have more dragons." "If only we made the game hyper-competitive, everyone would like it more." The pivot meeting process says, "We are not going to have that conversation now. We will have the conversation at the pivot meeting." It can be liberating to have a few, defined problems to solve, rather than an infinite possibility space.

At the meeting, there are three possible outcomes.

- You carry on as before, with the plan.

- You kill the project.

- You change direction, also known as pivoting.

Pivoting can be major or minor. At the extreme, it could mean throwing away a Base Layer. "We were making a first-person shooter, but we've found the strategic gameplay we built into the Retention Layer compelling, and it would complement a squad-based tactical shooter better. Let's pivot." More usually, it involves making a minor change. A team may have thought that their game works best with a progression map like *Candy Crush Saga*'s, but concluded that a simpler XP levelling system would work better. Or they might replace a grind-driven technology-tree with a luck-driven loot box system, and so on.

At the end of the pivot meeting, you should set *the next pivot meeting*. Again, agree on the question and what you need to learn and set out to learn it. The process repeats itself.

If you are applying the pivot meeting to a company strategy ("Should we be making mobile games or games for Steam?"), then a six-monthly cadence is reasonable. In the prototyping process, you can set yourself objectives on a daily basis. More likely, you will have made meaningful progress in a month. Set your schedule accordingly.

One fear about the pivot process is that it lacks consistency, because participants keep changing their minds. The first pivot meeting might obsess about minute-to-minute gameplay, the next on achieving good retention, the third on building social features and so on. There seems to be a lack of consistency. That is true, but only from a certain point of view.

The consistent objective is to identify the next most important thing to learn and then to learn it. Once you have learned it, find the next most important thing and learn that. A prototype is an attempt to eliminate a risk. Once you are satisfied that your game has enjoyable, minute-to-minute gameplay, it is sensible to move on to the next most pressing issue.

The prototype and the pivot are two of the most useful tools for rapid, iterative development. Next, we need to look at the nature of the production schedule and when you should move from one phase to the next.

CHAPTER 12

Production

THERE ARE MANY DIFFERENT stages of game development. My favourite way of describing development is shown in Figure 12.1.

For me, there are five major phases: concept, production, launch, live and sunset. These can be broken down further as shown in Figure 12.2.

Phase 1 is concept, which encompasses the idea, pitching and prototyping. This phase may be long if you need to demonstrate significant development progress or produce lots of pitch material to earn funding for your project. It may be short, if you are an indie developer who can greenlight projects on your own.

Phase 2 is production, split between pre-production and production. Service games tend to have longer pre-production cycles, relative to the production cycle, than product games because there is more that is unknown. Some elements of the game, such as level design, art creation and audio, may enter production before the rest of the game has exited pre-production. This is fine, but problems emerge if you go too far down the production roadmap with major unknowns still outstanding in the design track.

Phase 3 is launch, consisting of the quality assurance and submission phase, soft-launch, hard launch and initial post-launch activities. In a service game, this phase is often much longer than phases 2 and 3.

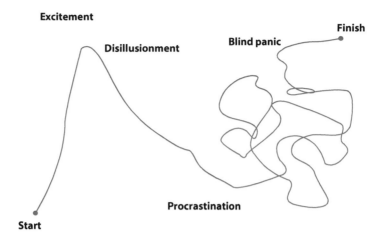

FIGURE 12.1   The phases of creative development.

Phase 4 is the Live Agency phase, a concept I explore in detail in this chapter. The launch phase and live phase sometimes overlap, as the development team transitions from creating the game to operating it.

Phase 5 is the sunset phase, which is not discussed in this book. The sunset phase occurs when the game is longer developed, but is operated with a skeleton crew to keep the players satisfied and to keep earning money.

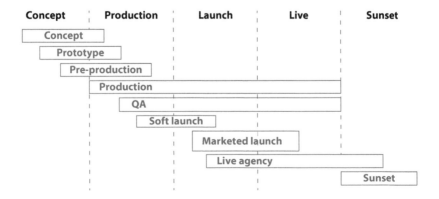

FIGURE 12.2   The phases of game development.

PHASE 1: CONCEPT

This is not a book about concepting, so I will cover this area briefly. During the concept phase, you need to come up with the idea for the game, get support for it and start proving that you can make it. The requirements for this phase vary with each company. Some companies need to raise external finance. Their pitch will require lots of polish and pizzazz. If they are pitching to sophisticated game financiers, they may need a prototype or a vertical slice. If the pitch is to unsophisticated ones, they will need a whizzy idea. Tim Schafer, in the Kickstarter campaign for *Broken Age*, merely promised to make "a classic point-and-click adventure."[1] This is no longer possible as Kickstarter has matured, but it used to work.

Prototyping is about proving out the ideas that you need to test, to eliminate risk, while being prepared to throw away code once it has achieved its purpose. Pre-production is the next phase. Gameplay risks have begun to be eliminated. Now it is time to start focusing on production risks. We start seeing schedules and milestones or more Agile methodologies of Sprint plans and backlogs, or Must, Should, Could, Won't (MoSCoW) prioritisation.

At this point, production starts for some teams before pre-production is completed in others. Some work streams are ready for production, whereas others still need experimentation. For example, perhaps the Base Layer has advanced to a stage where the team is happy with it, but producers are worrying about delivery schedules. The team needs to start creating character art and animation, trees and scenery or building whole levels. Teams generally need few artists to focus on pre-production, so the studio has skilled resource standing by with nothing to do. This never lasts long; they are set to work making assets.

This is normal and not a problem, provided the pre-production and even prototyping continues apace. The team needs to keep iterating and experimenting to solve thorny problems while allowing the asset creators and production team to keep moving towards the eventual ship date. At some point, the pressure to make rather than to experiment has become overwhelming, and the game is finally in production.

PHASE 2: PRODUCTION

The production phase often combines both pre-production and production. Parts of the team are on a treadmill, producing known assets or providing five levels of detail (LoDs) of an object. Others are still experimenting and iterating to find the fun. As this phase continues, pre-production needs to stop. A designer tweaking the speed of a monster, for example, starts to break the animation that has already been produced so the monster can appear to be lurching towards the player, not striding. At some point, the advantages to be gained for the project by the rapid iteration of pre-production are outweighed by disadvantages caused by the communication flow and disruption of dependencies in the team.

Exactly when this moment will occur is hard to predict. Remember that your overall ambition is to learn, as fast and as cheaply as possible, how to make a game that fits your vision, brings joy to your audience and earns you money. Then you must make it. The danger of going into production too early is that you make a game that doesn't satisfy your audience or that underperforms on too many key metrics. The danger of going too late is that you spend too much time and money on your game for it ever to be profitable.

PHASE 3: LAUNCH

The purpose of the production phase is to get to the launch phase. This is not the end of development. You should create your Minimum Awesome Product and, after a period of user testing and quality assurance, release it to a large but limited group of real players, often called a *soft launch*. From soft launch, you have a marketed launch and then your game will switch into a live mode, where you will continue to maintain and love it for many years to come.

PHASE 4: LIVE

The live phase is where the focus of the development team switches to getting the best out of the existing game. There is a smaller possibility space, and more restrictions on the changes that the team can make to the game. Development tasks are likely to be shorter, and focused on events or repeatable content to satisfy the existing community. Most of the rest of this chapter is focused on the live phase.

PHASE 5: SUNSET

Eventually, the opportunity cost of maintaining the game may be higher than the revenues that you can generate from it. You may be able to find a buyer for it, or you may need to shut it down. There is no need to plan for this from the beginning, but once you are deep in the launch phase, it starts to become a consideration.

WORDS TO BAN #3: ALPHA AND BETA

I dislike words that confuse instead of clarify. Alpha and beta tests are two such words. In the days of boxed product development, or the release of online games on PC, the terms had clear meanings

- Alpha meant "feature complete" All the features, systems and core technology were in place. The purpose of the alpha test was to eliminate the system design and technical risks.
- Beta release meant "content complete." Levels, characters, missions and narratives were all in the game. The purpose of the test was quality assurance, bug testing, load-balancing the servers with large numbers of players and so on.

Alpha and beta tests are relics of the era of production-centric design. They fit well with milestones, with deliverables, with contracts that specify exactly how many levels are needed, with what content and by what date. They fit well when the design paradigm is that a game is complete when it is launched. Updates come in discrete packages, like the dinosaur-themed expansion for *Zoo Tycoon* that was originally sold in physical packaging in retail stores, or the *Wrath of the Lich King* expansion for the most successful massively multiplayer online (MMO) game in the world, *World of Warcraft*.

We now operate in a different paradigm. We live in the era of the Minimum Awesome Product (MAP). We are continually releasing new updates for the game. We consciously aim to keep the initial product as small as possible so we can test the key performance indicators (KPIs) in a soft launch. We are never feature-complete. We are never content-complete.

We could attempt to adapt the words *alpha* and *beta* to this new world. We already have the distinction between closed alphas, typically internal only, and open alphas, which are (probably, possibly, I'm never sure) open to a limited number of members of the public, feature complete but lacking in content.

The danger is that when you use these words, every person listening hears a different meaning, usually the one that is more useful for them. You end up with a test where the team can't agree what success looks like. I prefer to use new terms: *technical test*, *soft launch* and so on, which I explain in Chapter 14.

Use *alpha* and *beta* if you must. But make sure you define them, and check with your team often to confirm they are trying to achieve the same thing that you are.

DEVELOPMENT AGENCY versus LIVE AGENCY

By now, you have read a lot about the difference between the Lean approach to operations, which I have also referred to as startup behaviour. We have also discussed corporate-style approaches. I have implied that corporate-style structures are most suited to product games and startup-style structures are more suited to service games.

This is only partially true. As your high-school physics teacher may have told you, "it's not as simple as that."

Startup skills and tools are best used when you are trying to eliminate uncertainty. Corporate tools are best used when you are trying to do something that is already known, but optimising to do it better, cheaper or more profitably.

I worked with a client some years ago trying to make the transition to mobile F2P games. The company culture focused on AAA production values, and they were very good at making those games. We iterated to make a base-defence strategy game with a 1960s vibe. It had a lovely art style, but the game didn't deliver the key performance indicators (KPIs) that we needed. We killed the project.

Some months later, the same client told me that he had chatted with three separate publishers who said, "Of course you didn't hit the KPIs. You didn't have the daily login bonuses and live events and continuous updates that a successful F2P game needs. That's why you failed."

The publishers are wrong.

The soft launch this client released was a Minimum Viable Product (MVP). It didn't yet have enough content to be a Minimum Awesome Product, but it was sufficient to start learning. As I explained to my client, the soft launch exists to answer the question: *Is the lifetime value of my customers good enough to justify spending my scarce marketing resources on this title?*

Many developers focus on testing the First-Time User Experience (FTUE) completion rate, retention statistics like D1, D7, D30 and monetisation metrics like conversion rate and Average Revenue per Paying User (ARPPU). They also throw in a laundry list of features that have no place in a soft launch:

- Daily rewards

- Daily quests

- Achievements

- Sharing to Facebook or posting to Twitter

- Dozens of others

There are always exceptions to the rules above, but this is the principle: You want to test the fundamental retention (and subsequently) monetisation of the game. Features like daily rewards are retention techniques that can work on any game. They are not a big element of risk in your design. You want them in your game before you spend your marketing resources, but by putting them in your soft launch, you are delaying learning whether the core of your game has good retention.

Actually, it's worse than that. By putting in systems like login bonuses or achievements, you can obscure the true retention metrics of your game. A game like *Crossy Road* or *Flappy Bird* doesn't focus on these retention techniques because they are just so fun. Even games like *The Simpsons: Tapped Out* or *Fallout Shelter* need to draw users back because of the intrinsic fun of playing the game, not because of the extrinsic rewards of getting your login bonus every day.

The publishers mentioned were not thinking about Minimum Viable Products. They were not focused on finding the fun. They were thinking, "Assuming that this game is fun, what tools and techniques do I need to improve retention and monetisation." Those publishers were not Dev Agents; they were Live Agents.

LIVE AGENCY versus DEVELOPMENT AGENCY

Live Agents have been handed a game that works. They are no longer, in Eric Ries's words, "operating under conditions of extreme uncertainty."[2] The Dev Agency has created a Minimum Awesome Product. It has passed the KPI test with flying colours. The game is now launched worldwide with a successful marketing strategy (See Chapter 14: Marketing Your Launch). The key uncertainty—that players will not enjoy the game—has been eliminated. The Live Agency now has the responsibility to deploy every weapon in its arsenal to improve player enjoyment, retention and monetisation. All the usual suspects, from daily logins to push notifications to ambitious live events, are on its roadmap. Live Agency teams are required to make the game meet or beat its KPIs. My client's sparse base-defence game, lacking all the bells and whistles of a modern F2P game, must have looked strange to a Live Agent.

Dev Agents have a different brief. They are trying to eliminate uncertainty. They are measured not by revenue and profits but by validated learning. Revenue and profits are the end goal, but not the near-term one. When you are, in Steve Blank's words, searching for a repeatable and scalable business model, you need to be agile, and you do that best by avoiding bloat.

To a Live Agency team, adding daily login bonuses is a high priority. It will nudge retention metrics up by a few percentage points. That makes a difference to a Live Agent's results. As do sales, seasonal events, and so on. To a Dev Agency, these features use up scarce development cycles and testing time to test features *that we know work*. We know that they can nudge the KPIs upwards. What they can't do is compensate for a weak Core Loop, a Base Layer that is dull and a Retention Layer that doesn't pull players back for more. They are distractions and should be developed after soft launch.

This disconnect between Live Agency publishing staff and Dev Agency development staff is going to get stronger as the service-game industry matures. In the early days of service games, the developer and the publisher were the same entity, whether it was CCP creating and publishing *EVE Online* or Playfish launching *Restaurant City* on Facebook. There was a close connection between the development, the marketing and the monetisation of the game. For many of the most successful service companies, that is still true. Think of Riot with *League of Legends*, Supercell with *Clash of Clans*, King with *Candy Crush Saga*, Electronic Arts with *FIFA Ultimate* Team, or Valve with *Team Fortress 2*.

Increasingly, we are seeing publishers working with external developers. This phenomenon is driven by two structural challenges. The first is that many developers do not have the marketing muscle to stand out in a competitive environment. They need marketing partners to amplify their games on Steam, on mobile stores and elsewhere. The second is that some publishers have found that they are unable to change the DNA of their product-centric development and marketing teams. The only way that they can get F2P expertise into their organisation is to hire it from external teams.

There are many challenges with this approach—enough to fill a book of its own. The main challenge is avoiding a misalignment of incentives. When the developer is also the publisher and the financier, it has one group to keep satisfied: the end user. Decisions are optimised to balance the financial health of the developer, the desires of the target audience and the technology resources available. When a publisher is funding development, the developer is now in conflict because its customer is the publisher, not the end user. Developers must walk a tightrope between satisfying the publisher who pays their bills and delivering the game that they think will best satisfy end users. When publishers are filled with Live Agency staff and developers with Dev Agency staff, there can be a gulf in understanding over prioritisation and feature set. This gap in understanding kills projects.

When a developer has sourced the financing for a game itself, but sought out a publisher to market it, the "financial risk versus operational risk" relationship, set out in Chapter 10: How to Develop a Service Game, comes into play. The marketing partner has every incentive to encourage developers to ratchet up financial risk by spending more money on the game. It makes their marketing job easier, but the publisher has little incentive to do a risk-reward analysis. The three publishers telling my client that his 1960s-themed base-defence game failed to hit the metrics because it lacked obvious retention features were making this mistake. They were encouraging my client to ratchet up the financial risk by adding features that did nothing to eliminate the operational risk: that players did not find the Core Loop compelling. When you have a corporate mind-set, this is the best route to go. When you have a start-up mind-set, it is foolishness.

Most organisations need *both sets of skills*. Steve Blank emphasises that a startup is a *temporary* organisation. Dave McClure argues that when a startup figures out what its product is, who its customers are and how it is going to make money, it ceases to become a startup and becomes a business. That is the objective of a successful game design process. When that happens, the Dev Agency's job is done. They can hand over to a Live Agency to start optimising and tweaking.

ngMoco did just that. Founder Neil Young argued that swapping out an entire team when the game went live was a sensible strategy, "because developers tend to get tired of a product soon after release."[3] Given the chance, the old team would probably spend the first six months of Live Agency building all the features that were dropped from soft launch for budget or time reasons. A new team can look at the game as it is, together with the feedback from the players and the analytics, and decide what to do next. It also means that you can put the right people in the right places: the startup problem solvers who are comfortable with uncertainty focus on Dev Agency, and the corporate types with an analytical, pragmatic approach can optimise the game thereafter.

LOCAL MAXIMA

A local, or relative, maximum is the maximum within some neighbourhood. It need not be the same as the global maximum.

In service-game design, finding the local maximum often implies using metrics and analytics to squeeze the last bit of performance out of the existing game systems. To find the global maximum, you may need to create whole new features.

Furthermore, a successful game will continue to have Dev Agency even after launch. While one team will be busy optimising the game for existing users and finding the local maxima, another team will be continuing to develop new features, often with extreme uncertainty, to add to the game to create a new global maximum. CCP calls this Live Operations and Feature Development, which is another way of framing the difference. Knowing the difference between the two approaches can make it much easier to understand how to manage your team through the three phases of production.

PRIC EVALUATION OR PRICE

In the old days of product games, developers would go to extreme lengths to defend their ideas to prevent them from being tagged LATER. LATER was a death knell. The brutal prioritisation that resulted in the agreed feature set for the final game turned LATER into OUT. If you had shown weakness in defending your idea, it would be culled. Some developers understood that this was necessary to be able to ship the game. Others took a different lesson: never, ever, ever admit that your idea or feature might have a weakness if you want it to appear in the finished game.

Most of us will have worked with someone who thinks like this and who won't let go of their ideas or admit to any flaws in their suggestion. Worse, they pounce on anyone else's admission of weakness in a design as an excuse to kill the feature, not as an opportunity to improve the design, the feature or the game. The problem is compounded if the person with this mind-set is senior. Then it becomes a HiPPO problem, the Highest Paid Person's Opinion.

This is dangerous for all games. I once worked on a game that had local multiplayer added over the objections of the entire development team who argued it would be an expensive, unnecessary feature that would have no noticeable impact on downloads, revenue or any other KPI. It was added because the CEO thought it would be cool. A 2016 PhD thesis explored the hypothesis that games with high-status leaders have a worse success rate. In his study of 349 video game projects with 179 producers from 17 companies, Hungarian researcher Balazs Szatmari of the Rotterdam School of Management found that games with high-status leaders have a higher variability of success; they were more likely to fail and more likely to be very successful than games with low-status leaders. The thesis concludes that perhaps high-status leaders get so much support and unquestioning obedience that no one is brave enough to challenge the decisions in the organisation or project, and a project where the leader is unchallenged no longer benefits from the diversity of views, skills and talents that an engaged and communicative team can provide.[4]

The IN/OUT mind-set is a relic of physical distribution on shiny discs. In service games (and product games with patches and DLC), we have replaced it with NOW/LATER. We no longer fight tooth and nail to keep an idea in soft launch in case it dies later; we focus our efforts on what we need to learn next. Ideas that are not critical for NOW get put into the LATER pile. (Keep a backlog of ideas in your favourite idea management system, whether that be a game development tool like Confluence or Jira, a task management tool like On-Time or Asana or an ideas management tool like Evernote. Tag them with their purpose—monetisation, onboarding, Return Hook, and so on—so that you can find them again when you are searching for solutions for a problem in the future.)

To evaluate whether a feature belongs in the core experience or in a later release, I recommend that you undertake a PRIC Evaluation.

- *Publicity*: Will adding the feature have a positive impact on your game in the eyes of players and the press? Will it have a negative impact?

- *Retrofit*: How easy is it to add this feature? Can it be added with little engineering difficulty? Is it embedded in the economy, the user interface (UI) or the progression system such that retrofitting will be hard?

- *Impact*: Will it have a significant impact on KPIs? Which ones? Mainly early game KPIs?

- *Cost*: How expensive is this feature to implement? Is it cheap to design but expensive to implement (a perennial problem with senior executives and external stakeholders)?

When you undertake a PRIC Evaluation, you are asking yourself whether the benefits of implementing this feature outweigh the disadvantages in development cost, launch delay and team distraction. You are trying to decide if a feature should be developed NOW, or if it should be put in the backlog marked LATER. The default assumption should be that a feature should be developed later, after you have more information from your soft launch.

To give some specific examples:

- Daily Login Bonuses? They have a small Impact on KPIs but are easy to Retrofit. LATER.

- An unproven feature, that is essential to the vision of the game. Impact could be significant. Part of validated learning. NOW.

- Boosts that affect gameplay. Negative Publicity if they are introduced after soft-launch; neutral if they are part of the game from soft launch. NOW.

- Challenge systems. If they are a core way of delivering currency and rewards to players, NOW. Otherwise, they are easy to Retrofit, so LATER.

- Social is tricky. If it is at the core of the game, like matchmaking in a PvP game, or in any MMO, the Impact is enormous, so NOW. If it is merely connecting with friends via Facebook, you are unlikely to want this to happen during soft launch anyway. LATER.

Of course, there are exceptions to the rule. If daily quests are at the absolute heart of your game, you need them now. If your game is multiplayer only, then maybe you need Facebook to provide liquidity for your players. If your economy doesn't function without the drip feed of resources through the daily login bonuses, add them now. The basic rule is that if the reason you are putting a feature in is because it's "best practice," or because Apple won't feature you without it, or because everyone else does it, leave it for later.

This is about putting the minimum into Minimum Awesome Product. It will save you time and money. It may even save your game.

DON'T DO SEASONAL EVENTS

Don't make seasonal events like Halloween specials, Christmas treats and Diwali delights.

But don't all successful games have them? Can't you just get bundled into a Steam Halloween promotion simply by putting a few hollowed-out pumpkins onto the heads of your battle-weary space marines?

Yes, and no. I heard of a developer that was desperate for money. It pinned all its hopes on a last roll of the dice and made special items to celebrate Easter. Like many game projects, the date slipped. They shipped their update on Easter Monday and filed for bankruptcy later that week.

Seasonal events are a great idea as the icing on the cake of your success. Once you know that you have an enjoyable, successful game that reliably gets players coming back, playing more and spending often, run all the seasonal events that you can.

Until then, seasonal events are a Band-Aid. They are easy for an executive or a designer to request. They take time and effort to build. Time and effort that would be better spent figuring what is wrong with the core of your game, not applying minor tweaks around the edges.

They are dangerous because a studio can become addicted to them. Instead of doing the hard, grinding work of nudging KPIs upwards, through endless iterations and a better understanding of your customers, you can have a seasonal sale, watch the numbers skyrocket for a week or so and drop back from a roar to a trickle. You then decide that you must do it again and again, each time to less effect.

Focus your efforts. If you must do events, do ones that are repeatable. Design events that can happen whenever you want. Don't do seasonal events because everyone else is doing them: do them when you have run out of other, more enduring and more systemic updates for your game.

CHAPTER 13

Managing Creativity

C REATIVITY IS BROKEN.
Our scientific, rationalist approach taught through schools, colleges, universities and businesses is broken. I blame Socrates.

In 1985, Edward de Bono published *Six Thinking Hats*. De Bono argued that, "the basic idea behind Western thinking was designed about 2,300 years ago by the Greek 'Gang of Three' and is based on argument."[1] De Bono reckons that in 80% of the dialogues in which Socrates was involved, as recorded by Plato, "there is no constructive outcome at all." Socrates saw his role as being to point out what was "wrong." Plato and Aristotle added their philosophies and, de Bono argues, "as a result, Western thinking is concerned with 'what is', which is determined by analysis, judgement and argument. That is a fine and useful system. But there is a whole aspect of thinking that is concerned with 'what can be,' which involves constructive thinking, creative thinking and 'designing the way forward'."[2]

Six Thinking Hats was de Bono's attempt to address the challenges of traditional Western thinking. De Bono contended that we are all capable of bringing a variety of different thinking approaches to any problem, but thanks to Socrates, Plato and Aristotle, we have been trained to believe that only one critical approach works: the logical, destructive one.

You will have been on the receiving end of a critical or logical analysis. You put forward an idea in a team meeting. The team shoots it down. "It's too expensive." "It will be a huge performance drain." "We'll have to rebalance the entire economy." The team is, in its own way, attempting to help. It is evaluating the proposal in the only way it knows how: it attacks. As hard and as viciously as it can. If the idea is still standing at the end of this brutal assault, it was a good idea and deserves to be implemented. It is survival of the fittest, red in tooth and claw.

The problem with this approach is that few people relish being on the receiving end of such harsh criticism. After you have been subjected to this barrage once or twice, you become reluctant to stick your neck out again. The creative spark leaves the room. The only people still prepared to put forward ideas are the thick-skinned, the narcissistic or the foolish. That is not a recipe for getting the best creative work out of a team.

The proponents of the criticism approach will defend their actions by arguing that an idea needs to be evaluated. If it is a bad idea, or will be difficult to implement, it deserved to die. They are right. It is their timing that is wrong. We need to create environments in which creativity flourishes. This is best done by fostering an environment in which people are prepared to put their ideas forward. In this chapter, I will explore how best to do that.

HOW TO FOSTER IDEAS AND HOW TO KILL THEM

There is no need to kill most creative ideas with analytical thinking. Most ideas will wither on the vine long before that.

As I discussed in Chapter 10 in the section about the Minimum Feasible Product, we have moved past the "Can we do it?" phase of technology into the "Should we do it?" phase. Although there remain a handful of games that are pushing the technological envelope, for most studios any technological problem can be solved with sufficient time and money. That is not to disregard the skills and expertise of those people who have to solve the difficult problems. Those people remain an important competitive advantage for a games studio. The point instead is to say that if the team jumps straight to evaluating all the reasons why a particular solution might be difficult to implement, it has made an implicit assumption: that the idea should be implemented, if only it can be. Instead, we need techniques that allow the team to explore the purpose and value behind the idea. We need to encourage creativity and a positive working environment. We need to allow ideas to flow, and *then* we need a structure to evaluate ideas for feasibility and practicality.

De Bono addressed the problem with his *Six Thinking Hats*. The guiding principle is that humans have many different skills and approaches to bring to bear on problems. De Bono described each thinking hat by its colour, which he related to its function.

White Hat: White is neutral and objective. The White Hat is concerned with objective facts and figures.

Red Hat: Red suggests anger, rage and emotions. The Red Hat gives the emotional view.

Black Hat: Black is sombre and serious. The Black Hat is cautious and careful. It points out the weaknesses in an idea. (This is the Socratic-Platonic-Aristotelian approach)

Yellow Hat: Yellow is sunny and positive. The Yellow Hat is optimistic and covers hope and positive thinking.

Green Hat: Green is grass, vegetation and abundant, fertile growth. The Green Hat indicates creativity and new ideas.

Blue Hat: Blue is cool, and it is also the colour of the sky, which is above everything else. The Blue Hat is concerned with control, the organisation of the thinking process and the use of other hats.[3]

It is human nature to respond to a new idea with Black Hat thinking. New is risky. We need to evaluate it for the risk. The aphorism "everyone's a critic" resonates because it feels true. It is easier to be a critic than it is to create. This is dangerous in a creative organisation. We need to find the time to create, find the time to critique and to do it in a way that works for the team.

De Bono's key advice is that the whole team should be using the same hat at the same time. It is no good to assign one person (often a programmer or a lawyer) to a Black Hat, one to Red Hat emotions, one to Green creativity and so on. The whole team must work together, looking at the same problem from the same point of view. If an issue becomes one of facts, where different members of the team believe they have conflicting information, adopt the White Hat and figure out what the facts are. When someone is thinking positively with a Green or Yellow Hat, everyone should be doing it. When it is time to do the critical analysis, and that time *always* comes, everyone dons the metaphorical Black Hat.

De Bono believes that humans like to show off. Much of our self-esteem and ego is tied up in being right. Combine that trait with a Black Hat approach to thinking and you get a roomful of people arguing each other's ideas into extinction as each one tries to prove that they are the best, most thoughtful, most comprehensive thinker. By forcing the whole team to adopt, say, a Yellow Hat, you can subvert this desire in support of creativity. As de Bono says, "team members show off by performing better as a thinker than others in the meeting. The difference is that this type of showing off is constructive. The ego is no longer tied to being right."[4] People "win" by being the most creative in this discussion, not the most critical.

The *Six Thinking Hats* approach was trendy towards the end of the 20th century, although its star has waned. I find the concept useful, but it has its flaws. The main problem is the number of hats. I use the Black Hat phrase all the time, but I can never remember what the Blue Hat is for, and no one ever remembers the difference between the Green and Yellow hats. The key for me is understanding that Black Hat thinking has its place *but not at the start of the process.* The truth of creativity is that most of our initial ideas suck. They don't stack up; they are dull, derivative or fail to achieve our objectives. They deserve to die. The question, then, is what is the best way to kill them.

PLUS IT

Ed Catmull is a talented man. In 1974, he invented texture mapping, the technique for wrapping a 2D image around a 3D object that is a core element of video game development today. He coined the term *Z-buffer*, pioneering the approach of "assigning a depth to every object in three-dimensional space, then telling the computer to match each of the screen's pixels to whatever object was the closest."[5] In 1986, with the help of Steve Jobs, he founded Pixar with the goal of making the first animated movie made with nothing but computer graphics. In 1995, he achieved his ambition with the launch of *Toy Story*. It is a stellar career.

Having achieved his lifetime ambition with *Toy Story*, Catmull set himself a new ambition. He wanted to become an excellent manager of creative people. He wanted to make Pixar into a shining example of how to assemble teams that work together to blend technology and creativity to make, in Steve Jobs' words, "insanely awesome products." The string of hits from Pixar—*Finding Nemo, The Incredibles, Monsters, Inc.*, among others—show that Catmull was able to achieve this objective and, to steal the subtitle of his book, *Creativity, Inc.*, to "overcome the unseen forces that stand in the way of true inspiration."[6]

The world of computer animation and the world of video game development have much in common. In both cases, we can experiment, iterate and prototype in a way that is much harder for a live action movie to manage. For example, during the production of *The Incredibles*, writer/director Brad Bird was struggling with a scene in which Bob Parr (Mr. Incredible) sneaks back into his house late at night after doing some illicit superhero moonlighting. He is caught by his wife, Helen (Elastigirl), and a row ensues. Bird showed the scene to an internal group at Pixar known as the "Braintrust." Initial feedback on this scene was that it felt all wrong.

> "Bob was yelling at Helen, and the note I got [from the Braintrust] was, 'God, it seems like he's bullying her. I really don't like him. You've got to rewrite it.' So I go in to rewrite it, and I look at it and think 'No, that *is* what he would say, and that *is* how she would respond.' I don't want to change a damn thing, but I know I can't say that, because something's not working. And then I realise the problem: Physically, Bob is the size of a house and Helen is this tiny little thing. Even though Helen is his equal, what you're seeing on the screen is this big, threatening guy yelling and it felt like he was abusing her. Once I figured that out, all I did was have Helen stretch [because Elastigirl's superpower is to be stretchy] when she holds her ground and says, 'this is not about you!' I didn't change any dialogue, I just changed the drawings to make her body bigger, as if to say, 'I'm a match for you.' And when I played the revised scene, the Braintrust said, "'That's much better. What lines did you change?' I said, 'I didn't change a comma.' That's an example of the group knowing something was wrong, but not having the solution. I had to go deep and ask, 'If the dialogue is not wrong, what is?' And then I saw it: Oh, *that*."[7]

You can make that change cheaply for an animated movie. Less so if you must get Tom Cruise and Emily Blunt back to the soundstage to re-shoot an entire scene for a live action flick.

Catmull's success at Pixar lay in encouraging a team to focus on making great products. He fought against what he termed "The Beast," the natural tendency as a company gets larger for processes to ossify, for departments to do what is best for them and for individuals to fall into ruts of doing things the way that they have always done. He made it a clear objective to *protect the new.*

> "When someone hatches an idea, it may be ungainly and poorly defined, but it is also the opposite of established and entrenched— and that is precisely what is most exciting about it. If, while in this vulnerable state, it is exposed to naysayers who fail to see its potential or lack the patience to let it evolve, it could be destroyed. Part of our job is to protect the new from people who don't understand that in order for greatness to emerge, there must be periods of not-so-greatness. Think of a caterpillar morphing into a butterfly—it only survives because it is encased in a cocoon. It survives, in other words, because it is protected from that which would damage it. It is protected from the Beast."[8]

Think back to the chapter on prototyping. You may remember that I said that there are some people who are less skilled at evaluating prototypes than others, particularly the Retention Layer prototypes that are abstract and long term. The executive who wants something visceral and exciting, the marketing specialist who wants a checkbox list of features and a video that makes you go wow, and the playtester who comments that there is no smoke when the wheels spin on the rally car and that there is a typo on the loading screen are all part of Catmull's Beast. They think that they are trying to protect the project. They are demonstrating that they care by their attention to detail or focus on the needs of the market. They also risk killing the project.

In *Creativity, Inc.*, Catmull gives a long list of recommendations and tips on how to manage creative teams. The heart of his message is that the purpose of all constructive criticism is to move the project *forward.* If it does not do that, it is not fulfilling its role. (Note that sometimes you have to kill a project. We covered that topic in the pivot section in Chapter 11. Giving constructive criticism to move the project forward does not preclude anyone from recommending that a project be killed at the appropriate time.)

The simplest way to think about this technique is to call it *plussing.*

Plussing is originally attributed to Walt Disney. In his production meetings, instead of just shooting down ideas, every criticism had to come with a "plus," a new idea or suggestion for strengthening the original.

It turns the emotional energy of the meeting on its head. If you don't like something, ignore it. Pick a bit of the idea that you do like, and run with it. Try to make it better. Bounce ideas backwards and forwards. The time for evaluation and analysis is soon, but not yet. Right now, we are trying to run with ideas and make them better.

Pixar added a principle drawn from improvisational comedy: accept every invitation. An improv comic may not know where his comic partner is going with his idea but when the two of them are standing on stage, and a line is thrown in his direction, he does his best to catch it. They both look better, have more fun, entertain their audience and do better creative work when they trust that their partner is doing the damnedest to catch them, to take their ideas, plus them and send them back. It doesn't always work because failure is an inevitable part of trying something new. On the other hand, the only way to be certain that you will never make something new is not to try.

Making plussing part of your working life is joyous. Switching from a Black Hat view of the world that focuses on all the reasons why change is difficult or can't be done to a plussing-centric view where you treat every new idea as something to be built upon and improved makes day-to-day life more fun. It strengthens your relationships with colleagues who start to trust that if they throw an idea at you, you will catch it. The bad ideas or the difficult-to-implement ideas that you would previously have spent time and energy dismissing get left behind because it turns out that there is a better, more interesting way of solving the same problem. You reached this place without having to go through the negativity of shooting every-one's ideas down.

Adapting to a plussing environment can be hard. I spent a year working with a client to encourage them to embrace this new way of working. One day, in a design meeting, an idea was put forward and the lead program-mer said, "That idea is shit!"

I had been working on plussing for a while and was delighted when every person in the room turned to the lead programmer and said, with vehemence, "Plus it!"

The lead programmer was silent as he thought. Then he enunciated, "Our game would be much better without your shit idea in it!"

Not everyone gets it. People whose professions have trained them in seeking out weaknesses and edge cases—coders and lawyers, for example—often struggle to make the transition. Stick with it. Help them believe that there is a time for plussing and a time for Black Hat thinking.

THE HEMINGWAY METHOD

Ernest Hemingway knows how to write pithy sentences. His writing advice is short:

Write drunk. Edit sober.

I take this advice to heart. Write drunk because the greatest enemy of creativity is the critic. We've discussed the danger of the team applying Black Hat thinking too early, which leads to people not putting ideas forward because they fear the reaction they will get, often with good reason. The danger doesn't only apply to external critics. The inner critic—that part of your own brain that finds fault in everything you do, think or say—is always present. Left to its own devices, it will censor, criticise and challenge until you never put forward any ideas at all. The inner critic has a role. The important skill to learn is when to listen to it and when to ignore it.

When I wrote this book, I sat down and went at it. I didn't go back and re-read it as I went along. I wrote it out over the course of a couple of months to get a first draft of 100,000 words. Through having written several books (published, self-published and very much unpublished), I have realised that there are two processes I need to go to. The first process is to create. The second process, editing, comes later.

The most inspirational piece of writing advice I have ever received is this: "The first draft is perfect, because its only job is to exist."[9] The inner critic is frightened. It wants to pre-empt the Aristotelian challenges it expects to receive. It worries and it analyses and it prevaricates. It will stop you doing great work.

Hemingway's advice is simple. Write drunk. Get the ideas out of your head and into the world: on paper, in drawings, in code. I usually treat his advice as metaphorical, although I suspect that Hemingway treated it as literal. Sometimes going to the pub is a good solution to a knotty problem though.

Editing sober comes next. Writing this book was hard. Editing was brutal, but somehow easier than staring a blank sheet of paper. The time for Black Hat thinking is when you shape and correct and reject and analyse the work to turn it from an ungainly, poorly defined idea into a thing of elegance and beauty.

I use this approach with my clients all the time. I often set up a meeting as being a "Write Drunk, Edit Sober" meeting. We will spend the first half of the meeting writing drunk. No Black Hat thinking allowed. If you think an idea might be difficult to implement, ignore that thought or write it down for later. Plus the idea and run with it. Before long, the original idea has gone. Not because it was analysed into oblivion but because the group has moved on. It has thought of something better. The ungainly, poorly defined idea takes shape. It grows with input from all different perspectives. You do better creative work.

Then take a break. Have a cup of coffee. Stretch your legs to get fresh air into your lungs and into the room. Regroup with the energy of the previous session and start focusing on what you *can* do. This is the time for Black Hat thinking to turn the creative thoughts into practical, executable tasks.

Combining the iterative, validated learning approach of the Lean movement with the positive creative environment encouraged by de Bono or Catmull gives your studio the best chance of doing great work.

And once you have finished great work, you need to launch it.

CHAPTER 14

Marketing Your Launch

THE OVERALL STRATEGY OF a marketing campaign is to focus your scarce marketing resources on the task of acquiring customers who will stay engaged in your game. The broad approach, particularly on mobile, is this:

> On the day of launch, harness the power of your brand to get featured, and if possible, covered by the relevant press. Rise up the charts, gaining free organic users as your visibility increases. Use your frenemies to send you traffic, amplifying the benefits of this visibility. Keep getting lots of users for free, who, if they are engaged and enjoying your game, will stay and spend money, allowing you to re-invest some of your revenues into the cash marketing that you need to stay visible in the charts, getting more free users. Repeat *ad infinitum.*

It is not easy. Marketing games has always been hard, and it has recently got tougher. But if you have a coherent strategy for your marketing, you will have a much better chance of succeeding.

The financial strategy of a marketing campaign can be expressed as a simple equation. Much like Charles Dickens's Mr. Micawber, happiness for a service-game company comes when the lifetime value of a customer exceeds the cost of acquiring the customer.[1]

LTV > CPI

CPI is the cost per install: how much it costs you to acquire a player. LTV is lifetime value: how much you expect the customer to spend with you over their lifetime in your game. It is a combination of how long they stay playing your game, how often they spend and how much they spend each time. A successful marketing strategy focuses on satisfying this equation. Marketers need to understand this equation because if your game is free, all customers are not created equal. In the product world, a customer who bought the game represented money in the bank, whether they liked the game or not. In service games, it is possible to acquire customers cheaply, but if those customers do not stick around or do not spend, the return on investment may be very low. I will discuss more about how to determine Lifetime Value (LTV) in Chapter 15: Metrics. For now, it is enough to say that you need to keep CPI less than LTV. Soft launch is a key tool in this process.

The purpose of soft launch is to determine whether you should use your scarce marketing resources to hard launch your game. Let's talk about some definitions:

- A **technical launch** is a test of the core technology of the game. If you come from AAA development, you might call these a closed beta, or even a closed alpha. This launch tests if the technology works. It is particularly important for a game with significant online functionality, such as a Player versus player (PvP) game with matchmaking like *Hearthstone* or *Clash of Clans* or for an MMO when it is important to test whether the technology will scale well.

- A **soft launch**, or commercial test, is focused on commercial viability. It focuses on retention, first-time user experience (FTUE) completion rates and monetisation metrics like conversion and average revenue per user (ARPU). It is designed to answer one question: *Is the lifetime value of my users good enough to justify a marketed launch?* On mobile, this is most often managed country by country, while on PC it may be closer to an old-style beta test, where a limited number of players are invited to register for exclusive access.

- A **hard launch** is the main event, the moment you have been working up to. It has two components:

  - A **global** or **worldwide launch** is when you flip the switch in the online stores to make your game available to a global audience.

  - A **marketed launch** is when you deploy your scarce marketing resources to promote the game. This is where you pull the trigger on whatever marketing support you have for your title. It might be a platform feature from Apple or Google. If you have a strong brand like *Plants vs. Zombies* or *Angry Birds*, it is simply making the game available globally. It might mean cross-promotional support from other titles in your network, or it might mean spending $1 million on a user-acquisition campaign. Whichever marketing tools you have at your disposal, you want to maximise the chances of a strong, marketed launch.

The global and marketed launch often, but not always, coincide. To understand this point, we should look at the marketing resources that you can bring to bear.

WORDS TO BAN #4: TUTORIAL

Whether you call it the FTUE, initial experience or onboarding, the first experience a player has with your game is a crucial part of your retention, particularly in a F2P game. If the game is paid, players have already made a $60 commitment to the game; they are prepared to invest some additional time to learn the ropes. The same is not true of free players.

If a team is asked to create a tutorial, the team members will think about the meaning of the word: A tutorial's job is to teach. They will identify all the things that the player might need to learn and try to teach them that in an efficient, fun way.

But the purpose of the FTUE is not teach; it is to demonstrate the fun of the game to players who may not yet be engaged. Demonstrating the fun might include learning—as Raph Koster argues in *A Theory of Fun*, fun = learning; learning = fun—but learning is not the purpose.[2] The *Plants vs. Zombies* campaign is a great example. See Figure 14.1.

Ban the word Tutorial and focus on delivering the fun to earn the next 30 seconds of Playtime, and the next, and the next.

Figure 14.1   The whole of *Plants vs. Zombies* campaign mode is a FTUE.

MARKETING STRATEGY

Strategy can be defined as the application of all your resources in a co-ordinated effort to achieve your objective.[3] The objective of the marketed launch is to get as many high-quality players—those who are likely to enjoy your game and go on to spend time and money in it—for as little cash outlay or human effort as possible.

This is not easy.

More than 4,000 games were released on Steam in 2016, 40% of all the games that have *ever* been released on Steam. For mobile stores, we are seeing more than 4,000 games a month, sometimes as many as 500 in a single day.

Service games also have long lives. I can reasonably predict the top games of 2018 by copying and pasting the list of the top games of 2017. There are always some surprises: *Kim Kardashian: Hollywood* was an unexpected hit in 2014, and *Pokémon Go* surprised in 2016, but I would be confident of getting seven or more of the top ten right. You don't see that in lists of best-selling movies, books or boxed games.

This means that the competition for attention is fierce. To fight through the noise, you have a range of resources that can be divided into five categories.

Marketing Resource 1: Brand

One of the best ways to ensure that your game sells well is to be successful already. *Angry Birds Go!*, a title that I worked on and the first *Angry Birds* title that was not a catapult game, saw 100 million downloads in the first year. When Electronic Arts (EA) released *Plants vs. Zombies 2*, the sequel to PopCap's acclaimed and popular game *Plants vs Zombies*, they saw 16 million downloads in the first five days and 25 million in the first two weeks.[4] This is a double-edged sword. In many ways, *PvZ 2* was not ready to receive such a huge influx of players. Despite time in soft launch, EA may have had too many players through the door in the first few weeks, who played and then left, never to return. If the game had received new players at a slower pace, they may have been able to iterate on the initial experience to keep more players for longer.

If you are not lucky enough to already own a global brand, you can always licence one. Glu Mobile had a reasonably successful lifestyle role-playing game called *Stardom Hollywood* in 2013. Eighteen months later, after licensing Kim Kardashian and launching a game based on the same engine called *Kim Kardashian: Hollywood*, the company had a huge hit on its hands. *Forbes* reported that the game generated $71.8 million revenue in 2015.[5]

Brand endorsements like this do not come cheap. Kardashian's earnings in 2016 were estimated to be $51 million. Forty per cent of that came from her cut of game revenue. If you pay for a brand endorsement like this, it should be considered as part of your marketing expenditure, whether it involves cash up front or payments later in the form of a revenue share. In return, you hope that the endorsement will generate free downloads for you through press coverage or brand recognition in the store, or you are betting that the Cost Per Install for a branded game will be lower than the CPI for an unbranded game. The brand can also help drive retention and monetisation, depending on how you integrate it into your design.

It doesn't always work. As we've seen, Scopely pulled its *Breaking Bad* game from soft launch, presumably because it was not hitting the key performance indicators (KPIs) necessary to make a soft launch viable. The *Little Britain* licence led to one of the worst products in video game history. *Enter the Matrix* contributed to the collapse of Atari. Licences are not a panacea, and they come with a "brand tax." The brand tax is not just the cash payments that you have to make, but the approvals process, the brand expectations, and so on. If you licence a car brand, for example, are you allowed to let it get dirty? Damaged? Deformed? Can you ever show the vehicle in a bad light or let it lose a race to a model from one of its competitors? Will a movie star demand final approval over all visuals of the game? Must you negotiate every little change with the brand owner for whom your game is a tiny part of their overall business? Will you have to ship the game too early to meet an external deadline imposed by the opening night of a movie, the launch of a new toy or the start of a music tour?

From a marketing perspective, brand is not a tool that you can switch on and off as you wish. You either have it or you don't. A brand can be powerful, but it often leads to a strong influx of players on the first day of launch. This is often not what you want for a service game.

Marketing Resource 2: Featuring

The second resource you have is "relationship with the gatekeepers."

The gatekeeper for a PC game is Steam. The gatekeepers for a mobile game are Apple and Google. Larger companies often have a competitive advantage because they have direct relationships with the platform holders. They have a human they can speak to discuss launch plans, to learn about upcoming changes to the platform and to increase the chances that they get featured in Editor's Choice or Midweek Madness sales.

This route is open to independent developers, but it is harder. You must spend some of your scarce development time on cultivating relationships with platform holders. You may need to attend conferences or visit their offices, which costs money and time spent away from development.

Featuring, like brand, is hard to turn on and off. Platforms tend to promote new things because they are trying to showcase the best products and the most interesting games to their audience. They don't care about *your* game. They care about the overall experience on their platform. If you help them to do that, great. If not, don't expect any help.

For mobile devices, one piece of guidance is to "work on things that the platform holders care about." For a while, it was tablet-centric not smartphone-centric games. Sometimes it has been about visual fidelity and resolution or using platforms such as iCloud to store progress across devices. New technology is currently at the fore, with Apple focusing on ARKit and Google on its virtual reality experiences. The best advice is to pay attention to the announcements coming out of the platform holders. If your game aligns with their strategic goals, you are much more likely to be featured.

Featuring, however, is a spike. It is not long-lasting. It can help to kick-start your success, but it is ephemeral. You need additional elements as well.

Marketing Resource 3: Cash

Cash is a marketing resource. You can buy installs. Most successful game companies buy lots of installs.

One reason for that is that if you have the money to buy customers, you have a competitive advantage. You can disadvantage your competitors by outspending them. Activision has harnessed this approach for years. Its senior ranks are filled with executives from fast moving consumer goods (FMCG) industries who understand how to distribute, sell and market physical products. Part of Activision's competitive advantage has long been its great relationships with physical retailers and with advertising channels. It could outspend its competitors on launching a new brand or supporting an existing franchise. The middle tier publishers—THQ, Majesco, Atari—struggled to compete and overstretched themselves financially as they tried. This is part of the dynamic of concentration in the videogame industry, where the big get bigger, the niche thrives but the middle tier die.[6]

Spending cash on customers is expensive. It can cost you $1–3 or more to buy an install on a mobile device, rising to $8–10 at Christmas. It can require as many as 100,000 downloads a day to get into the top free charts on iOS in the United States. If you were buying all those customers, you would need to spend $300,000 or more. Per day.

The big players are spending lots of money. In its last financial statement before it was acquired by Activision, King's marketing budget was reported as more than $400 million. Supercell's revenue grew significantly before it was bought by Tencent, but its profitability grew more slowly, implying that marketing costs grew faster than revenue.[7] Spending your way up the charts is a strategy for the large, the brave or the foolish.

One of my clients refers to cash marketing as a "parachute." If you are lucky enough to appear in the charts through your brand, your feature or other techniques, you get free, organic downloads from the improved visibility that the chart position gives you. You can now consider spending money to *stay* in the chart. You are not trying to brute-force your way into the charts, but you are trying to slow your inevitable descent. This is a virtuous circle for you: the longer you stay in the charts, the more free downloads you get, and those new users are more likely to be high-quality users who will be interested in your game. This gives you more cash to spend on the parachute to slow your descent out of the charts. This virtuous circle is why we see a market dominated by a few, large mobile games companies. To the winners go the spoils.

HIGH QUALITY USERS

Not all users are created equal.

A user from a rich country who downloaded your game because they saw it advertised on Facebook and love the genre is likely to be a higher-quality user than one from a poor country who downloaded the game to get 100 free gems in another title. A high-quality user, from a marketer's point of view, is one who spends time and money in your game. A low-quality user either churns out early or stays without spending money (although, as we've seen, they can add value to your game as freeloaders).

Eric Seufert, author of *Freemium Economics*, points out that the one thing that you know about a user you purchase with marketing money is that the user was put up for sale. Someone decided that the user was worth more to them as CPI revenue than as a potential convert to spending money in their game in the future.[8]

Your marketing objective is to acquire users who will stay with your game and choose to spend money in it. To marketing teams that are more used to worrying most about the initial purchase, and very little about ongoing engagement, this can be a new discipline that takes time to develop.

Current best practice suggests spending your marketing money on Facebook campaigns first. Facebook is highly targeted but hard to scale. After that, you can move to trackable forms of advertising, whether on mobile or on the web. There are many third-party suppliers of tools to help you with user acquisition. Only after you have exhausted the possibilities of trackable advertising is it worth moving to untrackable advertising such as billboards or television.

On mobile, at least, it is hard to buy customers for anything other than free-to-play games. As you know by now, F2P is a variable pricing model. Some players spend very little or nothing. Others spend an enormous amount, in the thousands or tens of thousands of dollars. Successful F2P games can keep players engaged for weeks, months or even years. In this model, it can be quite easy to solve the marketing equation of whether LTV > CPI. If you can keep players for many years, spending several dollars a month on average, you can afford to pay a lot for the initial install.

If you are a paid game, you don't have this luxury. A mobile paid game is unlikely to retail for more than $4.99, and it is likely to be lower. Your ability to find enough impressions, at a cost-effective rate, to buy customers for a game where the maximum potential lifetime value is just under five bucks is limited. Large corporations, seeking to market blockbuster franchises with retail prices of $50 or more can afford brand-building marketing, the sort of television or outdoor campaigns you see for *Destiny* or *Call of Duty*. They are playing a different marketing game, one that is product-centric, not service-centric, and outside the scope of this book.

Not all customers are created equal. You might be able to acquire customers cheaply, but they will leak out of your funnel, they won't make it to D1 and they are unlikely to spend. Sophisticated marketing techniques involve not just understanding how cheaply you can get your users but also how valuable they are. The ambition of a user acquisition specialist is to deliver the highest-quality users at the lowest possible price, because this helps make the LTV > CPI equation work. Chasing volume at the expense of quality can improve your chart position but have little (or negative) impact on your cash balance.

The real value of cash, particularly for mobile and PC games, is that it is one of the few marketing resources that you can control. You can turn the spigot on or off at short notice. Your brand is a one-shot weapon: you launch a game with the brand attached and—boom!—you have gained most of the value. The feature is ephemeral. It gives you value, then it's gone. Spending cash on marketing is difficult to do well, but you are in control of when and how to do it. This is its unique benefit.

Marketing Resource 4: Press and Influencers

The value of press relations (PR) in service games varies. Some audiences engage heavily with the specialist press. PC and console gamers are avid readers of gaming news, and a good review on *Rock Paper Shotgun*, *Kotaku* or *IGN* can make a big difference to your success. This is more true for paid games than service games. With Steam, the ability to build a following, to communicate with your community and to re-promote your game to people who have expressed an interest in the games you make is valuable.

In mobile, not so much. The sad truth is that PR for mobile is almost, but not entirely, pointless. Which is the worst of all possible worlds.

Mobile gamers don't seek out reviews, particularly of F2P games. Why bother wasting your time reading the review when you can just download the game and check it out.[9] People who play games on mobile are less likely to self-identify as "gamers." Games are not a part of their identity, any more than most people would describe themselves as "readers," or "moviegoers." There is a sub-culture of gamers, a group fiercely defensive of any attempt to widen the reach of games outside power fantasies of battle and conflict, and there is a much wider audience of people for whom games are just part of their entertainment mix. Possibly a large part of their entertainment, but not enough to have them poring over the latest review of a game, or even caring about the name of the publisher or developer who made the game they liked. (In just the same way that few people care about a movie being made by Paramount or enjoy a novel more because it is published by Penguin.)

Busy developers might be breathing a sigh of relief that they can claw back some time to develop their game by abandoning PR. Not so fast. There is still value in doing press work. The reason is simple: there are a handful of important people who do read the press for announcements and reviews of games that matter. Not the audience; they don't bother. But the editors, influencers and reviewers who decide whether to feature your game or give it additional promotion *are* influenced by the press. They read Touch Arcade and Pocket Gamer and other sites. If they see journalists whom they respect recommending your game, or even saying that they are excited about it, they are more likely to notice your game when you submit it. They will argue for its inclusion in a feature because it's an anticipated title. They will fight on your behalf because they have external validation that this game is good, or at the very least, is anticipated. The purpose of your PR strategy is to reach the two or three people at Apple or Google in each territory who get to decide whether your game is featured.

You may think that this is cynical. It's also how advertising works. Any advertising buyer in the brand world will find out where his client's CEO and the marketing director live. He will make sure that the CEO sees billboards on the freeway on her way into work or at the train station. Oxford Circus station on the London Underground is always filled with advertisements for video games. The fact that PlayStation's European headquarters are just outside the station is just a coincidence, I am sure.

I've done it myself. When I was the CFO of a dotcom, we were trying to raise money in the City of London. We realised that the offices of almost all the investors we wanted to talk to lay on the route of the number 11 bus. We bought ads on the side of the buses. We bought billboards on the bus shelters outside their offices. We went into meetings, and were told, "You must be doing well, we see your ads everywhere."

"Yes," we replied. "Our targeted advertising is working perfectly."

If you have a strong relationship with decision makers at the major platforms, you have less need to use the press to get you noticed. Even so, there is a role for the press, in gaining initial audiences, in amplifying your success and in surfacing otherwise hidden gems. On the other hand, it is not a panacea. With so many new games being released every month, there are only so many titles they can cover. For many games, particularly mobile ones, your target audience probably don't read reviews anyway. The editors who select which games to feature are not going to feature your game just because it was mentioned on a popular website. You may conclude that there are other, more-effective strategies that you can use to get your service game noticed.

The important thing to remember is that your objective is to reach potential players as cost effectively as possible, to draw them into the game and to engage as many of them as you can. There is no silver bullet. For most service games, particularly on mobile, I suggest that press outreach is something that you have to do, but it will not drive significant installs. Its value lies in the quotes you get to use in your own marketing, the validation from trusted third parties and bringing your game to the attention of editors and influencers.

Ah, influencers. A topic that is growing in importance day by day. As the importance of game review magazines and websites has waned, so the role of influencers has waxed. Influencers come in many stripes, and you need to think about whether how to harness support from influencers.

Influencers are part of the video generation. The term often is used synonymously with YouTubers because video is their preferred medium. Influencers come in many varieties. *Let's Players* play the game. They might be trying to record a how-to or a speed run, or just playing for the fun and drama of it. The heart of the experience is watching someone else, usually with dramatic flair or an entertaining personality, play the game. *Streamers* stream their gameplay experience live via Twitch. This is an unfiltered feed. You are watching someone else play and getting the experience at the same time that they do. *Vloggers* talk to camera, perhaps making jokes or discussing some arcane element of gameplay. Many YouTubers are all three.

The games that get successful attention from influencers like this are often games with high levels of unpredictability. They have gameplay that can surprise the video star, leading to moments of unscripted, emotional content. Rogue-likes, multiplayer games and card battlers like *Hearthstone* have all benefited from influencers. If you are going to spend marketing money on above-the-line marketing, a term that usually means "money that is not focused on driving a specific, trackable action," it makes increasing sense to commission a YouTuber of some form to review, play or vlog about your game, rather than to spend money on banner advertising around the web.

As always with this book, there are no right answers or rules to follow. The world is evolving too fast. Current rules of thumb are that if you are making a paid game, cash marketing is hard to make work unless you are an enormous publisher; if you are making a F2P game, spending your scarce marketing resources on chasing elusive press and influencer coverage may not be the most effective use of your time and effort.

HOW TO REACH INFLUENCERS: NICK TANNAHILL, FIREFLY STUDIOS

Video games have huge passive audiences who are just as vital to your success as active players. Developers and product managers are now purveyors of entertainment, a completely new role that requires showmanship. Let's Plays may have been around since 2007, but we are only now creating games that audiences want to watch as much as streamers want to play. More people than ever are watching.

Put yourself in the shoes of a content creator, as many of the principles and considerations overlap. Channels thrive off interactions that promote content on their platform of choice, just as games that can be interacted with or even played are more attractive to viewers. These interactions foster unexpected and entertaining reactions from the content creator, which is both fun to watch and play. These reactions should also emerge naturally from gameplay. Streamers should not have to rely on audience participation to entertain, especially on platforms where interaction takes place after content is uploaded and stored online.

Considering available resources, you may also want to consider designing for a specific platform. Procedural, randomised elements found in rogue-likes make it easy for someone who loves your game to create a video series and upload regular, lengthy videos to YouTube. This boosts watch time and thus visibility on the platform, one reason why titles like *Nuclear Throne* perform so well. For Twitch, you should be more concerned with boosting concurrent viewers. Introduce obstacles or even benign interactions that audiences can affect, impacting the gameplay and giving viewers a role to play in the stream. A great example would be Telltale's "Crowd Play" mode, which allows audiences to vote on and determine the outcome of player scenarios in its adventure games.

You could of course simply create a multiplayer title that is just as thrilling to watch as it is to play. Failing that, it is important to identify low hanging fruit when it comes to design and reflect honestly about how fun your game is to watch. However you choose to go about creating the next hit just remember you now have two audiences, each demanding to be entertained in their own unique way.

Although reviews from the press have fallen in importance, reviews from players continue to matter. Getting above 4.5 stars on Apple and Google or "Mostly Positive" on Steam give players the confidence to download or try your game. This provides an important and difficult counterbalance to the Minimum Awesome Product. You need to ship as early as possible to start validated learning, but by the time you market the launch of your game, you need review scores to be high. Balancing this issue is key to your success. (By the way, review scores are just as important for books as for games. If you have found this book helpful, it would be great if you could review it somewhere, either on the site where you bought it or a review site like Goodreads.)

Marketing Resource 5: Cross-Promotion

You don't have a brand. You are not already successful. You don't have any money and getting coverage in the press for your mobile game would be great, but you don't expect it to drive significant downloads. What else can you do?

Cross-promotion is a successful strategy. Nimblebit launched *Tiny Tower* with cross-promotional activity in their other hit game *Pocket Frogs*. They reached a million downloads in just four days.[10] Blizzard gives *Hearthstone* players a new skin for the Paladin hero, Lady Liadrin, if they develop a new character to level 20 in *World of Warcraft*. Iron Maiden collaborated with Rovio to bring the heavy metal band's iconic mascot, Eddie, as a playable character into *Angry Birds Evolution* for a Halloween promotion to promote the band's *Iron Maiden: Legacy of the Beast* mobile RPG.[11] This strategy requires you either to be successful already or to forge commercial relationships with successful companies. Or you can turn to a publisher.

Marketing is one of the four major commercial roles that publishers undertake. (The others are sales, distribution and finance.)[12] Many developers therefore turn to publishers to market their title, even if they have self-financed development. Publishers have multiple games in the market. They can cross-promote. They can spend cash on marketing. They have relationships with the mobile and digital stores to get you noticed and promoted. Publishers are a viable route, but be careful of their promises. Don't give up too much in return for a promise of "getting featured." You might have been able to get that feature anyway. Wherever possible, extract an agreement that focuses on actual cash spent on marketing as part of your contract.

There is another way. That is to turn to your frenemies. We've established that most games are not in competition with each other. They are a series of little monopolies. If I am making an idle city builder, the fact that you are selling in-app purchases in your tennis game is not competitive with me.

THE VALUE OF REVIEWS

Reviews on the relevant store are a valuable source of traffic. More accurately, a low or middling review score can make it much harder to drive downloads.

Current best practice suggests that you should remember to ask the player to leave a review *at a time when you expect them to be enjoying the game.* Many people leave reviews when they are feeling frustrated or annoyed with a service; fewer leap to write a review when they are having a good time without a prompt.

Best practice is constantly evolving. Some companies pop up an in-game message asking if players are enjoying the game. If they are, they send them to the store review page. If not, they divert them elsewhere: to a feedback page or simply to a page that says, "I'm sorry to hear that."

The value of the review prompt is that it increases the proportion of your reviews left by people who enjoy your game but might not have bothered to give you a rating. If that can drive your rating up from 3.5 to 4.5 stars, that is worth doing.

(Remember that this may not belong in your Minimum Awesome Product, though. It is a feature that could be developed during your soft launch.)

In many parts of the world, independent developers know and are supportive of one another. They go to the same meetups, they help each other out with knotty problems. They are part of a local gaming community. If you are part of your local community, harness your combined strength.

The basic deal is that you ask your fellow game developers to send traffic to your new game at launch. You promise to repay the favour when they launch. I have talked to several developers who have done this successfully, helping each other and gradually improving the audience size of all parties over time. If you try this, don't make it contractual: I will send you x players if you send me y back. If you want to be formal, spend money and use a CPI network. This form of cross-promotion is a karmic approach that works best with an element of trust and flexibility. One participant may hit luckier than others. So be it.

A NOTE ON VIRALITY

When I first started giving my masterclasses on F2P games in 2008, it was titled *How to Make Money from Social Games.* The iPhone barely existed yet and the focus of this new business model was the social network. In the West, that meant Facebook.

In those early days, virality was everything. Zynga got an early head start by harnessing the power of the social network. We were not yet inured to plaintive requests to rescue a lost sheep or to offers of free cherry trees. We still thought it quaint if someone posted a status update to their wall saying that they had just reached Level 5. Zynga had not yet destroyed virality.

It didn't take long. In his book, *Influence*, Robert Cialdini describes how successful salespeople can harness and subvert positive human behaviours to good ends. One such technique is to harness *reciprocity*, the human desire to repay favours that someone else has done for you. When a salesperson offers you a cup of coffee or buys you lunch, he is not acting out of the goodness of his heart. He is trying to create an obligation from you to him so that, at a subconscious level, you will feel uneasy until you have repaid the favour.

I once gave a prospective client a copy of my book, *The Curve*, as a gift when we first met. He instantly left the room and returned carrying a copy of his own (much larger and more expensive) book, a coffee table book about *il Palio*, a horse race run twice each year in Siena, Italy. It had nothing to do with the subject in hand, but he cleared the obligation immediately. This is an experienced negotiator.

In the early days of *Farmville*, Zynga harnessed that sense of reciprocity. They realised, unlike Playfish, that when you are dealing in virtual goods, you have an unlimited supply. When a player sends a gift to another player, the logical thing might be to add the gift to the recipient's inventory but subtract it from the donor's. Zynga realised it could just magic a duplicate copy into existence. Before long, Facebook was full of people sending each other fences and cherry trees and lost brown cows, and the Facebook wall disappeared under a sea of *Farmville* messages—for a while at least.[13]

Then two things happened. The first is that players started to realise that this was a ju-jitsu move, an unwelcome harnessing of a positive social relationship. Players realised that these were not real gifts. The donor had lost nothing in the giving. It moved from feeling like a gift to feeling like spam, an unwelcome intrusion and the creation of an artificial obligation. Not only that, but it also made people cross to have their good natures exploited in this way.

In *Influence*, Cialdini gives the example of the Hare Krishna sect, which grew rapidly during the 1970s and 1980s. The sect harnessed reciprocity by pressing unwanted flowers or religious books on passers-by, insisting that it was a gift and refusing to take it back, but then asking for a donation. Over time, people began to object to the technique and took against the Krishnas. Passers-by would cross the street to avoid them. Airports would announce that Krishnas were soliciting or restrict them to certain areas. In one memorable scene in parody movie *Airplane!*, Captain Rex Kramer refuses to speak to any of the missionaries and instead punches his way through them on his way through the airport.[14]

The second thing that happened was that these feelings started to make people feel cross *at* Facebook. They complained or stopped using the service. Facebook had to act. In a series of moves they reduced the ability of games to access the newsfeed, the wall, the profile and the notifications system. *Farmville's* early competitive advantage—its ability to spam Facebook better than others—went away.

It hasn't entirely gone. In 2015, Mark Zuckerberg, the CEO of Facebook, held an Ask Me Anything in India. He solicited questions from the 1.5 billion monthly users of Facebook. They could ask him any question they liked. The top question, with 7,500 likes, was, "I don't want any more invitations to *Candy Crush*. How can I stop them?"[15]

Technical virality as an acquisition technique has largely vanished from the strategy of service games. I discussed social techniques as Return Hooks in Chapter 6, but those are retention techniques, not acquisition techniques. When was the last time that you downloaded a game because a notification from it appeared in your newsfeed? Or because someone tweeted about it?

There is still room for virality. Good old word of mouth is a form of virality. People play games because their friends recommend them or because they see other people playing. Some entertainment products break out and go global suddenly. In 2012, Korean singer Psy had a sudden global phenomenon in "Gangnam Style," with a pop video that was so successful that it broke YouTube's view counter. Interviewed on Jonathan Ross's UK chat show, he was phlegmatic about his success. "I cannot call this success, because this is called phenomenon. Which means I didn't do anything. People do it, right? It was by people, not by me. So, on the next one, what if people don't do it again?"[16]

Virality on the web is often a matter of paying for it. Many "viral" sensations are actually paid-for marketing campaigns. Agencies such as Unruly and GoViral spend their clients' money to promote a viral message, using their knowledge of Internet marketing and influencers. The same is true of games. Although there are some spontaneous viral sensations, more often success comes from a combination of a good game with a clear marketing strategy and strong execution, plus a hefty dose of luck.

Your marketing strategy should be a coherent set of actions that support each other in raising awareness, increasing downloads and helping you to find the users who will go on to be your Superfans. It is hard, unpredictable work. Use all the tools at your disposal—your brand, relationship with stores, cash, press and influencer relationships, cross-promotion and more—to give your game the best chance of standing out in a crowded marketplace.

CHAPTER 15

Metrics

IT IS HARD TO write a book about free-to-play (F2P) games without a discussion of metrics. Metrics are a vital tool for game designers. Used badly, they are damaging to both your game and to your business.

Many people use metrics as benchmarks. Like the sales director in Chapter 9 trying to forecast the revenue from a free-to-play game, many people want to use metrics to create a financial forecast to see how much money their game will generate. Financiers need this. Executives need this. If it's your own business, you need this. My experience as an investment banker and a CFO has taught me the value of a forecast. I also know that it is usually wrong.

The job of a financial model is not to provide certainty. It can't do that. There are too many unknowables. Spreadsheets give the impression of certainty, but they provide precision, not accuracy. They are frequently wrong to three decimal places. They are still useful. The value of a financial spreadsheet is to help you understand what you must do to deliver the users, the revenue and the profit that you need to justify investing in the game. The model is an *analysis* tool, more than a forecasting tool.

The basis of a revenue forecast for a F2P game is:

How many players download your game × how long do
they stay × how much do they spend

As we start to unpick those concepts in the rest of this chapter, you will see how some of the numbers that we use in a forecast are *levers*: metrics that we can influence directly to deliver the results that we need. Others are not. They are either *compound metrics*, made up of two or more levers, which can't be influenced directly or *external metrics*, driven by factors outside our control. In some cases, the distinction is blurred. For example, the number of free, organic users we get is a combination of store placement, word of mouth, advertising that we can't track, reviews and so on. It is essentially external, but we have some influence over it.

To illustrate this point, consider average revenue per daily active user (ARPDAU). It is calculated by dividing your revenue on a given day by your active users on that day and is typically quoted in cents. Ranges might be 1–20 cents for a word or puzzle game, with a strategy or role-playing game (RPG) game pushing up to 50 cents or higher.[1] It is tool beloved by analysts and publishers. It is a good way of comparing the performance of different genres or of different games in the same genre. It is an excellent shorthand for "this game is monetising well (or badly)."

I don't think it is useful for designers. As a consultant, I have no idea how to push ARPDAU up. No human player directly influences ARPDAU. How do I go about persuading the average player to move from five cents ARPDAU to six cents ARPDAU?

The problem is that ARPDAU is a compound metric. It blends conversion rate (the percentage of players that spend on a given day) with number of transactions and transaction size. As a designer, I can think of ways of encouraging my players to convert today, whether it be sales, nudges or simply continuing to make the game appealing in a way that gives them reason to want in-game resources and assets. I can influence transaction size by bundling, by merchandising techniques or, again, by making the game sufficiently compelling that players want more resources. I can think of ways of encouraging them to spend multiple times in a day.

I still don't know how to drive up ARPDAU.

The purpose of the financial model is to give designers and developers a clear picture of what they need to deliver to make the game more successful. By its nature, it can't capture the elusive variable of "is this game fun?" or, if that is too airy-fairy for you, "does it have the quality of making players enjoy playing it for a long time?" It can give you a framework to identify areas where you have not created a design that can achieve your commercial goals, and to diagnose where there are problems in your game.

THE FRAMEWORK

Before I dive into the metrics, let's remind ourselves of some first principles. We introduced the core equation for any business, LTV > CPI, in Chapter 14.

This equation is simplistic, and even if you achieve it, it does not mean that you have a successful game. Yet. Cost per install (CPI) is the *marginal* cost of acquiring a new user. That means that if I spend $1 to acquire a customer, and that customer spends $1 on my game, I broke even on the acquisition of the customer. This ignores many substantial costs. It does not capture the ongoing cost of supporting that customer: servers, bandwidth, customer support teams, and so on. It does not cover the original development cost or ongoing development. It does not cover the cost of financing the game, whether that is repaying the publisher advance, settling a loan or paying dividends to equity investors. It is a basic equation, but it is not sufficient.

Lifetime value (LTV) is similarly tricky. It is the total amount of money someone spends in your game. It is a compound metric consisting of how long they stay, how often they play, how often they spend and how much they spend. There are many different levers you can pull to increase lifetime value.

A financial forecast will cover the cost per install transaction. It will find some way to capture the lifetime value for your customers. Usually this means modelling retention to capture how long players will stay, and monetisation by estimating monthly or daily conversion and spend. Out of this you will be able to forecast the revenue of your game, and the metrics that you need to achieve to reach this revenue. You can find a sample revenue estimation spreadsheet at www.gamesbrief.com.

You should have a clear idea of your costs, both ongoing operating costs and the fixed costs of pre-launch development. Ideally, you will know the difference between your fixed costs, which are those costs that you must pay whether you have zero customers or a million, such as the development team's salaries, and variable costs, which rise with the number of players, such as bandwidth, servers or additional customer service or technical support staff.

KEY PERFORMANCE INDICATORS (KPIs)

I once walked into a client to be greeted by their analyst. "I'm so glad you are here. We are just agreeing which KPIs we should track. I have 157 already tracked. Can you think of any more we should add?"

KPIs are useful. The more of them you have, the less useful they become. I like to focus on six, maybe seven. There are many other second-order metrics that can be useful to a design team to diagnose problems or to provide confirmation that a change has had a beneficial effect on the game. That does not make them key.

The problem with having too many metrics is that it becomes hard to separate out the signal from the noise. The data is important, but it is more important to get rapid, directional information from the analytics system. We are not scientists trying to find absolute truth in the universe. We are game makers trying to use all the tools at our disposal to make games that are more fun and more profitable. Analytics and KPIs are just another tool in our toolbox. Used well, KPIs can pull an entire team together behind the project. If the whole company knows which KPIs matter, they have clear direction about what it is needed for the game to be successful.

My time as a CFO took place during the dotcom boom at a comparison shopping engine called ShopSmart, an early Internet business that compared the prices of albums, games and movies to help you find the cheapest place to buy them online. In 2000, a senior group from the company travelled to the United States to meet with the executive team of a rival comparison shopping service.

As I stood in reception on a Friday morning, I noticed a ticker on the wall. It was counting up slowly and then in bursts. I don't recall the exact number, but it was in the tens, or hundreds, of thousands.

"What's that," I asked the receptionist as she filled out my details on the temporary security badge.

"It's the number of comparison searches that our customers have done in the last seven days. We are on track to beat our target of x this week." (I'm afraid I can't remember what x was.)

I was impressed that the team had managed to get knowledge of KPIs spread so widely that the receptionist—someone whose job was not focused on delivering KPIs—knew which metric was key to the business and what the weekly target was.

Later that same day, I was in the CFO's office as 4 P.M. approached. A line had started forming outside his door, cheerful employees chattering away outside our meeting. The CFO said, "Watch this, you'll enjoy it."

He stood up, walked to a wall safe and opened it. Inside was a stack of $100 bills. He lifted them out and placed them in neat piles on his desk. At 4 P.M., a bell rang, the line outside erupted into cheers and the CFO opened the door. Each employee walked in, collected a crisp $100 bill and left with a huge smile. The receptionist was one of the people in the queue.

I must have looked confused because, once the last employee had left clutching their $100 bill, the CFO explained what I had just witnessed. The ticker on the wall was the target for the number of searches on the site. The directors had determined this was *the* KPI, the metric that mattered above all. They set a weekly target and the technology team had wired up the analytics to broadcast that one metric to all staff via the ticker in reception. Each Friday, at 4 P.M., if the target had been hit, then every member of staff, from the most senior to a the most junior, received $100 in cash.

The clarity this provided was amazing. Every member of staff cared about the number of searches that users had carried out on the site. The content team were besieged with ideas for new articles or homepage features to drive users to perform more searches. The business development team were encouraged by the whole company to bring new partners into the comparison engine in the hope more retail partners would drive more searches. If the site went down, the technology team knew that the fate of the bonus for the whole office depended on them getting the site back up.

This is extreme. It is representative of dotcom hubris, not just KPI clarity. But being clear to your team which metrics matter is important if they are to stay focused on their objectives. I recommend dividing metrics into three groups.

- *KPIs.* These indicate the financial health of your business. There should not be many of these. Fewer than seven. Possibly only three. If you are really focused, one. These metrics should have a direct impact on your financial forecasts, so usually include active users, a retention metric and some monetisation metrics like conversion and average spend.

- *Performance indicators (PIs).* These do not contribute directly to the financial forecast but are useful indicators that you want to improve. They might include server uptime, length of time for queuing or matchmaking in an online game, Net Promoter Score or virality for the marketing team.

- *Diagnostics.* Every other metric is a diagnostic tool. It may not matter in which direction it moves. If Session length goes up or goes down, I don't care, provided that my KPIs are still doing what they should. Use these metrics to diagnose problems, to identify whether an experiment you are running is having a positive impact, and to help you form hypotheses about how to make your game more fun and more successful.

Imagine metrics as being like the battery of tests that a doctor has available to her. The KPIs are the basic vital signs that just need to be right: Is the patient breathing? Is his blood pressure normal? His heart rate? Is he bleeding on the linoleum? The KPIs need to be healthy for the patient to be healthy. The PIs are the next layer down: the patient is fine in the short term, but we want to check there are no chronic problems: Cholesterol levels. BMI. No sign of prostate cancer.[2] The doctor only turns to the diagnostic tools if the KPIs or PIs give her reason to do so. You should do the same: Use the KPIs and PIs to keep an eye of the health of your game. Don't sweat the small stuff, until the KPIs and PIs suggest you should do so, then use all the diagnostic tools at your disposal to figure out the problem and fix it.

You still need to think about the diagnostic tools in advance. When you identify a problem, it is wonderful to have all the diagnostic data you might need available. There is a cost to this. Every day you delay to code better telemetry and instrumentation is a day your game is not in soft launch getting invaluable feedback from live players. This is, as always, a trade-off. You are increasing financial risk by not launching, but decreasing the operational risk that you won't have the data that you need. Make a judgment based on your circumstances. Remember that although you will always wish that you had more data, you can't be sure what data you are going to need until you need it. If in doubt, ship once you can track the KPIs and players' progress through the first-time user experience (FTUE). You can always improve your telemetry later.

Sources of Design Input

There are three sources of input you can access as a designer, which are shown in Figure 15.1. There is your design expertise, drawn from instinct,

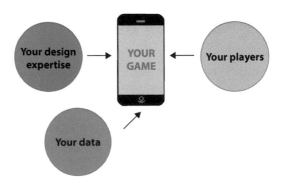

FIGURE 15.1   Sources of design input.

tempered with experience. There is the feedback that you get from your players. There is the information that you can glean from your data. All are useful, but all need to be used in the right way.

Let's start with players. Making the game that players say they want is likely to be mistake. As Henry Ford may or may not have said, "If I asked my customers what they want, they would have said 'faster buggy-whips.'"[3] Steve Jobs said, "People don't know what they want until you show it to them."[4] New product categories like the iPad or genres like the walking simulator or the MOBA don't emerge out of market research. They emerge from the imagination and invention of creative teams.

Many designers turn to forums to get feedback from their players. I hate forums. I understand their value and necessity, but they descend into pettiness and in-fighting quickly, and they provide an opportunity for the shouty minority to dominate the conversation. They can give developers a flawed impression about what matters in the game and this can cause real problems. One company I have worked with, which has a passionate audience for its online game, was bad at giving its development team feedback on how the game was performing, whether quantitatively (based on metrics) or qualitatively (based on senior management giving praise for the progress the team had made). As a result, the team sought validation for their work on the Internet: from forums, from Reddit and from reviews. The players who hang out in forums and on Reddit are not representative of the user base; they are a vocal minority who are often trying to influence the game to their tastes or to their benefit. With this company they often succeeded, to the detriment of the game and to the morale of the team.

If I could, I would ban forums (much like the president of Iceland would like to ban pineapple on pizza), although I have yet to find a good alternative that does the good things that forums do (foster community, provide support for players, create a good opportunity for reporting bugs and so on), without the weight of negativity that inevitably descends. Instead, I focus on using forums better.

My suggestion is that if you use forums or Reddit as forms of feedback, pay attention to the areas that the players are complaining about. They have probably found an area of weakness in your design. Never listen to their solutions. They are not game designers. They have no interest in the health of the game overall or the experience of other players. They are trying to manipulate the system in their favour, either because they think, possibly wrongly, they would enjoy it more or because it would give them more power. You can get enormous value out of listening to the players reporting the symptoms that they see in a game, much less from listening to their diagnosis and none at all from their suggested treatment.

To give an extreme example, when Hello Games *No Man's Sky* was published without multiplayer support, the Internet got cross. One player posted:

> "The thing that probably pisses people off the most is that the data is there, your position, what weapon you're using, your space ship (type/speed/position), etc. it would take max. one week for ONE employee to implement multiplayer vision. So it would be like *World of Warcraft* where you can see each other but not interact physically with each other."[5]

Although this may not be representative of how all players think, it does give an example of where a player has no idea of the complexities or consequences of implementing a feature. (Most experienced professionals would estimate many person-months for implementing multiplayer in a game). Listening to your players to identify weaknesses in your game is a great idea; implementing their solutions is not.

Using data without caution is similarly foolish. We've already seen what happened to Zynga when it decided that design mojo was not important and that everything could be designed according to the Playbook. Data can help you find a local maximum. It can't make giant leaps that enable real creative progress.

To take a foolish example, if I wanted to climb Mount Everest, I could travel to Nepal and follow a simple rule of "always go up." Before long, I would be standing on the top of the nearest molehill.[6] I need to take a leap of faith to go down and up again to reach the summit.

A clear example of local maximisation is the "shouty men in hats" phenomenon in iOS games, as shown in Figure 15.2. In 2016 and 2017, many of the top-grossing games—*Game of War*, *Clash Royale*, *Clash of Clans*, *Lords Mobile*—had icons that were remarkably similar.

I imagine that the user-acquisition experts at Machine Zone, Supercell and IGG ran a series of tests to see which icons ended up with the best click-through rates, the best engagement metrics once players were in the game and the best lifetime value. It is remarkable how similar they all ended up.

2. Game of War - F   3. Clash Royale   4. Lords Mobile   5. Clash of Clans
Machine Zone, Inc.   Supercell   IGG.COM   Supercell

FIGURE 15.2   Shouty men in hats. Four of the top-grossing iOS games in May 2017.

When design is driven by computers, and the algorithms are given a similar set of objectives, it is unsurprising that the results are similar. Car design in the 1990s went through this phase, as wind tunnels, aerodynamic modelling and computer-aided design led to a single, "optimised" design for efficiency. It ended the era of distinctive cars that varied widely by marque. Cars are still similar—computer efficiency and regulations designed to keep car occupants and pedestrians safe in accidents limit flexibility—but designers have started trying to inject some individuality into new vehicles.[7]

The reign of "shouty men in hats" may be coming to end. Supercell recently updated the logo for *Clash Royale* to close the mouth of its iconic character. That may be driven by dedicated testing, or it may be a designer's guess about what might attract people to their game. Either way, it appears that we have reached the local maximum and the only way to break out is to experiment with, admittedly minor, changes from accepted practice.

Being too designer-centric has its own risks. The games industry is littered with struggling games with an auteur at the helm. Perhaps the best-known developer who has suffered from this is Peter Molyneux, the founder of British studio Lionhead. Molyneux is an enthusiastic, optimistic developer who has proven to be a public relations dream (and nightmare) because of his habit of letting his enthusiasm take control of his mouth and make promises that no team could deliver.[8] Designers often push through expensive pet ideas which can jeopardise the entire game, or by seeking to be too ambitious, hurt the final product, as for Bioware's *Mass Effect: Andromeda*.[9]

My recommended approach is to use a blend of all three inputs. When creating a game from scratch, the designer's input remains paramount: there are no players to ask yet or data to analyse. The designer should be aiming to make the best possible game that blends artistic intent, fun and commercial success. I believe that the way to success is to build on the Lean startup principles of getting out of the building to talk to real customers (in our case, players) and for video games, that means building something playable.

Getting playtest feedback from real users as fast as possible is important. As the project progresses, the designer might identify and develop different tests. For example, a Base Layer prototype, consisting of an FPS deathmatch or a hidden object levels, works well for user testing: You ask a volunteer to play your game for between 15 minutes and an hour or so, and you can either observe the gameplay (which is more useful) or ask for feedback (which has many of challenges of the "feedback by Reddit" outlined previously). Retention Layer prototypes are better suited to longer-term tests because you are trying to determine whether players will stick at the game for a long time, not whether they enjoy the moment-to-moment visceral experience.

This is the cycle of successful development. Designer expertise, informed by metrics, directed towards areas where tests with real players are surfacing problems. As the game enters its Live Agency phase, it is even more important. Data become a resource to help identify weaknesses, as well as a way determining if the changes that you make achieved the result that you want. Data can be unhelpful if followed slavishly. For example, I often focus on the "promise of Session length," the idea that if players know that they can have a short, rewarding experience, like the 60-second level of *Bejeweled Blitz* or the 10-minute *Hearthstone* match, they are more likely to start playing the game. If the experience seems like it will take a long time—my children take about an hour to finish a *Skylanders* level, for example—players may choose an entirely different game to play. I'll often say that they can't play *Skylanders* if we only have half an hour before we need to go out, so my son chooses *FTL* and my daughter *Dragonvale*.

If I diagnose "promise of Session length" as a problem, I warn my clients that if they successfully treat this problem, the likely consequence is that session length stays the same, or even goes up. This diagnosis is an *On-Ramp* problem, not a *Playtime* problem. The likely outcome of successful treatment is that Session length stays the same or goes up, and the number of Sessions per day or per week—metrics that are influenced by players' perception of the On-Ramp—will rise. Slavish devotion to tweaking a single metric is unhelpful.

Game design exists in an enormous possibility space. There is so much we can do to make any given game bigger, more exciting or more awesome. Our objective as designers is to use all the tools at our disposal to reduce the possibility space until we have a tightly crafted, elegant game that delivers the vision of the developers to players in a way that is fun and profitable.[10] Design instinct, data and player feedback are key tools in the process.

KPIs: BY THE NUMBERS

The initial purpose of KPIs is to provide designers with a tool to identify the nature of their game and to design accordingly. Are they building a massive-audience, low-conversion, low average revenue per user (ARPU) game like *Candy Crush Saga* or *Farmville*, or are they building a more niche audience game with a lot of Superfans like *Clash of Clans*.

Note that *Clash of Clans*, although niche in its own way, also has an enormous number of monthly active users (MAUs). It is a massive-audience, high-ARPU business, which is why it makes so much money. In F2P, you can make a mass-market game and hope to get high ARPU, which is hard, or you can make a niche game that is likely to have high ARPU and try to reach a mass audience, which is hard. The hyper-successful games manage to combine big audiences with high ARPUs. It is viable to build a successful business without reaching these heady heights, while keeping the tantalising potential of making a blockbuster.

I have seen games that are successful enough for their creators with a conversion rate of 0.1%, and I've seen games with a conversion rate of 10%. That's a 100 × difference, or two orders of magnitude. Making financial decisions with that level of uncertainty is hard. Yet, with all my caveats, I know that you will, at some point, need to have a financial model that shows how your game is going to make money and how much money it will make. No matter what I say about the danger of benchmarks, you will be asked to provide some. In this section, I will give you some guidance on the key benchmarks you should consider.

Once the game is out of Dev Agency and into Live Agency, the purpose of the KPIs changes. They become financial and operational management tools. They have transformed from a useful roadmap that guides design instincts into a management tool with a lot more power, and the tyranny that comes with it. A Live Agency lives and dies by its ability to introduce features and run operations that improve the KPIs.

NICHOLAS'S GUESSING GAME

Nicholas's Guessing Game is a thought experiment that makes the design process faster and more efficient.

When you have identified a new feature that you want to build, ask team members to write down a guess for which metrics are likely to be impacted by this change and by how much. They don't have to be KPIs; they could by diagnostic metrics such as daily logins or "amount of hard currency used in our game per day." Guess whether the metric will go up or down, and by how much. "By 3%," "by 5 percentage points" (i.e., from 10% to 15%) and "from 5 to 10" would all be valid guesses.

The guessing game forces people to build a mental model of the game and of the consequences of making the proposed change. They form a hypothesis—or guess—about how the change will affect a metric they can measure. They observe the experiment, a key component of the scientific process.

Ask each team member to explain their reasoning. It will give you insight into how the team thinks about the feature. It will teach you something about the feature and often about the entire game. It will also surface differences of opinion within the team because of different understandings of the nature or purpose of the feature, which you can address.

Write the metrics down on a white board and take an average. You will see the team's perception of the consequences of a feature in this average. While working on *Angry Birds Transformers*, we were tasked with making a "Retention Update." After a two-hour brainstorming session, we had a bunch of feature ideas ready to pass to the production team to determine costs and timings. I forced the group to play Nicholas's Guessing Game, and every one of us—every one—guessed that all our ideas would drive up conversion and average spend but not retention. We kept all the ideas in the backlog for a future update and went back to the drawing board to work on retention.

Call it a Guessing Game, not forecasting, or estimating. (Feel free to call it [your name]'s Guessing Game, though.) If it is a forecast, people will refuse to play. They will say that they feel unqualified to participate or that the analytics team should forecast. *This is a big mistake.* The importance of the process is the formation of the mental model, the creation of a hypothesis and the discussion about the experiment. The value lies in the process, not the output. (Although the average from the Guessing Game is surprisingly often close to the experimental results.)

When the results come back, the people who guessed wrong won't remember what they guessed. It *is* amazing how often they remember their guess when they were right.

Cost Per Install (CPI)

The CPI is how much you pay to acquire an installation of your game. It has many variants. Sometimes you pay just for an install even if the user never opens the game. At the other extreme, you may only pay—but usually at a much higher rate—if they complete your First Time User Experience.

In 2018, you can expect to pay anywhere from $1 to $5 for a mobile user. That number soars higher in the run-up to Christmas because the big players are trying to dominate the charts on Christmas Day. That is the day when many new devices are opened, and users rush to the mobile stores to download some new content for their shiny toy. The large players want to get all those new users, so they invest heavily in the run up to Christmas and you can expect to spend $10 or more per install in certain markets at that time.

There is an important difference between CPI and effective CPI (eCPI). Let's imagine that I spend $100,000 on marketing my game and acquire 100,000 users directly from that marketing. My CPI is $1 per user. But I also get a lot of free users—from an Apple or Google feature, from my chart position, from great word of mouth and so on. So I have a total of 500,000 users. Was my CPI $1, or given that I spent $100,000 and have 500,000 users, was it $100,000/500,000 = $0.20?

The answer is both. Your CPI is that amount *you spent and can track* divided by *the users you acquired through that trackable campaign.* Many companies track CPI by marketing channel, by nature of advertisement and so on. Your eCPI is that *total amount of marketing spend* divided by your *total new users in that period.* On the cost side, it should contain the costs of all of your marketing activity including elements such as PR efforts or the salary of the marketing director. On the user side, it just contains all the new users you acquired.

In my modelling, I make a guess (and yes, this is a guess), that any given company will get 25% of its users through paying for them and 75% through organic or other means. That is iteration in the mathematical sense: You guess a starting number and then run iterative cycles or experiments to improve the accuracy of the guess. There are many things that you can do to influence that number. If you are able to secure store placement, you will get more free users. If you can cross-promote, you will get more free users. If your game is excellent, you will get more free users. For forecasting purposes, I suggest that a 25% to 75% split is a good sighting shot.

USER ACQUISITION IS LITTERED WITH TLAs

The terms used for how much it costs to acquire a customer are drawn from the marketing world. Many terms are used interchangeably. Make sure you know what you mean.

- CPI: Cost per install: The amount you pay for a single installation of your game.
- eCPI: Effective CPI: The total amount you spent on marketing/total number of users who signed up during that period.
- CAC: Customer Acquisition Cost: In practice, similar to eCPI.
- CPA: Cost per acquisition: Often used as CPI. Traditionally, CPA is focused on the cost of getting a *paying* customer, not a sign up or trial.
- CPC: Cost per click: An advertising term, where the marketer gets charged every time a user clicks on an advert.
- CPM/CPT: Cost per *mille*/thousand: The cost for 1,000 impressions of an ad. The marketer pays when an ad is viewed, not based on interaction or installs.
- CTR: Click-through rate: The percentage of viewers who click on an ad.
- TLA: Three-letter abbreviation.

It is also possible to pay for users only when they reach a certain threshold: complete the FTUE, reach level 8, spend 20 minutes in the game and so on. The amount you pay rises with each extra step needed. You pay least for an impression, more for a click, more again for an install and even more if the payment is triggered by an in-game activity.

Downloads

Downloads are a vanity metric. The number of downloads can only ever go up, and you learn little about your business by focusing on this statistic. Eric Ries, author of *The Lean Startup*, says "vanity metrics wreak havoc because they prey on a weakness of the human mind."[11] People believe that when the numbers go up, it was because of something they did, but when they fall or slow, it is someone else's fault.

The primary use of downloads is to feed into a metric that matters much more: your active users.

Do not confuse the vanity metric of lifetime downloads with the useful metric of Daily New Users (DNU). DNUs are the new users pouring into your acquisition funnel to replace the users who inevitably churn out later in the game. They are a key component of your active user base.

Users—MAU, WAU and DAU

The number of active users you have in a given period—daily active users (DAUs), weekly active users (WAUs) or monthly active users (MAUs)—is a function of how many new users you got in the period plus how many you retained from the previous period.

The number of new users is not fully in your control. As discussed in Chapter 14, you can turn cash marketing on and off, but the other elements of user acquisition are unpredictable. Will the reviews or word of mouth be good? Will I be featured? Will I be lucky enough to hit the *zeitgeist*? And so on.

For the purposes of modelling, I use a "halo" effect: by spending money on marketing, you hope for increased visibility, whether that be via mobile charts, increased number of reviews, Steam friend lists or word of mouth. You therefore model that for every new customer you get via marketing spend, you also get an increase in the number of organic users you get. This "halo" effect can be unpredictable, but it is a useful additional forecasting tool to help you understand the impact of your different marketing strategies.

Product games obsess about the number of new users. In a product mentality, all users have already paid to purchase the game, so the commercial imperative to make them stick around is low. In a service game, the opposite is true. Service games care most about how many users they retain. Retaining users is hard. Most mobile games lose 60% of their users from Day 0 to Day 1 and 90% from Day 0 to Day 30. That is quite a drop off. If you continued the trend of losing 90% of your users from month to month, your business needs a huge supply of new users to be viable.

In practice, that is not what happens. If a player gets to Day 30, she is now much more likely to get to D60, or D90. Many people play a single F2P game for months or years. A sophisticated model performs *cohort analysis*, lumping all the people who arrive in a single day or month into buckets and forecasting their behaviour over time.

A halfway house version is to model the behaviour of players in the first month (D1 retention, D7 retention and D30 retention, see discussion in this chapter) and then model that cohort as having a steady decay rate thereafter.

> **COHORT ANALYSIS**
>
> Cohort analysis is a technique that separates users into distinct groups, or cohorts, and looks at the behaviour of that group over time.
>
> In service games, the most usual cohort chosen is "Users who downloaded a game on a specific day." It is also possible to group users by their spend pattern (i.e., free players, low spenders, high spenders).

The number of users on a monthly or daily basis is a critical metric. You need to know how many players you are getting through the door and how well you are doing at keeping them. Some games use weekly because the development team feel that the rhythm of the game is weekly. I dislike using weekly because it makes it hard to compare with other games, and because it seems to me both too long to enable rapid iteration (unlike DAU) but too short to be a meaningful representation of behaviour in your game (unlike MAU).

Whichever active user metric you pick, remember it is a compound metric, not a lever. It is combination of two levers: new-user acquisition and existing-user retention.

Retention (D1, D7, D30 and D365)

Retention is the Holy Grail of service-game design. The industry has moved from being product-centric to being service-centric. For a service game, success comes from keeping the CPI low and the LTV high. CPI is heavily affected by your competition. In the late 2010s, competition for players of service games on mobile and PC is fierce, and many companies are bidding for players, pushing the CPI up. Retention, on the other hand, is an internal metric. It is within your control. That is why it has become such a key issue for so many game developers.

There are three benchmarks that are often quoted for mobile game developers:

- D1: Target 40% (that is 40% of people who played on Day 0 also played exactly one calendar day after their first session)

- D7: Target 20% (exactly seven days after their first session)

- D30: Target 10% (exactly 30 days after their first session)

This is the *40:20:10 rule of retention*, and I have seen instances of game publishers refusing to unlock marketing funds to drive user acquisition for a game until it has reached 40:20:10.

There are issues with this rule. The first is that it suits some styles of game better than others. It was popularised by Supercell, who make games that are designed to bring you back into the game multiple times a day for a short Session. With a game like that, a player who returns on D7 probably also returned on D6 and D8; if a player is expected to play every day, then the sampling error from picking a particular day is low.

Other games are not designed like that. A game like *Hearthstone* or *Fortnite Battle Royale* is not so focused on daily logins. The designers would probably be quite happy if a player came in a couple of times a week for a few hours. This means that the 40:20:10 rule is not helpful. If I download *Fortnite* on a Monday but only play it at weekends, I will never show up in D1, D7 or D30 statistics.

If you are making a mobile game with an expectation of players playing every day, or multiple times a day, this benchmark is helpful. If you are making a PC game or a mobile game with different expected play patterns, it may not be helpful to wrangle your game into matching this pattern.

Once we move past the first month, things get a bit tricky. Few people talk about their retention rate beyond the first month. Some games do well. For example, *EVE Online* is 14 years old and has no empty cohorts yet. There is at least one person still playing *EVE* who first started in each month between the launch in 2003 and now.

I suggest that you consider a 25% drop-off each month after D30 for your users for the purposes of forecasting.

I have a simple heuristic or rule of thumb when diagnosing a problem with month 1 retention for a game. In Figure 15.3, you can see the ideal rule of 40:20:10 in the top line. That is the target that most mobile games strive for.

The *FTUE issue* line underperforms the rule. On D1, it is 30% instead of 40%. It underperforms throughout the month with D7 at 15% and D30 at 7.5%. The shape of the graph is the interesting point. From D1 to D7, both the ideal and the FTUE issue retention percentages fall by half. The same happens from D7 to D30. This suggests that the issue might be with the FTUE: If we can raise the D1 percentage up to 40%, we can hope that we lift D7 and D30 by the same amount. We would now hit the retention rule.

The *Death by A Thousand Cuts* line is different. It does better on D1 with 35% retention but then falls to 10% on D7 and 2% on D30. The curve

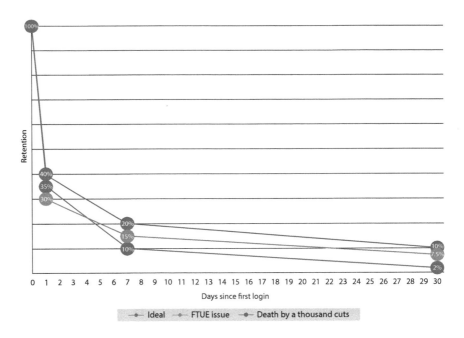

FIGURE 15.3   Diagnosing problems with retention for a service game.

is steeper. This is a much bigger problem: it means that you are losing players steadily throughout the month and is harder to fix.

In the FTUE issue case, I would focus my efforts on improving the First Time User Experience. Is the FTUE a tutorial that focuses on teaching players how to play? It should be laser-focused on showing them the fun (which may involve teaching them, but is not the purpose). Study your metrics to find where people drop out of the FTUE funnel. Perhaps there are obvious errors, such as forced account creation or unskippable cut scenes, or even just an action that is too hard. If you can't spot those, consider user testing. The metrics tell you where people drop off, and the user tests tell you why. By improving the FTUE completion rate, we move people further into our game and hope that the retention curve retains its shape after that. By moving the D1 retention percentage up, we may get improvements in D7 and D30 for free.[12]

Death by a thousand cuts happens when we don't keep players on the correct edge of their competence: competent enough to feel capable and incompetent enough to feel challenged. If you are losing players at a steeper rate than the 40:20:10 rule, then my default hypothesis is death by a thousand cuts. There are many little decisions or actions which the players don't understand, which mean they can't find the fun, which means they

THE IMPOSSIBILITY OF CUPHEAD

In 2017, *Venturebeat* journalist Dean Takahashi suffered the ignominy of failing the tutorial of StudioMDHR's homage to classic 2D platformers, *Cuphead* (as shown in Figure 15.4).[13]

The game has a First Time User Experience that is punishingly hard. As designer Jose Abalos explained in a blogpost,

> "the game says you need to press Y, [but] what you really need to do is jump back to the cube you just passed, make a running jump and perform an air dash in order to pass the cylinder. It's a simple puzzle, but one more than enough to perplex people who are just starting the game for the first time. Does it make sense? Yes, it does. Is it intuitive? No, it isn't."[14]

The developers should have made a better First Time User Experience. A good FTUE is always worth having. On the other hand, *Cuphead is* an intentionally hard game. Making the FTUE easier would just have postponed the point at which Takahashi dropped out of a game that was not aimed at him. (*Venturebeat* admitted that Takahashi was not a fan of platform games, but was the only journalist they had available to meet with the developers at Gamescom in Cologne). And *Cuphead* is a product game, not a service game. Commercially, it is more important that people buy the game than that they play it. Given that *Cuphead* sold 1 million units in its first two weeks, the difficulty seems to have worked out just fine.[15]

For a service game, the FTUE should be easy and intuitive. It should also reflect the nature of your game. Your objective is to keep high-quality users in your game for a long time, not merely to postpone the moment that disengaged players leave anyway.

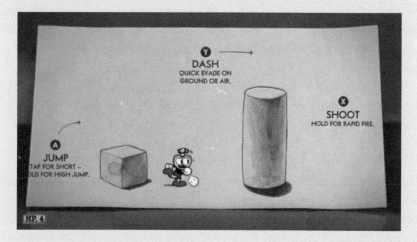

Figure 15.4   The tutorial in *Cuphead*.

leave. Maybe our FTUE is so hand-holding, with big green arrows pointing everywhere, that players can play through without ever understanding what they are doing. When we stop hand-holding, they feel overwhelmed, then stupid and then quit. Maybe we have introduced our complexity too fast. Instead of presenting it in layers, we have introduced in one lump, and again, players feel stupid and leave.

Steve Krug wrote a marvellous book on web and mobile usability called *Don't Make Me Think*. It is a great book and you should read it. It's short. The heart of Krug's thesis is that people are only prepared to invest so much effort into understanding a website or a mobile app (or a game). Each time you add additional cognitive load, you increase friction. If you increase friction too much, the user leaves.

Unlike websites, games are *supposed* to make you think, react or engage, but in a fun way. If the feedback the game is giving you doesn't ring true, it jars. If it jars too often, you will leave. It's why game designers spend so much time worrying about how to provide information to a player about whether that barrel will explode (or because gamers assume all barrels explode, why this one won't) or that, in this game, chickens are the most lethal predators. Communicating the rules of the game to the player is important.

You don't have to dumb down your game to avoid death by a thousand cuts and there is no silver bullet. The first pass is to revisit your game and look for ways to introduce *complexity in layers*.[16] Maybe you can introduce an element of the game later. Maybe you have been so busy teaching the player about all the cool things in your game you forgot to let them discover things for themselves.[17] Maybe you need to remember that the purpose of the first 30 seconds of the game is to earn the next 30 seconds, the first minute to earn the next minute and so on.

It is not easy. But the metrics can you give you a clue as to what the problem is. With a diagnosis, you can state your guiding principle for how to approach the problem and your coherent actions to do so.

Conversion Rate

Conversion rate is the percentage of users that spend money on your game in a given period. If you focus on DAUs, it's daily conversion rate; if you focus on MAUs, it's monthly conversion rate. It can also be calculated as the percentage of users who have ever spent money during the lifetime of your game, which I view as a vanity metric.[18] The lifetime version is a difficult lever to influence and should be avoided.

Many conversion rate benchmarks are bandied around, but they all vary. When Gabe Newell mentioned that *Team Fortress 2* had a 20%–30% conversion rate in 2011, he meant that 20%–30% of all people who had ever played the game had spent money on it. *Tiny Tower* developer Nimblebit quoted a 3.8% conversion rate based on the first six weeks of its lifetime.[19] Wargaming quotes a 30% conversion rate for *World of Tanks* and this is probably lifetime, but we just don't know.[20]

For mobile games, I tend to look at a conversion rate of 1%–3%. Higher conversion rates are possible, but it would be foolish to base your investment case on getting a higher number. If you ask me whether I mean that daily or monthly I will shrug and say, "Yes." If you are looking at daily conversion, I would go at the lower end of the range, for monthly at the higher.

If you are looking at a PC game, the percentages can get much higher. I have seen numbers as high as 20% of MAUs spending per month. I would be wary about forecasting higher than 10%, and for a PC game, I think it makes more sense to think monthly than it does for a mobile game. I would suggest 5%–10% monthly conversion rate is a sensible range.

Revenue Metrics

There are many different spending metrics. Know which one you are referring to, why it is useful and the strengths and weaknesses of it as an analytical tool.

> ARPDAU is Total Daily Revenue/Daily Active Users. Pronounced Arp-d-ow (as in "Ow! That hurt!")
>
> ARPU is Total Revenue/Total Users. It is important that the revenue and the users are from the same period. ARPU is usually calculated monthly and is therefore actually ARPMAU, although few people use this name. Pronounced Arp-oo.
>
> ARPPU is Total Revenue/Total Paying Users. Whereas ARPU looks at average spend across the entire user base, ARPPU only looks at the paying users. Pronounced Ar-pee-poo. (Stop sniggering at the back.) It is typically, but by no means always, calculated on a monthly basis, which makes it technically ARPPMAU, although few people use this abbreviation. If it is calculated on a daily basis, it would be ARPPDAU.

There are other metrics that can be useful. For example, the amount a player spends in a day is a combination of number of transactions multiplied by the size of the transaction, also known as *basket size*. Number of purchases and basket size are both levers that designers can pull to improve monetisation rates.

There is a direct mathematical relationship between ARPU and ARPPU, which is the conversion rate. Both numbers are based on the total revenue, but one is based on total users and the other is based on paying users. The metric that converts from total users to paying users is the conversion rate. If a game has 100,000 users, £1m in revenue and a conversion rate of 10%:

- ARPU = $1 million/100,000 players = $10

- ARPPU = $1 million/10,000 payers (100,000 users × 10% conversion) = $100

Remember the danger of averages! See "A Word about Averages" on p. 113 for a reminder, but all of these metrics are averages. They can make it difficult to understand whether you have a lot of small players or a few very large players.

I find it useful to "bucket" my users into four groups. This is not a deeply scientific or advanced method. Many of my techniques are focused on finding quick rules-of-thumb to understand the game, to diagnose its problems and to build a mental model of its player base. This is quick-and-dirty science, focused on getting actionable insights fast.

We can group our users into:

- Players: These are the people who play the game without spending. If the conversion rate (i.e., the percentage of payers) is 1%–3% then, by symmetry, the percentage of non-payers is 97%–99%.

- Payers: These are the people who play the game and choose to spend real money. They are split into three groups:

  - Tippers: Low payers, sometimes known as *minnows*.[21]

  - Fans: Middle payers, sometimes known as *dolphins*.

  - Superfans: High payers, sometimes known as *whales*.

I know, I know. I said I didn't like the term *whales* and I much prefer Superfans. Most of the time it is easy to swap out the terms with no confusion. However, when we are working on a definition of players which is financial-only, the term *whales* often creeps back in.

The idea behind the buckets is to gather the players into easy-to-understand groups so that you, as designers or analysts, can figure out how to move them from one bucket to another. There are two alternative ways of figuring out how many people are in each bucket.

- Percentages: Of your payers, the top 10% by spend are the Superfans, the next 40% are Fans and the bottom 50% Tippers. In this approach, you sort your users by spend in the period, put them in three buckets, calculate how much those payers spent and figure out the average spend for each bucket.

- Spend: The second way is to split your audience by dollar amount spent. For example, people who spend less than $5 per month are Tippers, people who spend more than $20 are Superfans and in-between are Fans. This model can be easier to query in a database, but your buckets can fluctuate significantly in size.

The purpose of this breakdown is to build a mental model and to learn the levers you need to pull. If your game has lots of Payers but no Superfans, maybe you need to develop better reasons for them to want to spend more money in your game. If you have all Superfans and no Tippers, maybe players do not understand the value of spending real money in the game until they are heavily invested.

In the end, the purpose of metrics is to enable you, as the development team, to make changes to the game that deliver long-term fun and profitability. Metrics are a set of tools that you can add to the many others in your development toolbox to help you make better games.

CHAPTER 16

Ethics

Byron Atkinson-Jones is an independent developer. After working at major studios like Lionhead and Sega, he went solo, releasing games such as *Blast Em!* and *Caretaker* via Steam and other platforms. Atkinson-Jones works to encourage young people to understand video games and what it takes to make them for a living.

In June 2017, Atkinson-Jones gave a speech to young people connected with the Prince's Trust, a charity that helps disadvantaged children to pursue careers or to start their own business. After his talk, he set the students a task: to design a video game that they would like to make.

The audience split into groups of three or four. They discussed their game ideas, the room buzzing with excitement and enthusiasm. Then each group was asked to present their ideas back to the room in a pitch session followed by questions and answers with their fellow students.

Every single game pitched was a F2P game. The questions from the audience revolved around the economy of the game and paywalls and whether you could earn currencies rather than just buying them. These students were not pitching remakes of beloved console games but variants on the games that they played on their smartphones.

Atkinson-Jones was surprised, but on reflection, realised he shouldn't be. A console is an expensive piece of kit. The games are expensive. Given the choice between owning a smartphone or owning a console, most young people would pick the phone first. And on those devices, F2P game are the norm. It is what these young people expected.[1]

Whatever you may personally think of F2P, it is ubiquitous and here to stay. It offers huge amounts of free entertainment to millions of people, from the 78 million core gamers who play *Fortnite* every month to the 93 million people who played *Candy Crush Saga* daily at its height. For the majority of players, this is one of the most cost-effective, easily accessible forms of popular entertainment.

Just because something is widely available and popular does not make it right. Roman citizens travelled to the Colosseum to watch gladiators fight to the death. Civilized societies have moved away from abhorrent notions like slavery, the absence of universal suffrage and capital punishment. The behaviour and mood of the mob is not a reliable guide to ethics.

On the other hand, let's look at this issue from the opposite direction. Imagine that we had never had paid games. All games were free and on smartphones. Sony comes along with a PlayStation, offering a new type of experience to anyone who can pay $300 for a console and $40 per game. Would some people take that offer? Absolutely. Probably tens of millions would. Choosing a paid game is a valid choice, as is choosing a free-to-play game. Neither is inherently evil, but both have advantages and disadvantages which we must weigh up as we consider the ethical boundaries of the new business model.

F2P IS NOT A CAUSE; IT IS A RESPONSE

F2P did not emerge out of nowhere. It emerged in response to changing commercial circumstances. The rise of the Internet as an enabler of cheap, digital distribution changed the economics of entertainment industries. Whether driven by piracy or competition, the price point fell towards zero. Businesses responded at first by complaint and litigation. Then smarter ones realised that what matters is *finding an audience*. Once you have found an audience that loves what you do, you have an opportunity—not a guarantee but an opportunity—to encourage them to give you money. Not every business succeeds at finding that audience. Not every business that finds its audience succeeds at keeping that audience. Not every business that finds and keeps its audience makes enough money to stay in business. But this approach—of finding an audience using free and then encouraging those who love what you do to spend lots of money on things they value—is a logical and sustainable response to the changing circumstances of digital distribution.[2]

The games industry is good at responding to disruptive challenges. There are many reasons for this. The first is that we are a technology industry and are not scared of new tech. When game makers hear about a new technology, their response is usually to go and play with it. The second is that we are a young industry. Seminal game *Pong* was released in 1972. Our industry is less than 50 years old. Many of the pioneers of the video game industry are still alive. Many of them are still alive *and running video game companies*. Although we often bemoan the corporate ethos of games giants, the truth is that the entrepreneurial spirit still runs through many games organisations. We have individuals whose approach to business is not just repeating what the previous generation did, or the generation before that, or before that. We have a higher proportion of entrepreneurs at senior levels than other industries.

Finally, the games industry realises that it must adapt. We saw what happened to music. We don't want to be next. Combine being comfortable with technology with entrepreneurial spirit with fear of revenues declining like music industry revenues have declined, and you have the recipe for a spirit of experimentation, and as economist Joseph Schumpeter would say, "creative destruction."

Schumpeter was an Austrian American economist writing in the 1950s. To him, the engine of growth of the capitalist system was the disruption caused by entrepreneurs innovating with new products or services at the expense of existing companies and workers who had carved out for themselves a position of power. That power might derive from market dominance, from political support, from logistical and distribution excellence or from technological advances. Flexible, adaptable entrepreneurs attempt to find better, cheaper or faster products that fulfil a market need while incumbents struggle to adapt.

F2P is an entrepreneurial response to changing market circumstances. Service gameplay emerged in different territories for very different reasons. In 1995, the South Korean government announced that it was going to create a knowledge-based society by, among other things, ploughing hundreds of millions of US dollars into building the world's best computer network. Up until then, Korea had been a weak gaming market. Access to much Japanese content was limited by a law passed after the Second World War banning the import of Japanese goods and cultural items. Western publishers did not see the value of investing effort in developing a relatively poor Eastern market. Much of the gaming culture in South Korea focused on Taiwanese knock-offs of Japanese products or PC titles pirated from the nascent Internet.

The turning point came when an IT firm called Samjung Data Service realised that people couldn't easily copy an online game, and even if they managed it, they would lack the infrastructure necessary to run it.

That would address the piracy issue. In 1994, they published *Jurassic Park*, a text-based Multi-User Dungeon (MUD). It was not a financial success, but it spurred entrepreneurs Kim Jung-Ju and Jake Song to form Nexon to create a better product: a massively multiplayer online (MMO) game with graphics. In 1996, they launched *The Kingdom of the Winds*. At its height, nearly one million people were paying a monthly subscription fee to play the game. Having established direct distribution networks, Korean companies started experimenting with selling virtual goods, not least because few Koreans had credit cards, but most had mobile phones which could be used to make small payments. The Korean market embraced online games and then micropayments as a way to get around the limitations of piracy, the lack of credit cards and the fact their users played on public PCs in cybercafés rather than on private ones in homes.[3]

In China, the challenge was a combination of piracy and platforms. China is not a country renowned for its respect for intellectual property and piracy is rife. By tying gameplay access to an account, it addressed the piracy problem. By enabling gamers to play on PCs in cybercafés, publishers could get around the problem that few in the population could afford their own computers. The Chinese market followed Korea's lead in embracing free-to-play games.

In Germany, the logic was different. My theory (and not everyone agrees with it) is that F2P emerged because Germany did not host global publishers of console or PC games. The United Kingdom had Eidos and Codemasters, as well as the European headquarters of nearly every major American game publisher. France had Ubisoft and Infogrames. Germany's publishers were much smaller and focused on PC titles. This is not an absolute blocker to success; there are successful game studios working from a variety of countries with no domestic publishing strength, but it has a subtle influence. Building relationships with publishers becomes harder and only studios that can afford dedicated business development efforts find it easy to get published.

Germany became the home of browser games companies. Bigpoint, founded in 2002, began life creating online sports team management games such as *Hockey-Manager* before moving on to more graphically impressive titles such as *Dark Orbit* and *Sea Fight*. *Tribal Wars*, a competitive real-time-strategy MMO was released by Innogames the following year. German companies embraced F2P as a route to market in the absence of existing publishers, unlike their British and US counterparts. Germany remains a major player in F2P games with companies like Innogames, Goodgame Studios and Wooga having international success.

The different experiences in these three territories highlight that service gaming, and the virtual goods economies that often follow, were driven by the competitive landscape and business circumstances. F2P is not the cause of gaming's financial woes. Quite the opposite. It is its saviour. Without the changing business model that has enabled companies like Riot Games, Supercell or Smilegate to create new ways of charging for gaming entertainment, the games industry might have gone the same way as the recorded music industry, which saw revenues collapse from $26 billion in 1999 to $15 billion in 2014.[4]

F2P may have saved the industry, but it also changed it. Just as arcade games were designed with the constraints of the one-more-go model in mind, and boxed games were influenced by the need to sell and market a $60 experience, so free-to-play games have adapted to the commercial needs of their distribution channels.

A successful free-to-play game gets players into the game, keeps them there and encourages them to spend money. There is enormous focus on retention amongst all F2P designers because if you keep a player in your game, you have the potential to make money from them, either directly in terms of purchases or indirectly through advertising. Monetisation is also important, with a range of options varying from cosmetic items, to progression, to outright power. We'll cover this in more detail in the next section.

As Chris Bateman, game designer and philosopher, says in *The Virtuous Cyborg*, "Money plays a role in the production of video games that is neither transparent nor neutral. The way games are designed relates to the way revenue is generated."[5] Bateman argues—and I agree—that there is nothing surprising about this, but we should still pause to consider the implications.

I believe there are three different elements to considering the ethics of F2P: How does it change game design? How does it use psychology to influence consumers and what are the consequences? And can games still be art with such substantial commercial influence?

CAN GAMES BE ART WITH SUCH COMMERCIAL INFLUENCE?

Of course, games can be art. So let's think about the commercial implications of free-to-play.

Commercial pressures have challenged artists for as long as art has existed. Michelangelo needed the patronage of the Medicis to paint the ceiling of the Sistine Chapel. Charles Dickens published *The Pickwick Papers* in 1836 as a serial. It was so successful that all of Dickens' subsequent novels were published as serials, with a significant influence on his storytelling rhythm. US television shows are 42 minutes long with multiple internal cliffhangers so that they can fill a 60-minute television slot with space left over for advertisements and an incentive for the audience to return.

The original arcade business model, seen by some core gamers as a purer form of gameplay, was designed to keep you reaching for another quarter. There was often a choice: add cash to continue or choose to let yourself die and spend more time in the game by starting from the beginning where the gameplay is easier. Multiplayer arcade games like *Gauntlet* or *Time Crisis* took the concept one step further. When you die, you can choose to add money to keep playing. Meanwhile your friend or gaming partner was screaming in your ear, "Come on! Put the money in! I'm on my own here! I'm dying!"[6] This looks like a conscious design decision to move the choice over whether to spend money in the game away from an economically rational one ("Will I get more utility from my money by paying to extend my session or by paying to restart the game from the beginning?") to a socially driven one ("Shall I spend my money, or shall I choose not to, which means my friend will die?")

The point is not to argue that the *Time Crisis* approach was better, although it was effective on me. It is that the business model *always* affects the content. A product game studio needs to invest its time and effort in securing the purchase, not the playing. That leads to a focus on visual fidelity rather than rich systems. It leads to a focus on the subcultures that demonstrably paid for games in the past (i.e., white males ages 15–30) and little focus on everyone else. It leads to games that are bloated with extra features to make the lives of marketing people easier.

Service games are more like television than movies, and as a result, are more focused on the enduring relationship with players than a one-off experience. This has, at least in the short term, made it harder for games with difficult themes to get funding. (Not that it was easy in the first place.) On the other hand, F2P has extended the reach of games outside the traditional demographic, leading to new types of gameplay for new types of audience. Art and commerce have always been uneasy bedfellows. Over time, I expect service games to push new artistic boundaries, just as product games have done.

DOES F2P CHANGE GAME DESIGN?

As I've argued, F2P is a *response* to changing technological and distribution pressures. It was not the cause of the change to the games industry; the environment changed, and F2P was a rational response. On the other hand, there is no doubt that F2P has changed game design, and particularly, the objectives of the design team.

In the old days, it was possible for the development team to be completely separate from the marketing and sales teams. A development team could pitch an idea, and if it made it through greenlight, not speak to the marketing and sales teams until the game was finished and ready to be sold in stores. That rarely happened, but it was possible. The role of sales was to generate demand from retailers and the role of marketing was to generate demand from players. The developers had to deliver the best possible game that they could within the constraints of time and budget to satisfy the estimated demand.

In a F2P game, that distinction is not just blurred, it is blown away. The game itself has become the place where the sale takes place. It is its own store. This is a major advantage, in that the game becomes a de facto monopoly: the only place to buy coins for *Homescapes* is in *Homescapes*. It also presents challenges for developers because, well, the whole game is a shop.

The best defence against this is consumers. Just as consumers will not shop in stores with predatory practices, so consumers will turn away from games with predatory practices. We saw this happen to Zynga. It believed that it had developed a Playbook that enabled it to deliver games that would deliver retention and monetisation key performance indicators (KPIs) over and over again.[7] Players got bored with the exhortations to spam their friends, the pain points and the repetitive gameplay and left in their droves. Zynga has yet to regain the heady heights of its early days.

Commercial business models *always* affect game design. Many of the changes are uncomfortable for players because they are unfamiliar. Some are uncomfortable because certain genres are harder to make work in this particular business model. Others believe, rightly, that F2P business models constrain elements of a game. For example, if your game design relies on a scarcity of resources, that is hard to reconcile with many F2P monetisation designs that allow players to buy resources.

However, a lot of these issues are about the *implementation* of F2P, not F2P itself. In 2013, I wrote an (admittedly inflammatory) blog post titled "Five Reasons Why FTL Is a Perfect Free-to-Play Game."[8] It engendered much discussion. Some of it was constructive, but much involved commenters inventing bad experiences that you could have if you made *FTL* free-to-play.[9] I agree that if we were to turn a title like *FTL* into a free-to-play game, we would try to do it in a way that wasn't rubbish. Many of the F2P criticisms are about execution, not principle.

What is indisputable is that in F2P game design, the game is the shop. Once a player has downloaded the game from Steam or the App Store or elsewhere, the designer aims to keep her inside the game. The player is no longer in the competitive environment of a games retail store where other games can grab her attention and her money. The designer is incentivised to keep the player in her game, and to encourage her to spend money. So F2P designers are no longer incentivised just to deliver fun. They must deliver retention and monetisation as well.

Of course, it is nonsense to think that designers were ever only focused on delivering fun. Game designers have always had to contend with marketing departments foisting the latest must-have feature onto them with the purpose of completing a checklist of extras on the back of the box. Sales teams have always pushed visual fidelity because it is easier to show off that feature than it is to demonstrate a complex upgrade and progression system that can provide hours of engagement. Senior executives look for features that they can understand and interact with in a few moments because that is the time they have available to understand the vertical slice. Designers have always had to deal with the conflicting demands of entertaining the player, delivering the game within technical and financial constraints and satisfying the commercial needs of the organisation.

The difference is now these pressures are more obvious and internal to the game.

(Note that one of the biggest challenges for a product-game company becoming a service-game company is adapting to these pressures. The senior executives, the marketing department and the sales team are all used to looking for easy-to-demonstrate success. This tends to focus on the Base Layer because the Base Layer is visual, visceral and offers rapid feedback. A successful F2P game needs a successful Retention Layer more than it needs a successful Base Layer. It is hard to demo a Retention Layer quickly because it needs a mental model of what a player wants to do and why; it requires a process of desire creation followed by desire delivery. To play a prototype requires a game-design imagination. To play the full Retention Layer requires plenty of time. These are not things that many senior executives have in abundance.)

The emergence of F2P games has pushed the commercial pressures of making successful video games deep into the realm of game design.

For some developers, this is unacceptable. That is their choice, and I respect it. For the rest of us, there are realities of both commercial and audience pressures: the Internet has made alternative forms of game distribution much harder, and, as the anecdote from Byron Atkinson-Jones at the start of this chapter shows, our audience is starting to expect free-to-play. When 78 million people play *Fortnite* every month, or 93 million people play *Candy Crush Saga* in a single day, it is hard to say that we are not responding to our audience demands.

F2P has therefore been both a benefit and a challenge for designers. It has elevated the design discipline above the production discipline in terms of delivering the retention that games now need. On the other hand, it has forced designers both to confront the commercial realities of their role and also to understand a whole new set of tools to drive fun, with a firm eye on the need to deliver retention and monetisation as well. Free-to-play has changed the role of designers. The key challenges are how do we use the tools of game design in the areas of retention and monetisation, and what new ethical questions arise from these new business models? The ability of video games to use human psychology as a tool more effectively than many other industries or products is the core of the issue.

HOW GAMES USE PSYCHOLOGY

All game design draws heavily on human psychology. All marketing draws heavily on human psychology. In F2P game design, the two disciplines are intertwined. This can lead to some challenges and conflicts. Ultimately, I believe that it will lead to F2P games being regulated, and we are already seeing this emerge in China, Belgium and the Netherlands and elsewhere.

Jamie Madigan is a psychologist who cares a lot about video games. In his book, *Getting Gamers*, he looks at the psychological tools that video-game developers use to entertain players and to get them to do the things that we—as game designers—want them to do.

We use "fear of loss" to keep players pumping quarters into an arcade machine when they die. We use the "endowed-progress" effect to encourage players to complete quests. We use random loot drops to keep players playing *Diablo* or *World of Warcraft* or any F2P game with a randomised reward system, often known as *gacha* or Loot boxes (see boxout). We create artificial scarcity to make working for a legendary item feel worthwhile or worth paying for. Madigan's book explains the many techniques, rooted in behavioural psychology, that game developers have been using for decades.[10] Similarly, if you read Robert Cialdini's seminal work on marketing and psychology, *Influence*, you can see the sales and marketing techniques that Cialdini identified in the mid-1980s being used throughout the games industry. The same is true for Dan Ariely's *Predictably Irrational*.

GACHA AND LOOT BOXES

Gacha is the name for random rewards delivered in games, particularly service games. The word is derived from the Japanese word *gachapon*, an onomatopoeia of "gacha" for the sound of turning a crank on a toy vending machine and "pon" of the sound of the toy capsule dropping into the receptacle. In the West, these rewards are often known as loot boxes or crates.

Gacha is at heart of many successful service games. The premise is that player rewards are randomised, much like the loot drops in *Diablo* or *World of Warcraft* but can be bought with real money. In *Marvel Contest of Champions*, players can purchase a crystal that contains a random character with two, three or four stars. They cannot purchase the character that they want; they must keep purchasing the crystal in the hope that luck will be on their side and they will get a specific character. In *Hearthstone*, the collectible cards are sold in packs of five, with randomised content. Games that include gacha mechanics include *Overwatch*, *Clash Royale*, *Fire Emblem Heroes* and many more.

Gacha mechanics work for many reasons. They create desires that players did not know they had. Abomination is not well-known character in the Marvel universe, but a 4* Abomination is much more desirable than a 2* Spiderman. They increase monetisation potential because players have a wide range of items to pursue. They are psychologically rewarding. They are ubiquitous.

We are seeing a backlash. Japan forced the industry to drop *kompu gacha*, a compound form of gacha where players had to be lucky enough to win multiple parts of a token to enable them to participate in a higher-level gacha system to get the item they actually wanted. China has forced publishers to publish drop rates and to keep records to demonstrate that they adhered to these drop rates. Hawaiian Senator Chris Lee described *Star Wars Battlefront II* as a "*Star Wars*-themed online casino, designed to lure kids into spending money."[11] A petition demanding that the UK government included loot boxes in gambling regulations received more than 10,000 signatures in less than a week.[12] In the months that this book has been in production, the gambling regulators in Belgium and the Netherlands have both stated that they view certain loot box designs in videogames such as *Overwatch*, *FIFA 18* and *Rocket League*.

If you design service-based games, you need to understand the principles of gacha. You also need to pay attention to legislation and ethics because the system is (rightly) coming under increased scrutiny.[13]

These techniques are used all the time by sales people. Yesterday evening, a pretty young woman knocked on the door of my London house (Pretty, a shortcut to "likeability," one of Cialdini's six marketing principles.) She said a cheerful "Hello" (more likeability). Her opening statement was, "We supply fresh cut flowers to many of your neighbours." (Social proof, Cialdini's first principle.) She then explained that I could sign up now, with no commitment, and get the first box of flowers for free. If I didn't want them, I could return them with no obligation to pay. (The endowment effect. The flowers would now be in my possession: I will value them more than I would similar flowers in a store, or in the salesperson's possession).[14] After noticing half a dozen more sales techniques, all of them rooted in behavioural psychology, I told the young lady that as a matter of principle, I did not buy anything on the doorstep. She tried one last time—"But then you won't be able to get this one-off offer," invoking scarcity, Cialdini's sixth principle. I stood firm.

The saleswoman on the doorstep was using her skill and judgement in a two-minute interaction to persuade me to take a free trial. A video game has days, weeks, months and years to learn the foibles of a player. It could identify, through trial and error or through pattern recognition, that I am a sucker for achievements and could be easy to manipulate through the achievement system, while another player is a sucker for time-sensitive "must-end soon" sales (to which I am mostly immune) and a third is hyper-competitive and will spend money like water to win. A game could, if it chose, optimise to become the most efficient money extraction machine that ever existed.

In practice, I don't think this would work. I talk about games being a monopoly, which is true within each game. But if the game becomes abusive or overbearing or obviously gouging, players will leave to rival games that do not have the reputation. I am still playing *Hearthstone* regularly, but I have two friends who have gone cold turkey on the game because they wanted to have more time in their lives for other activities: seeing their friends but also for playing other games. They saw *Hearthstone* becoming a monopoly, didn't like it and took action to change the situation.

Video games have always used psychological tricks to create fun in an artificial world and to capture players' attention. They are now being required to deliver fun, to capture attention and to capture money. They can also be infinitely personalised. Where a traditional marketing channel can use the psychological techniques that work, on average, for most people, a game can, over time, personalise its techniques to create a perfectly designed Skinner box targeted exactly at me, or you, your dad or your best friend. Each of us could be playing the optimum game designed to capture our attention and our money.

This, for me, is why the ethics of F2P game design is so important. I believe it is wrong to make a F2P game harder for payers (who have demonstrated that they will spend real cash to make a game easier) than it is for non-payers. I am not aware of games that do this. I am sure that, amongst the million games out there, some games do it. I think that publicising the drop rates of randomised gacha mechanics is a good thing. I also think it is a good thing if the publicised loot drops chance and the actual loot drop chance are the same.

My preference is for the industry to self-regulate. In the long run, I think this is unlikely. And that has a lot to do with the relationship between mainstream media and the video-game industry.

You don't have to spend long looking at the popular press to see how the mass media thinks about video games. They brand popular games like illegal drugs when players play them a lot (*Evercrack* and *Minecrack*). They seek out the dangerous edge cases. *"The mysterious death of a live-streaming gamer."*[15] *"Chinese gamer dies after playing World of Warcraft for 19 hours."*[16] They pretend that video games are just for children, so they can write "but-think-of-the-children" opinion columns to constrain and constrict a medium that they don't understand and don't like.

For many years, the games industry has fought back against censorship campaigns aimed at video games driven by (disgraced) Senator Lelland Yee in the United States or (disgraced) Member of Parliament Keith Vaz in the United Kingdom. It was right and sensible to fight against censorship and controls that would have limited the growth of a nascent and important medium.

Unfortunately, it has also trained many supporters of games to respond in vitriolic fashion whenever anyone challenges the behaviours of the industry, even when those critics might have a point. This is unhelpful when we need to discuss the appropriate ethical line to take with F2P game design. I have tried on several occasions to get a serious conversation about the ethics of F2P games at conferences. Every panel I've been on to discuss this topic, every attempt at a nuanced discussion, ends up in a shouting match between a subset of people that hate F2P so much that they will brook no discussion and supporters of the business model being forced to defend the very principle of F2P. We seem unable to have a sensible discussion about where and how we should draw the ethical lines.

It's all very well to say, "You should never use psychology to manipulate someone into doing something," but it is a pointless statement. Life does not work like that. Being polite is manipulative. Being likeable is manipulative. Running a sale is manipulative. There are shades of grey everywhere. I would like us all to start having a grown-up conversation about these ethics.

AN ETHICAL FRAMEWORK

Stanford psychologist B. J. Fogg is a key figure in the development of using computers as persuasive technology. In his book, *Persuasive Technology*, published in 2003, Fogg asks if persuasion is inherently unethical. His answer is that it depends. Some people believe that attempting to change a person's attitudes or behaviours is always unethical or at least questionable. Others believe persuasion is fundamentally good as part of ethical leadership or participatory democracy.[17]

Service games are not (generally) attempting to persuade in this sense. They aim to manipulate behaviours to entertain their players, to keep them engaged and to encourage them to spend money in the game. Fogg asks, "*Can* persuasion be unethical?" His answer is neither yes or no. It depends on how persuasion is used. "Because persuasion is a value-laden activity, creating an interactive technology designed to persuade is also value-laden."

As we debate the ethical boundaries of video games, it will be helpful to have tools to frame the debate that enable us to get beyond the "Free-to-play games are evil/No, they're not" argument that dominate the current discussion. Fogg argues that the designer's intent, methods of persuasion and outcomes help to determine the ethics of persuasive technology.

Intent

Games are designed to absorb a player's time and a player's money in return for entertainment. Unlike product games, service games *need* to engage players for a long time to maximise revenue. In an anti-F2P blog post in 2011, *Canabalt* designer Adam Saltsman came out with a diatribe against video games that could be aimed at any title that becomes a time sink, from *Pong* to *Civilisation*, *Minecraft* to *Candy Crush Saga*. He rails against games that allow players to trade time for money, particularly those that, in his view, use extrinsic "checklists" to encourage progression despite limited intrinsic motivation within the game.

> "That's when [these games] step in, like a mafia godfather, and offer you a deal you can't refuse: you're a busy guy, you have kids, you have a job; if you slip me a little cash under the table, I'll help you level up a little faster, maybe get through that next part of the checklist by tomorrow. This is extortion in the worst way; this is extortion of the time we have left until we die, the sole resource of consequence for human life. Developers who deliberately engage in this kind of design should be ashamed of their creations."[18]

I disagree with Adam's characterisation. For most of video-game history, the games that have absorbed our time and attention have been the praiseworthy games, the ones that win Game of the Year awards and are remembered fondly from our childhood. Dismissing the idea of allowing players to buy their way to different experiences as extortion of time is not only hyperbolic, but it is essentially agreeing with those critics of video gaming who argue we should stop playing children's games and go and do something more meaningful instead.

I would like our discussion around the intent of service-game design to be more nuanced. Are we more bothered about games that take an enormous amount of time or a game that takes an enormous amount of money? Service games are designed to do both. Selling something enjoyable that people love spending time on and choose to spend money on is not inherently unethical. That suggests that we need to consider Fogg's next criterion: Method.

Method

Much of Saltsman's (and other critics') concerns revolve around the methods used to drive these desires. Fogg states, and I concur, that deception is always unethical. Tricking a player into purchasing virtual goods and currencies is unethical, and we should not do it. Although the press loves a story about a child who bought thousands of dollars of in-app purchases (IAPs) without parental permission, this is a rare occurrence. The industry has not reached its success and scale through outright deception, and platform holders are quick to refund money on the occasions when it has happened. I believe that all of us who want an ethical video-game business agree that deception has no place in our industry.

Fogg also identifies operant conditioning, described in Chapter 6, as a potential "red flag" when considering the ethics of a persuasive technology. Most games have elements of operant conditioning, and the variable nature of the rewards that we get from our repeated attempts are part of the joy of video gaming. Fogg argues that operant conditioning "can be an ethical strategy when incorporated into a persuasive technology if it is overt and harmless." In other words, are players aware of the operant conditioning, and does it cause them any harm?

How you react to these questions may depend on the culture you espouse. Western culture, and particularly that of the United States, values individual freedom and self-determination over collective power or social paternalism. In that mind-set, an adult should be free to do what they like, provided it does no harm to others. It is hard to see how spending lots of time or money in a game is a direct, societal harm. Different societies hold different views about the boundary between individual responsibility and where government should intervene. As service games operate on a global basis, the industry is likely to get caught between competing cultural visions of what is appropriate.

That is all well and good, but "won't someone think of the children?" as I'm sure journalists and politicians have asked on many occasions. It is incumbent on us to protect the vulnerable in our society without infringing unnecessarily on the rights of adults to make their own choices. I can foresee a scenario where this outcry leads to, for example, loot boxes and other systems that "look like gambling" leading to a Mature or 18 rating on video games. (I wrote this sentence in November 2017, six months before the Dutch and Belgian gambling regulators publicised their position on this topic.) This is an outcome I am keen to avoid, but it requires the industry to demonstrate that players of all ages understand what they are purchasing. It may require much more transparency over the likely cost of a game or the actual chances of getting a coveted item in a random purchase.

Outcomes

Is the outcome of playing a service game harmless? Again, this depends on your point of view. Is it ethical to make a game that is so engaging that a player can literally die while playing it? Is it ethical to make a game that encourages people to spend $60 on it? $15 a month? $1,000 on microtransactions? $1 million? Is it right that someone can fritter money away on virtual goods? What gives us the right to determine what a law-abiding adult chooses to spend his or her money on?

The intended outcome of service-game design is that players spend a lot of time and a lot of money on the game. The unintended (but predictable) outcome is that some players spend money that they don't have or spend so much time in the game that they neglect real-world obligations to the detriment of themselves or others around them. To what extent should government step in to protect people from themselves?

Fogg argues that "three parties could be at fault when the outcome of a persuasive technology is ethically unsound: those who create, distribute, or use the product. The balance of culpability shifts on a case-by-case basis."[19] Developers have responsibility for the outcomes of their design decisions. Platform owners such as Apple, Valve and Microsoft must shoulder the ethical responsibilities of making these technologies so widely available. (To be fair, they do, swiftly reimbursing users for large, mistaken transactions and discouraging bad actors from their platforms.) Users also have a responsibility and an ability to influence the long-term trends of the industry by choosing not to play and not to spend in games that they view as ethically questionable

I find Fogg's framework of intent, method and outcomes to be useful in considering my view of the ethics of service and free-to-play games. I see nothing wrong with designing a game that draws players in and tries to keep them playing for a long time. I prefer games that are respectful of my time, hence my recommendations for giving players a clear Off-Ramp and not trying to extend Session lengths. I prefer the free-to-play model that enables me to try many games for free, but only choosing to spend on those that I love, such as *Hearthstone*, that has absorbed most of my gaming budget for the past three years.

I am nervous of the operant conditioning method, like Fogg. It is a tool that has its place, but it is also the preferred tool of the Las Vegas casino operator to extract the maximum amount of money from players. The key question for me is how aware a player is about how much they spend.

When I totted up how much I had spent on *Hearthstone* for this book, it was roughly double what I expected. Would it be more ethical to display a prominent total of how much you have spent on the game so far in every service game or to require developers to require additional, informed consent when a Superfan goes on a spending spree?

THE FUTURE WILL BE REGULATED

In 2017, China started requiring games companies to publish the drop rates of their randomised loot drops, specifically those where players spend real money to buy a pack of cards, heroes or equipment, some of which is common and some of which is rare. To this Western writer, China has never been thought of as being at the forefront of consumer protection. Yet here it is, legislating to force companies not only to publish their loot drop rates but also to make the actual drop rates available to government officials to verify. The historian in me remembers that when a country passes laws banning a thing, it often means that the thing is a very common practice.[20] It may be that the need for consumer protection in this area is stronger than in the West, where we already have strong consumer protection laws and the threat of class-action lawsuits. Whatever the proximate cause, China has ended up bringing regulation and transparency to the F2P gaming industry. I expect similar regulation to start emerging across the world.

For most game developers, there are three major regions that matter, with three smaller regions. The key territories, in terms of regulation, are the United States, the European Union and China because of their size and economic potential. Then there are the three smaller regions of Japan, South Korea and, post-Brexit, the United Kingdom. Many companies will build their games to comply with the strictest rules to enable them to work on a global basis. In the near term, I suspect we will continue to have one build for the world excluding China and one for China, but over time, I suspect many of the regulations that emerge in China will spread to the Western world as well.

I believe regulation of F2P games is inevitable. The industry is visible, popular and, by its nature, manipulative. Politicians and lawmakers have not caught up with the power of the industry yet. In the near term, we may not need new laws. The existing frameworks of consumer protection or class-action lawsuits may provide the protection that consumers need. On the other hand, I suspect that there will continue to be egregious abuses of design that lead to consumers to be manipulated.

If regulation does come, I hope that it will be even-handed. I hope that it allows adults to spend their money on whatever they like—with informed consent. I worry about the dominance of gacha and loot boxes in free-to-play game design. I would like more transparency over drop rates, and evidence that these drop rates are borne out in reality.

Games have a peculiar ability to shape their manipulations to the personality of the player. I think F2P remains the saviour of the games industry and the reason that our industry is growing when so many other entertainment industries are shrinking in the face of declining barriers to distribution. We need to be more aware of the ethical consequences of the powerful psychological tools that we have at our disposal. We need to self-regulate, but because the incentives are misaligned here, I believe increased government intervention will happen. I look forward to more challenging conversations about where the ethical boundaries of F2P sit over the next few years.

CHAPTER 17

The Pyramid of Game Design Afterword

THE PYRAMID OF GAMES Design is a framework to help you make better, more profitable games. In this book, I have set out the principles of the Base Layer, Retention Layer, Superfan Layer and the Core Loop that connects them. I have highlighted the importance of the Session, the fundamental building block of service design and explored what people will pay for in a world where they are getting so much of their entertainment content for free.

I've looked at the changing nature of development, with a focus on how service games value iteration and validated learning over milestones and untested assumptions. I suggested additional techniques for driving creativity in an iterative environment. I've put forward some thoughts on marketing and set out the most important KPIs that you need to understand as you develop the game.

Throughout the book, I have emphasised that there is rarely a right answer and a wrong answer. Every decision you make involves consequences. You will need to decide which trade-offs are right for your game and which ones are not worth making.

My hope is that I have demystified some of the elements of service games and helped advance the games industry by codifying some terms, phrases and frameworks so that developers can work together to make better games. Thank you for reading. For more information, join the conversation at www.gamesbrief.com.

Acknowledgements

This book has been in gestation since I first started consulting on free-to-play game design in 2008. Since then, I have had dozens of clients asking me interesting, challenging questions about how to make successful service games. The frameworks and advice in this book were formulated in response to these questions and tested on live games. Thank you to all of the clients of GAMESbrief over the past ten years.

Many individuals helped me by answering questions or giving me a sounding board for my ideas. I am particularly grateful to Byron Atkinson-Jones, Nick Bardsley, Chris Bateman, Thomas Bidaux, Ben Fisher, George Foot, Jon Gibson, Nick Harper, Simon Harris, Jon Jordan, Philip Oliver, Mike Sherlock and Mark Sorrell.

Joost van Dreunen of SuperData Research provided the information on revenue generated by service games in 2016. Nick Tannahill wrote advice on dealing with influencers.

Enormous thanks to the industry luminaries who were prepared to read and comment on early drafts of the manuscript: Andy Beaudoin, Ben Board, Simon Bradbury, Daniel Cook, Jak Marshall, Andrew Smith, Rob Stevens, Paul Kilduff-Taylor and Jeferson Valadares.

Thank you to One Life Left, a radio show dedicated to video games that is broadcast on Resonance 104.4FM in London and is available as a podcast at www.onelifeleft.com. They've invited me on the show three times in the past few years, it's been a blast each time, and I promised that I would give them an acknowledgment in the book in return for a Marioke song. This is me keeping my side of the bargain.

Many people helped with the images and screenshots throughout the book. Thank you to Henry Ryder for the images of the Pyramid and the Session. He picked colours I would never have chosen, and the illustrations are all the better for that. Thank you to Joe Sargent for help with refining the look of the cover. Credits for the images are given in the endnotes, but for help in securing or giving permissions, I would like to thank Ian Marsh, Owen Goss, Nick Yee of Quantic Foundry, Jeferson Valadares, Michiko Kumagai, Steve Ellis, Neil Ralley, Lucia Gomez, Lance Priebe, Charlotte Crampton, Tom Farrell, Eli Cymet, Chris Petrovic, Nick Harper, Frank Goldberg, Devin Peek and Natalia Luckyanova.

Thank you to Sean Connelly at CRC Press/Taylor & Francis Group for commissioning the book and putting up with the delays (although by most author standards, I was pretty quick in delivering).

And finally, thank you to my family, Catherine, Alasdair and Lucy, for putting up with a year of distraction while I wrote this book. I love you all.

Glossary

AA: pronounced "Double-A", video games that don't quite reach AAA heights. Often means games with shorter experiences, or produced by independent studios with smaller teams. AA games can be extremely good, but they have lower budgets and, generally, less of the bombast associated with AAA games.

AAA: pronounced "Triple-A," video games with high production values and high values. The game industry's equivalent to movies' blockbusters.

Achievement: A task that can only be completed once, like the Trophies in a PlayStation game or Xbox Achievements, and recorded in an Achievement section of the game. They are different to Challenges (q.v.) which can be completed many times. See Chapter 3 The Retention Layer, Retention Layer 17: Achievements.

Agile: a form of software development that encourages rapid deployment, adaptability to change and iterative development. The technology partner of Lean.

Appointment Mechanic: a game design technique where the game allows players to initiate a task or process that requires them to return in a fixed amount of time to complete the task or claim a reward. An appointment mechanic gives players some control over when they choose to return to the game, which makes it different to a Tamagotchi (q.v.).

ARPDAU: average revenue per daily active user

ARPMAU: average revenue per monthly active user

ARPPU: average revenue per paying user

ARPU: average revenue per user

Base Layer: The moment-to-moment gameplay in a video game, often contained within a level. Examples include fighting a wave of aliens in *Space Invaders*, exploring a level in *LEGO® Star Wars*, completing a level of *Candy Crush Saga* and playing a match in *League of Legends*.

CAC: customer acquisition cost

CCG: collectible card game

Ceremony: also know as euphoria, pizzazz, Peggle time or Popcapification. A collection of techniques used by a video game to make a particular moment feel especially rewarding to a player on an emotional level. Can include music, sound effects, animation, time dilation and any other technique that amplifies the emotional reward for something that the player has done.

Challenge: a task or objective that a player can do many times, earning new rewards each time, in contrast to Achievements (q.v.) which can only be completed once. See Chapter 3 The Retention Layer, Retention Layer 16: Challenges.

CPA: cost per acquisition

CPI: cost per install

CPM: cost per mille; equivalent to CPT

CPT: cost per thousand

D1: Day-1 retention. The percentage of users who logged in on day zero who also logged in on day one.

D30: Day-30 retention. The percentage of users who logged in on day zero who also logged in on day 30.

D7: Day-7 retention. The percentage of users who logged in on day zero who also logged in on day seven.

DAU: daily active user

DLC: downloadable content

eCPI: effective CPI

Endless Runner: a game, typically on mobile devices, where players must keep moving forward along a route for as long as possible, avoiding hazards and trying not to die. Popular examples include *Subway Surfers* and *Minion Rush*.

F2P: free-to-play

Feature Phone: a basic mobile phone from before the era of smartphones such as the iPhone. Functionality included phone calls, texting and basic gameplay. Internet connection was limited. The archetypal game on a feature phone was Nokia's *Snake*.

FPS: first-person shooter

FTUE: first-time user experience

Gacha: a form of reward that involves random elements, such as loot boxes or loot crates.

Game Jam: a gathering of people for the purpose of planning, designing and creating a video game in a short span of time, usually between 24 and 72 hours.

GDC: Game Developers Conference, an annual gathering of over 25,000 video game developers held since 2005 in San Francisco

Hidden Object: a game genre where players must look for the objects hidden within a scene or image.

HiPPO: highest paid person's opinion

IM: Instant Messenger

IP: intellectual property, defined as intangible property that is the result of creativity including patents, artistic and creative works, trademarks and inventions.

KPI: key performance indicators

Lean: a management philosophy that focuses on validated learning to develop new products and services. The commercial partner of Agile.

LOD: level of detail

LTV: lifetime value

MAP: minimum awesome product

MAU: monthly active user

MDP: minimum desirable product

Metagame: everything outside the game. The ways in which a game is influenced by activities outside the core rules of the game. For example, poker is a very different game when played for high stakes in a casino compared with playing with your children using matchsticks as chips. Often used to refer to how a multiplayer online game evolves as players develop new strategies, leading to the development of counterstrategies, which means that the original strategies fall out of favour.

MFP: minimum feasible product

Min-maxer: a player who gets innate satisfaction from playing the game "optimally".

MMO: massively multiplayer online [game].

MMORPG: massively multiplayer online role-playing game

MOBA: multiplayer online battle arena. A multiplayer game where teams of players vie for control, such as *League of Legends*.

MTX: microtransactions

MUD: multi-user dungeon

MVP: minimum viable product

Off-Ramp: the element of the game that hints to players that now would be a good time to leave.

Oligopoly: control by the few. Often used to refer a situation where a few big players control an industry, such as the publishers in video games, movie studios in film and the big four of Facebook, Apple, Google and Amazon in technology.

On-Ramp: the element of the game that makes it easy for players to return to a game.

P2W: pay to win

Playtime: the time during a Session (q.v.) where players focus on having fun and making progress. Often involves engaging with the Base Layer (q.v.).

Popcapification: see ceremony

Pottering: playing a game with no immediate purpose or intensity. Examples include rearranging the inventory in a role-playing game, decorating a farm in a resource management game or crafting a new deck in a collectible card game.

PvE: player versus enemy. Gameplay that involves the player against computer controlled opponents.

PvP: player versus player: Gameplay that involves the player against computer-controlled opponents.

Retention Layer: the part of the game that gives the player long-term purpose, whether that be narrative, progress, achievements, beating high scores, etc.

Return Hook: a technique used by game designers to give players a specific reason to return to the game and start a new Session (q.v.).

RPG: roleplaying game

RTS: real-time strategy

SDT: self-determination theory, a framework for what motivates people to play games, or to work, encompassing competence, autonomy and relatedness.

Session: the building block of service game design. A single gameplay experience. A player can have multiple sessions per day.

Social Games: a term that has fallen out of fashion for games played on social networks such as Facebook.

Superfan: a committed player of a game, measured by time or money.

Superfan Layer: the part of the game that engages Superfans. Often, but not always, involves "me and my friends" playing against "you and your friends", i.e. groups of people competing against each other, whether for in-game resources, for status or directly in competitive play.

Tamagotchi: a virtual pet created by Bandai in 1996. Tamagotchis required players to return to the game regularly, at a time of the game's choosing, otherwise the virtual pet would die.

TLA: three letter abbreviation.

TTP: time to penis. The length of time before someone has created a phallic object in your game. It is small.

UGC: user generated content

UI: user interface

UX: user experience

Whale: a high spender in a video game. See also: Superfan

XP: experience points

Endnotes

CHAPTER 1

[1] Annual revenue numbers sourced from SuperData Research. Thank you to Joost van Dreunen for taking the time to answer my questions.

[2] I argued that the $7.5 billion valuation of King was too high and that the value was likely to collapse to closer to $5 billion. It did. See, Nicholas Lovell, *Why I think King's share price will fall by half*, *GAMESbrief*, March 25, 2014. http://www.gamesbrief.com/2014/03/why-i-think-kings-share-price-will-fall-by-half/

[3] Mike Minotti, *Pokémon Go passes $1.2 billion in revenue and 752 million downloads*, *Venturebeat*, June 30, 2017. https://venturebeat.com/2017/06/30/pokemon-go-passes-1-2-billion-in-revenue-and-752-million-downloads/

[4] It is generally a bad idea not to know what business model your game is targeting while developing the game. Michael McWhertor, "Why isn't Overwatch free-to-play, and what are Blizzard's plans for DLC?," *Polygon,* November 7, 2015. https://www.polygon.com/2015/11/7/9688324/overwatch-buy-to-play-blizzard-pricing-model-plans

[5] CFO Blake Jorgensen confirmed these numbers at the NASDAQ 37th Investor Program in December 2017. Sinclair, Brendan, "35% or more of EA Sports players spend on Ultimate Team," *GamesIndustry.biz*, December 5, 2017. http://www.gamesindustry.biz/articles/2017-12-05-35-percent-of-easports- players-spend-on-ultimate-team

[6] Gross margin is the revenue of a product or service, less the direct cost of goods for that product or service. It does not include sales and marketing, or the overheads of the company. For both physical and digital versions of a game, that cost of making the game is the same. But each new copy of the game is much cheaper in digital publishing, since it does not have physical production costs, making the gross margin of digital products much higher. Matthew Handrahan, *EA's Ultimate Team now worth $800 million annually*, *Gamesindustry.biz*, March 1, 2017. http://www.gamesindustry.biz/articles/2017-03-01-eas-ultimate-team-now-worth-USD800-million-annually.

7 "Unity's David Helgason joins UK studio Lockwood Publishing," *GamesIndustry. biz*, December 5, 2017. http://www.gamesindustry. biz/articles/2017-12-05-unitys-david-helgason-joins-uk-studiolockwood-publishing

8 This is one of the most important concepts in this book. It is explored in Chapter 7: The Superfan Layer and in more detail in my book *The Curve* (2013, Portfolio Penguin).

9 Matt Fernandez, "'Star Wars' Video Game Microtransactions Ignite Controversy," *Variety*, November 23, 2017. http://variety.com/2017/digital/news/star-wars-video-game-controversy-microtransaction-loot-box-1202621913/

10 Tristan Donovan, *Replay, The History of Video Games*, 261

11 Fred Wilson, "My Favorite Business Model," *A VC*, March 23, 2006. http://avc.com/2006/03/my_favorite_bus/

12 Blizzard has continued to add new heroes. There are currently 14 male and 8 female characters.

13 Kotaku has a great post from April 2013 on the dangers of relying on Metacritic scores as a measure of a quality and of its use as a tool by publishers in their negotiations with developers. It explains why so many games seem similar: "A developer's priority is sometimes not just to make a *good* game, but to make a game that they think will resonate with reviewers.... Game producers were thus encouraged to identify the elements that reviewers seemed to most notice and most like–detailed graphics, scripted set piece battles, 'robust' online multiplayer, 'player choice,' and more, more of everything," from Jason Schreir, "Metacritic Matters: How Review Scores Hurt Video Games," *Kotaku*, August 8, 2015. http://kotaku.com/metacritic-matters-how-review-scores-hurt-video-games-472462218

14 Wikipedia has a list of the worst video games of all time. There are some real stinkers in here. https://en.wikipedia.org/wiki/List_of_video_games_notable_for_negative_reception

15 For more, see Nicholas Lovell, *How to Publish a Game*, 51, 60–61 and "Ten reasons microtransactions are better than subscriptions," *GAMESbrief*, October 8, 2009. http://www.gamesbrief.com/2009/10/ten-reasons-microtransactions-are-better-than-subscriptions/

16 See Ernest Adams and Joris Dormans, *Game Mechanics: Advanced Game Design* on how to model game mechanics and how to distinguish between games of progression and games of emergence.

17 Larry Frum, "Five years on, millions still dig 'FarmVille,'" *CNN*, July 31, 2014. http://edition.cnn.com/2014/07/31/tech/gaming-gadgets/farmville-fifth-anniversary/

18 Video coverage of the 2010 Game Developer Choice award from GameSpot. Coverage of the Best New Social/Online Game begins at 23'50". http://www.gamespot.com/videos/gdc-2010-game-developerschoice-awards/2300-6253472/

19 Reported in Raph Koster's blog post, *What core gamers should know about social games* http://www.raphkoster.com/2010/03/18/what-core-gamers-should-know-about-social-games/

20 Raph Koster quotes Jesper Juul's definition: "a game is a rule-based formal system with a variable and quantifiable outcome, where different outcomes are assigned different values, the player exerts effort in order to influence the outcome, the player feels attached to the outcome and the consequences of the activity are optional and negotiable." Raph Koster, *A Theory of Fun*, p.13.

21 Raph Koster's blog, *X isn't a game*, https://www.raphkoster.com/2012/03/13/x-isnt-a-game/

22 Raph Koster's blog, *X isn't a game*, https://www.raphkoster.com/2012/03/13/x-isnt-a-game/. *What core gamers should know about social games* http://www.raphkoster.com/2010/03/18/what-core-gamers-should-know-about-social-games/

CHAPTER 2

1 Kent, Stephen L, *The Ultimate History of Video Games*, pp.39–45.

2 Ibid., p.44.

3 Ibid., p.53.

4 Nick Yee, "As Gamers Age, The Appeal of Competition Drops The Most. Strategy is The Most Age-Stable Motivation," February 10, 2016, Quanticy Foundry Blog, http://quanticfoundry.com/2016/02/10/gamer-generation/#post/0

5 This chart is taken from an updated presentation given at GDC 2017. Nick Yee, Quantic Foundry, *The Anatomy of Gamer Motivations*. https://quanticfoundry.com/wp-content/uploads/2017/03/GDC-2017-Slides-Quantic-Foundry.pdf

6 James Batchelor, "Ken Wong: 'Gaming's remit is up for us to challenge,'" *GamesIndustry.biz*, November 1, 2017. http://www.gamesindustry.biz/articles/2017-11-01-ken-wong-gamings-remit-is-up-for-us-to-challenge

7 Ernest Adams, *Game Mechanics: Advanced Game Design*, pp.2–3.

8 Richard Bartle, *Designing Virtual Worlds*, pp.130–141.

9 Richard Bartle, *Designing Virtual Worlds*, p.131.

CHAPTER 3

1 Internally, King has started referring to its Retention and Superfan Layers as the "Envelope" and has dedicated design teams working on it.

2 King S-1 Registration Statement, p.96, https://www.sec.gov/Archives/edgar/data/1580732/000119312514056089/d564433df1.htm

3 Note that the ongoing scrutiny of loot boxes in video games by gambling regulators in many territories is being influenced by this PopCapification. The visual allure of the loot boxes is one of the factors that, for example, the Dutch and Belgian regulators appear to have taken into account when evaluating a range of service games for possible gambling law violations.

4 Blizzard keeps tinkering with its ranking system. Many of the changes seem to be focused on making "ranking up" more forgiving and less time intensive. An example is the creation of rank thresholds that, once achieved, create a safety net for players. For example, they cannot drop back through Rank 10 as a result

of losing matches, only as part of the monthly reset. This encourages players to experiment with new decks when there have just past a safety threshold because there are few negative consequences of losing many games in a row.

5   Tristan Donavan, *Replay, The History of Video Games*, p.116.
6   Erik Hurt, Graduation speech at the University of Chicago, June 2016. http://review.chicagobooth.edu/economics/2016/article/video-killed-radio-star. The speech was based on research that was subsequently published. Mark Aguiar, Mark Bils, Kerwin Kofi Charles, and Erik Hurst, *Leisure Luxuries and the Labor Supply of Young Men*
7   See Chapter 6 in Jamie Madigan, *Getting Gamers*, for more on SDT, or Przybylski, Rigby, and Ryan, *Motivational Model of Video Game Engagement*.
8   You can find out more about gamer motivations at the Quantic Foundry website http://quanticfoundry.com/2015/12/15/handy-reference/
9   Nick Yee, "The Surprising Profile of Idle Clicker Gamers," *Gamasutra* http://www.gamasutra.com/blogs/NickYee/20160708/276661/The_Surprising_Profile_of_Idle_Clicker_Gamers.php (accessed June 12, 2017).
10 TV Tropes, http://tvtropes.org/pmwiki/pmwiki.php/Main/MinMaxing
11 Robert Cialdini, *Influence, The Psychology of Persuasion*.
12 Jamie Madigan, *Getting Gamers*, pp.93–95.
13 Adweek reported that 57.9% of the audience was female, and it tended to be middle aged. "When comparing *Farmville's* age splits with other top apps, the game has a more substantial percentage of users in the 26–35 and the 36–45 age ranges than most other titles we examined." Susan Su, "Who's Using Facebook's Top Apps? Demographic Data Indicate Diverse Audiences," *AdWeek*, June 1, 2010. http://www.adweek.com/digital/whosusing-facebook-top-apps-demographic-data-indicate-diverse-audiences/
14 Cialdini, *Influence, The Psychology of Persuasion*, Chapter 3, Commitment and Consistency.
15 Ian Bogost, "Video Games are Better Without Stories," *The Atlantic*, April 25, 2017. https://www.theatlantic.com/technology/archive/2017/04/video-games stories/524148/
16 Brianna Wu, Twitter, April 25, 2017. https://twitter.com/i/moments/856904137715453953
17 Quoted in Jane Cunningham and Philippa Roberts, *Inside Her Pretty Little Head*.
18 Any approach to allocating behaviours or tendencies to a "male brain" or a "female brain" is fraught with risk. Not all men are the same, nor are all women. Nevertheless, it is worth seeking alternative perspectives, particularly in the game-design discipline that is overwhelmingly staffed by men, and historically, making games for men. Now that the audience is more diverse in age and gender, understanding other motivations beyond the systematizing desire will be critical for commercial success. For initial thoughts on the differences between men and women, see Cunningham and Roberts, *Inside Her Pretty Little Head*.
19 Anna Anthropy, *A Game Design Vocabulary*, p.8.

20 Celia Brayfield, *Bestseller: Secrets of Successful Writing*, p.2.

21 Yuji Nakamura, "Nexon Surges to All-Time High as Annual Profit Outlook Doubles," *Bloomberg*, November 13, 2017. https://www. bloomberg.com/news/articles/2017-11-13/nexon- surges- to-all-time-high as-annual-profit-outlook-doubles

22 Quoted in Madigan, *Getting Gamers*, p.99.

23 Kevin Wong, "The 15 Most Twisted Video Game Achievements," *Kotaku*, January 29, 2016. http://kotaku.com/the-15-most-twisted-achievements-in-gaming-1755499258

24 I cover this issue in more detail in Chapter 14: Marketing Your Launch in the section titled "A note on virality."

CHAPTER 4

1 The description of Occam's Razor is from Wikipedia. The paraphrase is my own.

2 Christopher Vogler's *The Writer's Journey*, a must-read in Hollywood, is a practical guide to applying Campbell's principles in storytelling. Although it is aimed at screenwriters, it is useful for novelists and game designers too.

CHAPTER 5

1 Quoted in Chris Anderson, *Free* (Random House Business Books, 2009), p.180.

2 2017 global mobile consumer survey: US edition, Deloitte. https://www2. deloitte.com/us/en/pages/technology-media-and-telecommunications/articles/global-mobile-consumer-survey-us-edition.html

3 comScore Custom Survey, June 2013, presented at MMA Mobile Gaming, July 17, 2013, London, *Mobile Gaming Trends—UK Insights.*

4 "Who Plays Mobile Games and When?," *Verto Company Blog,* May 21, 2015. http://www.vertoanalytics.com/who-plays-mobile-games-and-when/

5 Ibid.

6 PopCap's franchise business manager for *Bejeweled Blitz*, Giordano Bruno Contestabile, revealed these figures in his 2012 GDC talk.

7 *Jagged Alliance 2* remains my favourite game of all time. I complete it about once a year. Thank you to everyone involved in making it.

8 Allen Rausch, "'World of Warcraft' review," *GameSpy*, http://pc.gamespy.com/pc/world-of-warcraft/571585p1.html

CHAPTER 6

1 I recommend books by Anna Anthropy and Naomi Clark, *A Game Design Vocabulary*; Katie Salen and Eric Zimmerman, *Rules of Play*; Jesse Schell, *A Book of Lenses*; and Raph Koster, *A Theory of Fun.*

2 Interview with female, mid-40s *Candy Crush Saga* player.

3 If you ever meet me in real life, I prefer coffee and walnut cake. It's too much of a mouthful to use as a metaphor.

4. Nicholas Lovell, "SP-elling it out. How balancing your players on an 'SP' knife edge is the secret to social games success," *GAMESBrief*, http://www. gamesbrief.com/2011/03/sp-elling-it-out-how-balancing-your-players-onan-sp-knife-edge-is-the-secret-to-social-games-success/

5. Nick Wingfield, "Free Video Games Say Pay Up or Wait, Testing Players' Patience," *New York Times,* July 5, 2015. https://www.nytimes. com/2014/07/06/technology/free-video-games-say-pay-up-or-wait-testing-players-patience.html

6. http://tvtropes.org/pmwiki/pmwiki.php/Main/MinMaxing

7. John Geirland, "Go with the flow." *Wired*, September, 1996. Issue 4.09. https://www.wired.com/wired/archive/4.09/czik_pr.html

8. Search YouTube for "pigeons ping pong" if you want to see a video of the original experiment.

9. Quantic Foundry has a handy reference guide to its Gamer Motivation Model on its website. https://quanticfoundry.com/2015/12/15/handy-reference/

10. $60 quinvigintillion is $460,000,000,000,000,000,000,000,000,000,000, 000,000,000,000,000,000,000,000,000,000,000,000,000,000,000. *Adventure Capitalist* has a weird relationship with money.

11. "Complexity in layers" is a key concept in my work, and Rule 4 in my book *Design Rules for F2P Games*.

12. Michael Katkoff's analysis can be found on his website at www.deconstructoroffun. com

13. Jon Jordan, "Carrots and sticks: How F2P designers should balance wither and daily rewards," *PocketGamer.biz*, November 26, 2014. http://www.pocketgamer.biz/mobile-mavens/60423/how-f2p-designers-should-balancewither-and-daily-rewards/

CHAPTER 7

1. "Swrve Finds 0.15% of Mobile Gamers Contribute 50% of All In-Game Revenue," *Swrve Company Blog,* February 26, 2014. https://www. swrve. com/company/press/swrve-finds-015-of-mobile-gamers-contribute-50-of-all-in-game-revenue

2. US median wealth figures sourced from the US Census 2011. Exclude pension and life insurance wealth as well as home furnishings and jewellery.

3. Jennifer Calfas, "The Richest People in the World," *Time*, November 27, 2017. http://time.com/money/4746795/richest-people-in-the-world/

4. "The Biggest Gamblers In Las Vegas History," *Vegas Guy.* https://www.vegasguy.com/casinos/high-rollers-whales/

5. In a heart-breaking article, the BBC suggests that Japan only continues commercial whaling because a bureaucracy has been created to support it even though there is little demand for whale meat in the country. Rupert Wingfield-Hayes, "Japan and the whale," *BBC*, February 8, 2016. http://www.bbc.co.uk/news/world-asia-35397749

6. Kongregate publishes many of its conference presentations and other research material on its developer blog at https://blog.kongregate.com/

7 Emily Greer, "Don't Call Them Whales: F2P Spenders and Virtual Value", March 4, 2015. https://blog.kongregate.com/dont-call-them-whales-f2p-spenders-and-virtual-value/

8 Not only are Killers easiest to monetise, they are often in positions of authority within the game industry. Competitive people often end up as CEOs, heads of sales or as investors. That is one of the reasons that there are so many games in existence that appeal to Killers: the executives who authorise the funds to make games are disproportionately Killers.

9 Ryan Rigney, "These Guys $5k Spending Sprees Keep Your Games Free to Play," *Wired*, November 1, 2012. https://www.wired.com/2012/11/meet-the-whales/

10 For research for the book, I tried to track down the original source of this anecdote. The only references I can find are to me telling the anecdote in presentations or interviews. If any reader can help to confirm the authenticity of the story, please get in touch.

11 I consulted to CCP on the transition from subscription to F2P.

12 Flora Graham, "The struggle among the stars," *BBC*, February 23, 2009. http://news.bbc.co.uk/1/hi/technology/7905924.stm

13 Richard Garfield, "Metagames," 2000. https://edt210gamestechsociety.files.wordpress.com/2013/09/2000-garfieldmetagame.Pdf

14 Chris Bateman, "Metagame versus Structure," International hobo blog, July 19, 2017. http://blog.ihobo.com/2017/07/metagame-vs-structure.html

CHAPTER 8

1 I cover much more about the role of virtual goods and social status in *The Curve,* particularly Chapter 8 on Gawkers and Chapter 9 on Superfans.

2 Source via Wikipedia. https://en.wikipedia.org/wiki/Decline_of_newspapers#cite_note-NAAdata-76

3 Tim Wu, *The Attention Merchants.* Wu has written an excellent book looking at how we, as a society, go through cycles of letting businesses dominate our attention—through new media channels ranging from outdoor advertising to television to the Internet—followed by a period of backlash. He argues that we are currently living through a period of backlash, and that the rising concerns about privacy, surveillance and that "if you are not paying for a product, you are the product" are symptomatic of this consumer revolt.

4 Thank you to Elizabeth Cunningham, Jay Margalus, Zoya Street, Rob Fahey, and Heather Cotton for being that help.

5 Elisabeth Donnelly, "How Amazon and 'Fifty Shades of Grey' Created a Golden Age for Self-Published Romance Authors—and Why It May Already Be Over," *Flavorwire*, February 13, 2015. http://flavorwire.com/504084/how-amazon-and-fifty-shades-of-grey-created-a-goldenage-for-self-published-romance-authors-and-why-it-may-already-beover

6 For more on the impact of the free price point in the App Store, see Nicholas Lovell, *The Curve*, Chapter 3: Competition, Economics and a Man called Bertrand.

7 Apple Press Release, January 5, 2017, "App Store shatters records on New Year's Day," https://www.apple.com/newsroom/2017/01/app-store-shattersrecords-on-new-years-day.html

8 Nicholas Lovell, *The Curve*, p.45.

9 Justin Davis, "The Ridiculous Launch of the iPhone App Store," *IGN*, July 17, 2012. http://uk.ign.com/articles/2012/07/18/the-ridiculous-launch-ofthe-iphone -app-store

10 Ibid.

11 Apple removed the top-grossing charts in iOS 11 as part of its redesign of the App Store.

12 When the App Store launched, only paid apps were able to include in-app purchases. Developers who wanted to offer a preview version of their app had to off a "Lite" version for a free and a separate, paid app to generate revenue. This made it hard to, for example, charge for an upgrade to a premium version, or to turn off advertising in the app. Apple relented in October 2009, leading to an explosion in the number of free and free-to-play apps. Erica Sadun, "Apple relents: In-app purchase for free apps allows demo-topaid" *Engadget*, October 15, 2009. https://www.engadget.com/2009/10/15/apple-relents-in-app-purchase-for-free-apps-allows-demo-to-paid/

13 For more on this topic, read Nicholas Lovell, *The Curve*, p.114, and Geoffrey Miller, *The Mating Mind*.

14 I use Facebook as a shortcut for all social networks, because it is the largest. The trend towards virtual goods emerged in many subcultures first: video games like *Maple Story*, chat rooms like IMVU, early messaging systems, etc.

15 This is a game developer. When he dresses up, he still wears jeans and a T-shirt.

16 Dude, Where's My Digital Car, *Business Week*, 2005, quoted in Nicholas Lovell, *The Curve*.

17 The spelling mistake, "deserv," was in the original.

18 "How to Charge $1,000 for Absolutely Nothing," Priceonomics, https://priceonomics. com/how-to-charge-s1000-for-absolutely-nothing/

19 "Doing Free to Play Wrong: How Bad Monetization Harms F2P Games," *Extra Creditz*, Series 8, Episode 9. https://www.youtube.com/watch?v=Mhz9OXy86a0

20 Rani Molla, "Mobile is driving most ad spending growth worldwide," *Recode*, September 14, 2017. https://www.recode.net/2017/9/14/16294450/mobile-ad-spending-growth-worldwide

21 For more on the value of freeloaders, see tools 17, 19, 38, 39, 41, and 42 in Nicholas Lovell, *The F2P Toolbox and Chapters 7 & 8 of The Curve*. For an

extensive discussion of why self-expression and altruism have evolutionary benefits, see Geoffrey Miller, *The Mating Mind.*

22 RockYou's strategy is to acquire games that are "past their apex" and to continue to run them, because these games have very long-lasting and dedicated user bases that monetize for years, making them very profitable over the long run, according to CEO Lisa Marino in a company blog post. She likens their strategy as being like a cable channel, acquiring older shows and giving them an additional lease of life, while freeing up content creators to invest in the next potential big hit. "The RockYou Solution to Gaming's One Hit Wonder Problem," RockYou Blog, April 3, 2014. http://rockyou.com/the-rockyou-solution-to-gamings-one-hit-wonder-problem

CHAPTER 9

1 Wesley Yin-Poole "The *Legacy of Kain* game that was cancelled three years in," *Eurogamer,* May, 27, 2016, http://www.eurogamer.net/articles/2016-05-27-the-legacy-of-kain-game-square-enix-cancelled-after-three-years-of-work

2 Jason Schreir. "Why Are Game Developer Bonuses Based on Review Scores?" *Kotaku,* March 15, 2012. https://kotaku.com/5893595/why-are-game-developer-bonuses-based-on-review-scores

3 Lee Bradley, "Punching below its weight: The making of Punch Quest", PocketGamer.biz, November 28, 2012. https://www.pocketgamer.biz/feature/46887/punching-below-its-weight-the-making-of-punch-quest

4 Jared Nelson, "Amid slumping revenue, *Punch Quest* switches to a paid game," *Touch Arcade,* November 14, 2012. http://toucharcade.com/2012/11/14/amid-slumping-revenue-punch-quest-switches-to-a-paid-game/

5 Eli Hodapp, "'Punch Quest' Review, a Flawless Free-to-Play Victory." http://toucharcade.com/2012/10/26/punch-quest-review/

6 Punch Quest reverted to free-to-play, on Android at least, in November 2014.

7 Kent, *The Ultimate History of Video Games,* pp.238–240. Kent is excellent on this phase of the video-game industry, with detailed interviews from senior executives from Atari at the time.

8 The full story is covered brilliantly in *Masters of Doom: How Two Guys Created an Empire and Transformed Pop Culture* by David Kushner, which I highly recommend.

9 Nicholas Lovell, "Top Turkeys from the Noughties—part 2," *GAMESbrief,* January 18, 2010. http://www.gamesbrief.com/2010/01/top-turkeys-fromthe-noughties-part-2/

10 Wesley Yin-Poole's detailed feature on Lionhead is an excellent read. I hope they turn his collection of long pieces like this into a book. http://www.eurogamer.net/articles/2016-05-12-lionhead-the-inside-story

11 Allegra, Frank, "Legacy of Kain spinoff Nosgoth is shutting down," *Polygon,* April 8, 2016. https://www.polygon.com/2016/4/8/11392984/legacy-of-kain-nosgoth-shutdown-date

12   It is common for a brand contract to require upfront payments. This might include a payment on signature and a payment when the game is launched (and, if the lawyers are smart, "launch" means hard launch, not soft launch.) My hunch is that Scopely looked at the performance of the game and decided that triggering a guaranteed payment to its brand partner, on top of the risk and cost of launching the game on a global basis, was not worth it.

13   Ben Fritz, "Video game borrows page from Hollywood playbook," *Los Angeles Times*, November 18, 2009. http://articles.latimes.com/2009/nov/18/business/fi-ct-duty18

14   According to David Anfossi, Studio Director, Eidos Montreal, quoted in https://www.gamesindustry.biz/articles/2018-05-11-eidos-montreal-wehave-to-try-new-models-for-single-player-games

15   http://supercell.com/en/our-story/

16   Hollywood is partially to blame for this, with movies like *The Social Network* focusing on who had the idea, as if that is the heart of startup success. If you want to watch a movie with a realistic portrayal of startup life, watch *Ghostbusters*.

17   Dean Takahashi, "How Supercell kills its darlings to focus on potential hits," *Venturebeat*, November 15, 2016. https://venturebeat.com/2016/11/15/how-supercell-kills-its-darlings-to-focus-on-potential-hits/

18   Eric Ries, *The Lean Startup*, 2011, Crown Business, p.27.

19   Steve Blank, "What's A Startup? First Principles," *Steve Blank blog*, January 25, 2010. https://steveblank.com/2010/01/25/whats-a-startup-first-principles/

20   Answer to the question "What is the proper definition of a startup?" on Quora. https://www.quora.com/What-is-the-proper-definition-of-a-startup/ answer/Dave-McClure?srid=InUP

21   William Goldman, *Adventures in the Screen Trade* (Abacus, 1996; first published in 1983). Goldman was the screenwriter of *Butch Cassidy and the Sundance Kid, Marathon Man,* and *The Princess Bride. Adventures in the Screen Trade* is a terrific read because Goldman punctures the myth that there are experts out there who really know what they are doing. Reading his book has helped me see that nobody knows anything. All we can really do is try to learn, as fast and as cheaply as possible.

22   You can read the details of the avatar system that no one else could see in Chapter 8, pp.139–140.

23   Ben Kuchera, "Leaks, riots and monocles: How a $60 in-game item almost destroyed Eve Online," *Ars Technica*, July 11, 2011. https://arstechnica.com/gaming/2011/07/monocles/

24   Justin McElroy, "Microsoft's checkered history of gaming acquisitions, from Bungie to Minecraft," *Polygon*, September 15, 2014. https://www.polygon. com/2014/9/15/6153109/microsoft-minecraft-acquisitions

25   Wesley Yin-Poole, "Lionhead: The inside story," *Eurogamer*, May 12, 2016. http://www.eurogamer.net/articles/2016-05-12-lionhead-the-inside-story

26   Matthew Handrahan, Garriott awarded $32m in NCsoft contract dispute, *GamesIndustry.biz*, October 26, 2011, http://www.gamesindustry.biz/articles/2011-10-26-garriott-awarded-USD32m-in-ncsoft-contract-dispute

CHAPTER 10

1. David Ogilvy, *Ogilvy on Advertising.*
2. Eric Ries, *The Lean Startup*, pp.38–47. *The Lean Startup* is an inspirational read, even though many of its tenets, revolutionary less than a decade ago, are now accepted in the mainstream of both technology development and startup management.
3. Eric Ries, *The Lean Startup*, p.41.
4. Ibid, p.47.
5. Ibid, p.47.
6. In January 2012, shortly after *The Lean Startup* was published, I was lucky enough to spend a day at a masterclass given by Eric Ries in Dublin as part of the Irish Government's Internet Growth Accelerator Programme where I was lecturing to their games cohort. Most of the information about *The Lean Startup* is drawn from the book but some is drawn from the masterclass.
7. Chris Wilkins and Roger M. Kean, *Ocean, the History*, pp.13–17.
8. Chris Wilkins and Roger M. Kean, *Let's Go Dizzy, The Story of the Oliver Twins*. For the background to *Fast Food*, pp.94–95. On page 77, you can see a Gallup chart with 5 of the top 10 games developed by the Olivers and published by Codemasters. The whole book is an excellent read on the history of 8- and 16-bit computing through the lens of one very prolific team. The book was crowdfunded, and I was a backer.
9. Gary Marshall, "App Store millionaires share their secrets," *TechRadar*, February 5, 2009. http://www.techradar.com/news/phone-and-communications/ other-phones/app-store-millionaires-share-their-secrets-524586/2
10. Brian X. Chen, "Coder's Half-Million-Dollar Baby Proves iPhone Gold Rush Is Still On," *Wired*, February 12, 2009. https://www.wired.com/2009/02/ shoot-is-iphone/
11. David Kushner, "The Flight of the Birdman: Flappy Bird Creator Dong Nguyen Speaks Out," *Rolling Stone*, March 11, 2014. http://www.rollingstone. com/ culture/news/the-flight-of-the-birdman-flappy-bird-creatordong-nguyen-speaks-out-20140311
12. Nicholas Lovell, *The Curve*, pp.18–19. There are many other examples of selfpublished authors whose output is similarly prolific.
13. Because most public companies are owned by institutional investors, and most institutional investors get the money they use to invest from our pensions and our insurance premia, it does in fact hurt ordinary people when companies are profligate like this. But the pain is so diffused and so far away from the decision makers that it is an ineffective feedback loop.
14. *Star Citizen*, the crowd-funded game that had raised more than $140 million by the start of 2017 without hitting a single release date it had set itself, hired all of these people for the trailer of its spinoff title, *Star Citizen Squadron 42*. See Paul Tassi, "Star Citizen" Lumbers into 2017 with $141 Million in Crowdfunding', *Forbes*, January 9, 2017. https://www.forbes.com/sites/

insertcoin/2017/01/09/star-citizen-lumbers-into-2017-with-141-million-in-crowdfunding/#5669f1c2ebc0 For full cast list, see IMDB, http://www.imdb.com/title/tt5194726/

15 This is not an actual quote. Although if you look through any number of failed attempts by AAA studios to make mobile or F2P games, you will find this attitude entrenched throughout all of their early press announcements.

16 Image courtesy of IDEO.

17 Jimmy Maher, "Elite (or, The Universe on 32K Per Day)," *The Digital Antiquarian*. December 26, 2013. http://www.filfre.net/2013/12/elite/

18 Brad King and John Borland, *Dungeons and Dreamers, The rise of Computer Game Culture from Geek to Chic*. Chapter 5 explores the origins of Doom. The whole book looks at the interlocking fortunes of *Ultima* creator, Origin Systems, and *Doom* creator, id software.

19 I fear the outcome of this project. I believe that *Star Citizen* may be the product that tests the edges of consumer protection in crowdfunding, as well as the edges of consumer faith. Funding *Star Citizen* has become a game in its own right, with achievements, levelling up, and leader-boards. Chris Roberts and his team have created a tsunami of anticipation for their product. If it fails to live up to its height, disappointed gamers are likely to howl with rage and then look for redress. I think that *Star Citizen* may become a test case for the courts in how the promises made during a crowdfunding campaign should be treated in law. If not *Star Citizen*, then another project. But my money is on it being *Star Citizen*.

20 At the time of writing, Garriott is back raising money. The Kickstarter and crowdfunding to date has been for the *development* of *Shroud of the Avatar: Forsaken Virtues*. Now he is raising further funds through equity crowd-funding, where backers own a stake in the company, rather than placing a pre-order on a product that has not been made yet, to *publish* the game, with a particular focus on marketing costs.

21 There is a good list of successful Kickstarters on Wikipedia at https://en.wikipedia.org/wiki/List_of_highest_funded_crowdfunding_projects. I have backed a number of successful video game Kickstarters including *Double Fine Adventure, Elite Dangerous, Torment, Tides of Numenera,* and *Terratech*. I have also very much enjoyed games that were Kickstarted, but I did not back, such as *FTL* (where Steam tells me that I have played for 396 hours) and *Convoy*.

22 Kickstarter Update #9, *Dizzy Returns*, December 12, 2012. https://www.kickstarter.com/projects/theolivertwins/dizzy-returns/posts/367677

23 Wesley Yin-Poole, "Oliver twins announce Dizzy Returns Kickstarter two decades after the last original Dizzy game," *Eurogamer*, November 23, 2012. http://www.eurogamer.net/articles/2012-11-23-oliver-twins-announ-cedizzy-returns-kickstarter-two-decades-after-the-last-original-dizzy-game

[24] Kickstarter Update #11, *Alpha Colony,* December 4, 2012. https://www.kickstarter.com/projects/dreamquest/alpha-colony-an-exploration-building-andtrading-g/posts/361744

[25] Ric Cowley, "Rovio cancels *Angry Birds Football* after seven months in soft launch," *PocketGamer.biz,* November 14, 2016. http://www.pocketgamer.biz/news/64419/rovio-cancels-angry-birds-football/

[26] Ric Cowley, "Rovio cancels Angry Birds Football after seven months in soft launch," *PocketGamer.biz,* November 14, 2016. http://www.pocketgamer.biz/news/64419/rovio-cancels-angry-birds-football/

[27] I wrote a detailed piece on the demise of *Real Time Worlds* on my blog in August 2010. Nicholas Lovell, "Hubris, ambition and mismanagement: the first post-mortem of *RealTime Worlds*," *GAMESbrief,* August 18, 2010. http://www.gamesbrief.com/2010/08/hubris-ambition-and-mismanagement-the-first-post-mortem-of-realtime-worlds/

[28] I originally wrote this in April 2014 on *GAMESbrief.* I have subsequently changed the definition of a Minimum Desirable Product from "a designer's definition" to "a marketer's definition." I think the focus on marketing is a more useful way of thinking about desirability. The designer should be focused on the Minimum Awesome Product. Nicholas Lovell, "Make a Minimum Awesome Product," *GAMESbrief,* April 1, 2014. http://www.gamesbrief.com/2014/04/make-a-minimum-awesome-product/

CHAPTER 11

[1] "Well Done!" messages are important. As a society, we are moving away from punishment, and towards rewards. As game designers, that is happening even faster. The instant death and painful restarts of early consoles and 8-bit computers have given way to endless retries and games that try not to kill you. Even games that do, like *Temple Run,* congratulate you with a "Well done!" just after it has played a death animation. A traditional arcade game would instead have hit you with a "Game over! You died! You suck!" message.

[2] SpryFox founders David Edery, Daniel Cook, and Ryan Williams gave a great talk on how to prototype at the Game Developers Conference in 2013. http://www.gdcvault.com/play/1018263/How-to-Make-an-Original

[3] Eric Ries, *The Lean Startup,* p.47.

[4] In 2005, Cook wrote a long post on his blog at Lost Garden titled *Common Game Prototyping Pitfalls.* The whole post is well worth reading. Daniel Cook, "Common game prototyping pitfalls," *Lost Garden,* August 21, 2005. http:// www.lostgarden.com/2005/08/common-game-prototyping-pitfalls.html

[5] https://en.oxforddictionaries.com/definition/scientific_method

[6] There are weaknesses in the method. Nobel-prize–winning physicist Max Planck said (in a famous paraphrase) that, "science advances one funeral at a time." In an academic paper, *Does Science Advance One Funeral at a Time?* (NBER Working Paper No. 21788), Pierre Azoulay, Christian Fons-Rosen,

and Joshua S. Graff Zivin examined the theory and found that research diversity and progress did indeed occur more rapidly and frequently after the early death of a "superstar" academic in the field.

7 Michael Arrington, "Zynga Accuses Playdom of Stealing Trade Secrets; Judge Issues Temporary Restraining Order," *TechCrunch*, September 10, 2009. https://techcrunch.com/2009/09/10/zynga-accuses-playdom-ofstealing-trade-secrets-judge-issues-temporary-restraining-order/

8 The hits were *Hay Day* (2012), *Clash of Clans* (2012), *Boom Beach* (2014), and *Clash Royale* (2016). Thank you to Jon Jordan for verifying this for me and for describing Supercell's approach: "It ruthlessly killed its non-hits before they became failures."

CHAPTER 12

1 KickStarter, *Double Fine Adventure*, February 9, 2012. https://www.kickstarter.com/projects/doublefine/double-fine-adventure

2 See Eric Ries, *The Lean Startup* for the principles of the Lean movement and Ries, Eric, *The Startup Way* for how to apply the principles of entrepreneurship in large organisations.

3 Mike Schramm, *GDC 2010: ngMoco's Neil Young on how freemium will change the App Store World*, *Engadget*, March 15, 2010. https://www.engadget.com/2010/03/15/gdc-2010-ngmocos-neil-young-on-how-freemium-will-change-the-ap/

4 Balazd Szatmari, "We Are (all) the Champions: The Effect of Status in the Implementation of Innovations." *ERIM Ph. D. Series Research in Management.* Erasmus University Rotterdam, 2016. http://hdl.handle.net/1765/94633

CHAPTER 13

1 Edward De Bono, *Six Thinking Hats,* pp.1–3.

2 Ibid., p.2.

3 Ibid., pp.13–14. The de Bono company runs courses and training in Six Thinking Hats approaches.

4 Ibid., pp.8–9.

5 Ed Catmull, *Creativity, Inc.*, pp.18–19.

6 Since I wrote this section, John Lasseter, Catmull's cofounder at Pixar, has left Disney in the wake of the #MeToo campaign. *Variety* wrote a detailed, sourced article suggesting that the issues with Lasseter had been known for 20 years. My respect for Catmull's creative management skills has diminished given that he was complicit in a culture that may have done great creative work, but also enabled a difficult, challenging environment for women. I still recommend reading *Creativity, Inc.,* but the context has changed. See Gene Maddaus, "Pixar's John Lasseter Was the Subject of a 'Whisper Network' for More Than Two Decades," *Variety*, November 21, 2017. https://variety.com/2017/film/news/john-lasseter-pixar-disney-whisper-network-1202620960/

⁷ Ed Catmull, *Creativity, Inc.*, pp.102–103.

⁸ Ibid., p.132.

⁹ The quote is attributed to US novelist Jane Smiley, whose novel *A Thousand Acres* won a Pulitzer Prize in 1992.

CHAPTER 14

¹ "Annual income twenty pounds, annual expenditure nineteen [pounds] nineteen [shillings] and six [pence], result happiness. Annual income twenty pounds, annual expenditure twenty pounds ought and six, result misery," Charles Dickens, *David Copperfield*.

² I paraphrase. You should read Koster's book, *A Theory of Fun*, if you want to know more.

³ The best book I have read on strategy is Richard Rummelt's *Good Strategy, Bad Strategy*. He argues that a successful strategy needs a clear kernel of three parts: a *diagnosis* of the problem, the *guiding principle* that you are going to adopt in addressing the problem, and *coherent actions*, the specific steps that you are going to take to address the problem. He emphasises that you need all three elements to form a strategy, and the actions need to be *coherent*: they need to work together to deliver on the main goal. I have found using all three layers of Rummelt's kernel has clarified the problem for dozens of my clients.

⁴ "Plants vs. Zombies 2 Sprouts Big Numbers," *Electronic Arts Company website*, August 30, 2013. https://www.ea.com/news/plants-vs-zombies-2-sproutsbig-numbers

⁵ Natalie Robemed, "Kim Kardashian West's Earnings: $51 Million in 2016," *Forbes*, November 16, 2016, https://www.forbes.com/sites/natalierobehmed/2016/11/16/kim-kardashian-wests-earnings-51-millionin-2016/#51f12f8d6a5b

⁶ In 2010, I predicted the industry would shake out into three parts: A few blockbuster publishers, plenty of service-game companies, and a renaissance of indies. Eight years later, that's looking like a pretty good prediction. Nicholas Lovell, "The future of the games industry? It's in three parts." *GAMESbrief.* October 13, 2010, http://www.gamesbrief.com/2010/10/the-future-of-the-games-industry-its-in-three-parts/

⁷ Nicholas Lovell, "Free-to-play marketing costs rise and profitability falls at King and Supercell," *GAMESbrief*, March 24, 2015, http://www.gamesbrief.com/2015/03/free-to-play-marketing-costs-rise-and-profitability-falls-atking-and-supercell/

⁸ Eric Seufert, *Freemium Economics: Leveraging Analytics and User Segmentation to Drive Revenue*, pp.218–219.

⁹ There is a good reason to read reviews before you download a game. Our time on this planet is scarce, and although we can replenish our finances, we can't get back hours spent finding a game we like. Unfortunately, most of society seems to value money over time, which seems like an odd prioritization to me. Maybe it is worth reading a review for a couple of minutes, rather than investing an hour to see if you like a game. Few people seem to do this though.

10 Mike Schramm, "Tiny Tower picks up a million downloads in four days," *Engadget,* June 28, 2011. https://www.engadget.com/2011/06/28/tiny-tower-picks-up-a-million-downloads-in-four-days/

11 "Iron Maiden Mascot Eddie Invades Angry Birds Evolution," Rovio press release, October 16, 2017. http://www.rovio.com/news/iron-maiden-mascot-eddie-invades-angry-birds-evolution

12 I covered more on these topics in Nicholas Lovell, *How to Publish a Game.*

13 The first example of this gifting may have been *(lil) Green Patch,* a simple farming game that went to #1 on Facebook in 2008. Brett Terrill, "How to Make a Successful Social Game: Use Gifting," *Brett on Social Games,* September 25, 2008. http://www.bretterrill.com/2008/09/how-to-makesuccessful-social-game-use.html

14 You can see a 30-second clip of *Airplane!* showing this scene on YouTube. https://www.youtube.com/watch?v=qse_wf57tZM

15 Hannah Jane Parkinson, "'Candy Crush(ed)': Zuckerberg pledges to halt Facebook game invitations," *The Guardian,* October 28, 2015. https://www.theguardian.com/technology/2015/oct/28/candy-crush-zuckerbergfacebook-game-invitations

16 Interviewed on *The Jonathan Ross Show,* November 10, 2012. Psy's next single was called *Gentlemen.* The people, they did it again—a bit.

CHAPTER 15

1 These parameters are drawn from Quora in 2016 and may not age well. The industry has done well at moving metrics upwards. It may be that in five years, these estimates will look laughably low. https://www.quora.com/Whats-the-range-of-typical-ARPDAU-for-mobile-games

2 Sorry.

3 All the evidence suggest Henry Ford never said this. *Harvard Business Review* says so. Patrick Vlaskovitz, "Henry Ford, Innovation, and That 'Faster Horse' Quote," *Harvard Business Review,* August 29, 2011.

4 Chunka Mui, "Five Dangerous Lessons to Learn from Steve Jobs," *Forbes,* October 17, 2011. https://www.forbes.com/sites/chunkamui/2011/10/17/five-dangerous-lessons-to-learn-from-steve-jobs/#63852d4b3a95

5 Ben Kuchera, "Adding multiplayer to a huge video game takes longer than a week," *Polygon,* August 17, 2016. https://www.polygon.com/2016/8/17/12504244/no-mans-sky-multiplayer-difficulty

6 Do they have moles in Nepal? They seem like quintessentially British mammals to me, probably due to the character of Mole in *Toad of Toad Hall.*

7 Joseph Stromberg, "Why cars went from boxy in the '80s to curvy in the '90s," *Vox,* August 29, 2016, https://www.vox.com/2015/6/11/8762373/car-design-curves

8 Molyneux could get more column inches that almost any other game developer due to his unparalleled ability to know what the press wanted to hear, followed by grovelling apologies and self-flagellation when he could not deliver on his ideas. This skill is less important in the era of diminished press relevance.

9 Jason Schreier, "The Story Behind Mass Effect: Andromeda's Troubled Five-Year Development," *Kotaku*, June 7, 2017. https://kotaku.com/the-story-behind-mass-effect-andromedas-troubled-five-1795886428

10 I am not arguing that games need to be small. Although some games, like *Portal* or *Dear Esther*, are short experiences, others can be vast and expansive. All can benefit from high-quality feedback to smooth out the rough edges, and to tighten the links between the different gameplay systems or mechanics to create a richer, more satisfying experience.

11 Eric Ries, *The Lean Startup*, p.143.

12 This is worth doing, but is not guaranteed to work. You may simply move the churn moment later. Sometimes, a player is just not into you.

13 "Cuphead Gamescom Demo: Dean's Shameful 26 Minutes of Gameplay," *YouTube*, August 24, 2017. https://www.youtube.com/watch?v=848Y1Uu5Htk

14 Jose Abalos, "Common Pitfalls in Game Tutorials," *Gamasutra*, September 5, 2017. https://www.gamasutra.com/blogs/JoseAbalos/20170905/304995/Common_Pitfalls_in_Game_Tutorials.php

15 "Cuphead Goes Platinum," *Studio MDHR blog*, October 13, 2017. http://studiomdhr.com/cuphead-goes-platinum/

16 For more on complexity in layers, I recommend my e-book *Design Rules for F2P Games*, which I wrote with Rob Fahey and is available on Kindle or via www.gamesbrief.com.

17 For more on this topic, read Raph Koster, *A Theory of Fun*.

18 As Ries says in *The Lean Startup*, "For a report to be considered actionable, it must demonstrate clear cause and effect. Otherwise, it is just a vanity metric." As your game gets older, it will get ever harder to identify the cause of increases in your lifetime conversion. Daily or monthly conversion is a more useful analytical tool. Ries, *The Lean Startup*, p.143.

19 http://www.gamesbrief.com/2011/11/conversion-rate/

20 I capture a lot of conversion rate metrics on GAMESbrief at http://www.gamesbrief.com/2011/11/conversion-rate/

21 Hat tip to Jak Marshall of Electric Square for this naming suggestion.

CHAPTER 16

1 Byron Atkinson-Jones, "Opinion: The Kids Are F2P," *Develop*, June 21 2017. http://www.develop-online.net/opinions/opinion-the-kids-are-freeto-play/0233697

2 The whole of my book *The Curve*, published in 2013, was about this topic.

3 I am indebted to Tristan Donovan's marvellous book *Replay, The History of Video Games* for information on the development of the Korean and Chinese gaming markets.

4 Tim Ingham, "Global record industry income drops below \$15bn for first time in decades," *Music Business Worldwide*, April 14, 2015. https://www.musicbusinessworldwide.com/global-record-industry-income-dropsbelow-15bn-for-first-time-in-history/

5 Chris Bateman, *The Virtuous Cyborg*, Chapter 1.

6 This may just have been my experience in the pub. When I was a student. I recall that the first £1 coin of each game lasted for a long time. The next four or five would disappear in a heartbeat.

7 See discussion of Zynga's Playbook in Chapter 11, pp.198.

8 Nicholas Lovell, "Five reasons why FTL is a perfect free-to-play game," *GAMESbrief*, January 30, 2013. http://www.gamesbrief.com/2013/01/five-reasons-why-ftl-is-a-perfect-free-to-play-game/

9 For the record, I love *FTL* as a paid game, and Steam has logged that I have spent more than 400 hours playing it.

10 Jamie Madigan, *Getting Gamers*. I won't reference a single chapter here because Madigan's entire book is about this issue.

11 Luke Plunkett, "Hawaii Wants to Fight the 'Predatory Behavior' of Loot Boxes," *Kotaku*, November 21, 2017. https://kotaku.com/hawaii-wants-to-fight-the-predatory-behavior-of-loot-1820664617

12 Official petition hosted by Parliament. "Adapt gambling laws to include gambling in video games which targets children." https://petition.parliament.uk/petitions/201300. The UK government responded in detail, and concluded, "The government recognises the risks that come from increasing convergence between gambling and video games. The Gambling Commission is keeping this matter under review and will continue to monitor developments in the market."

13 Since this book was written, publishers included Square Enix, Activision Blizzard, Valve and NCSoft have either removed loot boxes from games in Belgium, or removed the games from the Belgian market entirely.

14 Dan Ariely gives a great example of students queuing to be part of a lottery to get tickets for basketball at Duke University. The winners of the lottery were not prepared to sell their tickets for less than $2,400. The losers were not prepared to buy for more than $175. The disconnect that possession created was enormous. Dan Ariely, *Predictably Irrational*, 127–133.

15 35 year-old father-of-three Brian Vigneault, known as Poshybrid, died during a 24-hour-long gaming marathon, playing World of Tanks to raise money for charity. Kayleen Devlin, "The mysterious death of a livestreaming gamer," *BBC*, March 11, 2017 http://www.bbc.co.uk/news/blogs-trending-39232620

16 *Daily Telegraph* headline, March 4, 2015.

17 B. J. Fogg, *Persuasive Technology: Using Computers to Change What We Think and Do*, 214–215.

18 Adam Saltsman, "Contrivance and Extortion: In-App Purchases & Microtransactions," *Gamasutra*, October 18, 2011. https://www.gamasutra.com/blogs/AdamSaltsman/20111018/8685/Contrivance_and_Extortion_InApp_Purchases__Microtransactions.php

19 Chapter 9, The Ethics of Persuasive Technology in B. J. Fogg, *Persuasive Technology*.

20 I once commented to my history tutor that the fighting orders such as the Knights Hospitaller were law-abiding, because they had issued so many rules forbidding gambling, drinking and whoring. "If they are so law-abiding," he asked, "why did the authorities feel the need to keep issuing the rules?"

Bibliography

Adams, Ernest, *Fundamentals of Game Design*, Third Edition. (New Riders, 2014).

Adams, Ernest and Dorman, Joris, *Game Mechanics: Advanced Game Design* (New Riders, 2012).

Anderson, Chris, *Free* (Random House Business Books, 2009).

Anthropy, Anna and Clark, Naomi, *A Game Design Vocabulary* (Addison-Wesley, 2014).

Ariely, Dan, *Predictably Irrational* (Harper, 2009).

Azoulary, Pierre, Christian Fons-Rosen, and Joshua S. Graff Zivin, *Does Science Advance One Funeral at a Time?* (NBER Working Paper No. 21788).

Bartle, Richard, *Designing Virtual Worlds* (New Riders, 2003).

Bateman, Chris, *The Virtuous Cyborg* (Eyewear, 2018).

Braon-Cohen, Simon, *The Essential Difference* (Perseus, 2003).

Brayfield, Celia, *Bestseller: Secrets of Successful Writing* (Fourth Estate, 1996).

Campbell, Joseph, *The Hero with a Thousand Faces*, Third Edition. (New World Library, 2012).

Catmull, Ed, *Creativity, Inc* (Bantam Press, 2014).

Cialdini, Robert, *Influence: The Psychology of Persuasion*, Revised Edition. (Harper Business, 2007).

Csikszentmihalyi, Mihaly, *Flow: The Psychology of Optimal Experience*, First ed., (New York: Harper & Row, 1990).

Cunningham, Jane and Roberts, Philippa, *Inside Her Pretty Little Head* (Marshall Cavendish, 2006).

De Bono, Edward, *Six Thinking Hats* (Penguin Life, 2016).

Dickens, Charles, *David Copperfield* (Wordsworth Editions, 1992).

Donovan, Tristan, *Replay* (Yellow Ant Media, 2010).

Eyal, Nir, *Hooked* (Portfolio Penguin, 2014).

Fogg, Brian J., *Persuasive Technology: Using Computers to Change What We Think and Do* (Morgan Kaufman, 2003).

Goldman, William, *Adventures in the Screen Trade*, Revised Edition. (Abacus, 1996).

Hornby, Nick, *High Fidelity* (Penguin, 1997).

Hunt, John, *Palio* (Archimedia, 2015).

Kahneman, Daniel, *Thinking Fast and Slow* (Penguin, 2011).

Kent, Stephen L., *The Ultimate History of Video Games* (Prima Life, 2001).

King, Brad, and Borland, John, *Dungeons and Dreamers* (McGraw-Hill, 2003).

Koster, Ralph, *A Theory of Fun* (Paraglyph Press, 2005).

Krug, Steve, *Don't Make Me Thin* (New Riders, 2014).

Kushner, David, *Masters of Doom,* New Edition. (Piatkus, 2004).

Lovell, Nicholas, *The Curve* (Portfolio Penguin, 2013).

Lovell, Nicholas, *Design Rules for F2P Games* (GAMESbrief, 2012).

Lovell, Nicholas, *The F2P Toolbox* (GAMESbrief, 2014).

Lovell, Nicholas, *How to Publish a Game* (GAMESbrief, 2010).

Lovell, Nicholas, *Ten Ways to Make Money in a Free World* (Portfolio Penguin, 2013).

Luton, Will, *Free-to-Play: Making Money from Games You Give Away* (New Riders, 2013).

Madigan, Jamie, *Getting Gamers* (Rowman & Littlefield, 2016).

Miller, Geoffrey, *The Mating Mind,* New Edition. (Vintage, 2001).

Ogilvy, David, *Ogilvy on Advertising* (Toronto: John Wiley & Sons, 1983).

Przybylski, Andrew, Rigby, Scott, and Ryan, Richard, *A Motivational Model of Video Game Engagement. Review of General Psychology* 13, no. 2 (2010): 154–166, [doi: 10.137/a0019440.]

Ries, Eric, *The Lean Startup* (Portfolio Penguin, 2011).

Ries, Eric, *The Startup Way* (Portfolio Penguin, 2017).

Rumelt, Richard, *Good Strategy, Bad Strategy.* (Profile Books, 2017).

Salen, Katie and Zimmerman, Eric, *Rules of Play: Game Design Fundamentals.* (MIT Press, 2003).

Schell, Jesse, *The Art of Game Design* (CRC Press, 2014).

Seufert, Eric, *Freemium Economics: Leveraging Analytics and User Segmentation to Drive Revenue* (Morgan Kaufman, 2014).

Stanton, Rich, *A Brief History of Video Games* (Robinson, 2015).

Veblen, Thorstein, *A Theory of the Leisure Classes*, Reissue Edition. (Oxford University Press, 2009).

Vogler, Christopher, *The Writer's Journey* (Pan Books, 1999).

Wilkins, Chris and Kean, Roger M., *Let's Go Dizzy, The Story of the Oliver Twins.* (Fusion Retro Books, 2016).

Wilkins, Chris and Kean, Roger M., *Ocean: The History* (Revival Retro Events, 2013).

Wu, Tim, *The Attention Merchants* (Alfred A. Knopf, 2010).

Wu, Tim, *The Master Switch* (Alfred A. Knopf, 2016).

Softography

A list of all games referred to in the text, together with the developer, publisher and year of release. If only one company name is listed, the developer and publisher were the same entity.

- *Adventure Capitalist*, Hyper Hippo Productions, 2014.
- *Alpha Colony*, Dreamquest, unpublished.
- *Alphabears*, Spry Fox, 2015.
- *Age of Wulin / Age of Wushu*, Snail, 2012.
- *Angry Birds*, Rovio, 2009.
- *Angry Birds Go!*, Exient, Rovio, 2013.
- *Angry Birds Transformers*, Exient, Rovio, 2014.
- *APB*, Realtime Worlds, 2010.
- *Assassin's Creed*, Ubisoft, 2007.
- *Avakin Life*, Lockwood Publishing, 2014.
- *Auto Assault*, NetDevil, NCSoft, 2006.
- *BattleTech*, Harebrained Schemes, Paradox Interactive, 2018.
- *Beasts of Balance*, Sensible Objects, 2016.
- *Blast Em!*, Xiotex Studios, 2014.
- *Boom Beach*, Supercell, 2014.
- *Brawl Stars*, Supercell, 2017 (soft launch).
- *Breaking Bad: Empire Business*, Scopely, 2015 (soft launch).
- *Broken Age*, Double Fine Productions, 2014.
- *Bubble Bobble*, Taito, 1986.
- *Bubble Witch Saga*, King, 2012.
- *Call of Duty 4: Modern Warfare*, Infinity Ward, Activision, 2007.
- *Candy Crush Saga*, King, 2012.
- *Caretaker Sacrifice*, Xiotex, 2016.
- *Chain Chronicle*, Sega, 2013.
- *Charley's Angels*, Neko Entertainment, Ubisoft, 2003.
- *Choices: Stories You Play*, Pixelberry Studios, 2016.

- *Cityville*, Zynga, 2010.
- *Civilisation*, MPS Labs, Microprose, 1991.
- *Clash of Clans*, Supercell, 2012.
- *Clash Royale*, Supercell, 2016.
- *Clicker Heroes*, Playsaurus, 2014.
- *Counterstrike: Global Offensive*, Hidden Path Entertainment, Valve Corporation, 2012.
- *Criminal Case*, Pretty Simple, 2012.
- *Crossfire*, Smilegate, Tencent, 2007.
- *Crossy Road*, Hipster Whale, 2014.
- *Crusader Kings II*, Paradox Interactive, 2012.
- *Crusaders of the Lost Idol*, Codename Entertainment, 2015.
- *CSR Racing*, Boss Alien, NaturalMotion Games, 2012.
- *Cuphead*, Studio MDHR, 2017.
- *Daikatana*, Ion Storm Games, Eidos, 2000.
- *Dark Souls*, FromSoftware, Namco Bandai Games, 2011.
- *Darkwind*, Psychic Software, 2007.
- *Dear Esther*, The Chinese Room, 2012.
- *Depression Quest*, The Quinnspiracy, 2013.
- *Destiny*, Bungie, Activision, 2014.
- *Diablo III*, Blizzard Entertainment, 2012.
- *Disco Zoo*, Milkbag Games, Nimblebit, 2014.
- *Dishonored*, Arkane Studios, Bethesda Softworks, 2012.
- *Disney Infinity*, Avalanche Software, Disney Interactive Studios, 2013.
- *Dizzy Returns*, Blitz Game Studios, unpublished.
- *Doom*, id Sofware, 1993.
- *Dragon Age: Origins*, Bioware, Electronic Arts, 2009.
- *Dragon City*, Social Point, 2012.
- *Dragonvale*, Backflip Studios, 2011.
- *Draw Something*, OMGPop, 2012.
- *Dungeon Fighter Online*, Neople, 2005.
- *Dungeon Master*, FTL Games, 1987.
- *Elite*, David Braben & Ian Bell, Acornsoft, 1984.
- *Elite Dangerous*, Frontier Developments, 2014.
- *Enter the Matrix*, Shiny Entertainment, Infogrames, 2003.
- *Episode*, Pocket Games, 2014.
- *E.T., The Extra-Terrestrial*, Atari, 1982.
- *Europa Universalis IV*, Paradox Interactive, 2013.
- *EVE Online*, CCP Games, 2003.

- *Eve Valkyrie*, CCP Games, 2016.
- *Everquest*, Sony Online Entertainment, 1999.
- *Fable Legends*, Lionhead, Microsoft, cancelled.
- *Factorio*, Wube, 2014.
- *Fallen London*, Failbetter Games, 2009.
- *Fallout 4*, Bethesda Game Studios, Bethesda Softworks, 2015.
- *Fallout: New Vegas*, Obsidian Entertainment, Bethesda Softworks, 2010.
- *Fallout Shelter*, Bethesda Game Studios, Bethesda Game Studios, 2015.
- *Farmaway*, Futureplay, 2015.
- *Farmville*, Zynga, 2009.
- *Fast Food*, Oliver Twins, Codemasters, 1987.
- *FIFA*, Electronic Arts, annually, 1993-present.
- *Flappy Bird*, dotGEARS, 2013.
- *Football Manager*, Sports Interactive, Sega, 2004-2017.
- *Fortnite*, Epic Games, 2017.
- *Frogger*, Konami, 1981.
- *FTL: Faster Than Light*, Subset Games, 2012.
- *Game of War*, Machine Zone, 2013.
- *Gardens of Time*, Playdom, 2011.
- *Gardenscapes*, Playrix, 2016.
- *Golf Clash*, Playdemic, 2017.
- *Grand Theft Auto*, DMA Design, BMG Interactive, 1997.
- *Hay Day*, Supercell, 2012.
- *Hearthstone*, Blizzard Entertainment, 2014.
- *Homescapes*, Playrix, 2017.
- *Ingress*, Niantic, 2013.
- *iShoot*, Ethan Nicholas, 2009.
- *Jagged Alliance 2*, Sir-Tech, TalonSoft, 1999.
- *Jetpack Joyride*, Halfbrick Studios, 2011.
- *Kart Rider*, Nexon, 2004.
- *Kim Kardashian: Hollywood*, Glu Mobile, 2014.
- *Kingdom of the Winds*, Nexon, 1996.
- *Kingdom Rush*, Ironhide Game Studio, Armor Games, 2011.
- *League of Legends*, Riot Games, 2009.
- *Legend of Grimrock*, Almost Human, 2012.
- *LEGO® Star Wars: The Video Game*, Travellers Tales, Giant Interactive Entertainment, 2005.
- *(lil) Green Patch*, Green Patch, 2008.
- *Little Britain: The Video Game*, Gamerholix, Blast! Entertainment, 2007.

- *Manic Miner*, Matthew Smith, Bug-Byte, 1983.
- *Maple Story*, Wizet, Nexon, 2003.
- *Marvel Contest of Champions*, Kabam, 2014.
- *Marvel Strike Force*, Kabam, 2018.
- *Mass Effect: Andromeda*, Bioware, Electronic Arts, 2017.
- *Medieval II: Total War*, Creative Assembly, Sega, 2006.
- *Minion Rush*, Gameloft, 2013.
- *Mobile Strike*, Machine Zone, 2015.
- *Modern Combat Versus*, Gameloft, 2017.
- *Monument Valley*, Ustwo Games, 2014.
- *My Horse*, NaturalMotion Games, 2011.
- *NonStop Knight*, Kopla Games, Flaregames, 2016.
- *Nosgoth*, Psynonix, Square Enix, 2015 (Early Access).
- *Nuclear Throne*, Vlambeer, 2015.
- *Overwatch*, Blizzard Entertainment, 2016.
- *Pac-Man*, Namco, 1980.
- *Pandemic Legacy*, Matt Leacock, Z-Man Games, 2015.
- *Papers, Please*, 3909 LLC, 2013.
- *Pearl's Peril*, Wooga, 2013.
- *Peggle*, PopCap Games, 2007.
- *Pillars of Eternity*, Obsidian Entertainment, Paradox Interactive, 2015.
- *Pirate Kings*, Jelly Button Games, 2015.
- *Planescape Torment*, Black Isle Studios, Interplay Entertainment, 1999.
- *Plants vs. Zombies*, PopCap Games, 2009.
- *Plants vs. Zombies 2*, PopCap Games, 2013.
- *Pokémon Go*, Niantic, 2016.
- *Pong*, Atari, 1972.
- *Potion Pop*, Delinquent Interactive, MAG Interactive, 2015.
- *Red Dead Redemption*, Rockstar Games, 2010.
- *Restaurant City*, Playfish, 2009.
- *Rockstar Presents Table Tennis*, Rockstar Games, 2006.
- *Rodeo Stampede: Sky Zoo Safari*, Featherweight Games, 2016.
- *Runescape*, Jagex, 2001.
- *Schoolgirl Strikers*, Square Enix, 2014.
- *Shenmue III*, Neilo and YS Net, Deep Silver, planned for 2019.
- *Shroud of the Avatar: Forsaken Virtues*, Portalarium, 2018.
- *SimCity*, Maxis, 1989.
- *Skylanders*, Toys for Bob, Activision, 2011.
- *Sonic Dash*, Hardlight, Sega, 2013

- *Space Invaders*, Taito, 1978.
- *Star Citizen*, Cloud Imperium Games, may never release.
- *Star Citizen: Squadron 42*, Cloud Imperium Games, may never release.
- *Stardom: Hollywood*, Blammo Games, Glu Games, 2013.
- *Stronghold Kingdoms*, Firefly Studios, 2012.
- *Subway Surfers*, Kiloo, SYBO Games, 2012.
- *Summoners War*, Com2US, 2014.
- *Super Hexagon*, Terry Cavanagh, 2012.
- *Tabula Rasa*, Destination Games, NCsoft, 2007.
- *Team Fortress 2*, Valve Corporation, 2007.
- *Temple Run*, Imangi, 2011.
- *Tetris*, Alexey Pajitnov, 1984.
- *The Last of Us*, Naughty Dog, Sony Computer Entertainment, 2013.
- *The Simpsons: Tapped Out*, EA Mobile, 2012.
- *The Stanley Parable*, Galactic Café, 2013.
- *The Walking Dead*, Telltale Games, 2012.
- *The World Ends with You*, Square Enix, 2007.
- *Time Crisis*, Namco, 1995.
- *Tiny Tower*, NimbleBit, 2011.
- *Tomb Raider*, Core Design, Eidos Interactive, 1996.
- *Tomb Raider: Relic Run*, Simutronics, Square Enix, 2015.
- *Torment: Tides of Numenara*, inXile Entertainment, Techland Publishing, 2017.
- *Triple Town*, Spry Fox, 2010.
- *UFO: Enemy Unknown*, Mythos Games, Microprose, 1994.
- *Ultima Online*, Origin Systems, Electronic Arts, 1997.
- *Uncharted*, Naughty Dog, Sony Interactive Entertainment, 2007.
- *Virtual Villagers*, Last Day of Work, 2006.
- *Wasteland 2*, inXile Entertainment, Deep Silver, 2014.
- *Wing Commander*, Origin Systems, 1990.
- *Wonky Tower*, Firefly Studios, 2016.
- *Words with Friends*, Newtoy, 2009.
- *World of Warcraft*, Blizzard Entertainment, 2004.
- *World of Warcraft: Wrath of the Lich King*, Blizzard Entertainment, 2008.
- *X-Com: Enemy Unknown*, Firaxis Games, 2K Games, 2012.
- *X-Wing*, LucasArts, 1993.

Index

Note: Page numbers followed by f and t refer to figures and tables respectively.